HUMAN VALUES IN EDUCATION

•

W. Ray Rucker

Dean, Graduate School of Leadership and Human Behavior
U.S. International University

V. Clyde Arnspiger

Professor of Sociology, Emeritus
East Texas State University

Arthur J. Brodbeck

Professor of Psychology and Social Science
Pennsylvania State University

KENDALL/HUNT PUBLISHING COMPANY
DUBUQUE, IOWA

Library of Congress Catalog Card Number: 79-78559

ISBN 0–8403–0378–5

Printed in the United States of America

Preface

The purpose of this volume is to introduce and promote a value-oriented education in a free society which includes comprehensive consideration of all human needs and aspirations. Suggested practices are designed to contribute increasingly to the wide distribution of human values to all people who accept responsibility for participating in value sharing as the basis of a humanistic way of life. Both teachers and parents are expected to participate with students in achieving wide access to these values which contribute to the overriding objective of the free society—the realization of human dignity on a grand scale.

To give adequate recognition to contributions of the many teachers and students at all levels of education in the United States and in other countries of the free world would not be possible. Scores of practicing classroom teachers have created and used techniques of classroom instruction designed to contribute to the emergence of mature personalities, who in turn share human values with others and thus have enhanced the human resources of our society.

Recognition is accorded our distinguished colleagues, Professors L. Varney Lieb and Elmer C. Ellis, who have served on three continents in the guidance of classroom teachers toward the employment of practices of value shaping and sharing as presented in this volume.

The curriculum project at Santee, California, in the creative use of *The Human Value Series* (Elementary Grade Texts)* under the direction of Superintendent Charles Skidmore and his colleagues, Dr. Kenneth Venn and Mrs. Jimmie Phelps has resulted in the creation of significant techniques for introducing new materials and methods into a value-sharing environment.

Professors Kenneth Evans, B.B. Bryant, O.L. Campbell, Allen H. Kavanaugh, L.V. Lieb, Everett M. Shepherd, and Wathena Temple of East Texas State University, and Warren Hamilton, William Clarke, and Francis Drag of the United States International University have provided creative sponsorship and assistance to advanced students in their institutions who have conducted research involving human values in education. Advanced studies leading to theses at East Texas State University have been conducted by Stanley P. Hobson, Lewis E. Lemmond, L. Blair, Carole W. McMillan, Helen B. Harwell, Rose Mary McGrill, Mary C. Wheeler, and Melba B. Wood. Dissertations at U.S. International University were also contributed by John Kerby, Elizabeth Higgins, James Saxon and Macy Abrams.

*Arnspiger, Rucker and Brill, *The Human Value Series* Steck-Vaughn, Austin, Texas, 1967-69.

The outstanding work of supervisors and teachers of the Fannindel, Texas School District in the Year of the Non-Conference project on value sharing in the classroom led to the creation of many significant practices reported in this volume. The Year of the Non-Conference was sponsored by the U.S. Office of Education and the National Commission on Teacher Education and Professional Standards of the National Education Association. The Fannindel School was one of the demonstration centers of this nationwide project directed by Superintendent Floyd C. Burnett.

The value-sharing project conducted jointly by the National College of Education, Richard K. Johnson, President, and the Chicago Public Schools, Benjamin C. Willis, General Superintendent, was supported by a grant from the Wieboldt Foundation for a period of five years. This project provided for the creation and use in pilot classrooms of Chicago, of practices designed to facilitate the wide distribution of human values, many of which are presented in this volume. The authors who served as consultants in this project, gratefully recognize the many contributions of the following supervisors and classroom teachers in the creation of democratic procedures in teaching and learning. Helen Challand, of the National College of Education, served as coordinator, and Marie Frank as director of the project for the Chicago Schools. The members of the National College staff included Dean Lewis Troyer, Elizabeth Brandt, Jeannette Branch, Oneida Cockrell, Avis Moore, Gregory Moore, Richard Panek, and Mary G. Williams. Members of the staff of the Chicago Schools who led initially in the creation of the strategies of the value-sharing project at the first pilot school were Grace Holt, Mattie Hopkins, D. Huffmon, Nerissa Johnson, Wanda Kuberski, Gwendolyn La Roche, Mildred Lavizzo, Verdel Saunders, Paula Simpson and Doris Zollar.

Harold D. Lasswell also served with great distinction as consultant in the Chicago Project. The authors having collaborated with Professor Lasswell for many years, gratefully acknowledge his creative contributions to the movement toward shaping and sharing human values in education and in other institutions of the free world.

The Authors

San Diego, California
January, 1969

Introduction

When the subject of values is introduced into education, it is often taken as a signal that one is about to engage in a long-winded discussion of all the abstruse and complicated matters that self-appointed experts have made part of the "conventions" and "norms" associated with the subject of values. As a result, one never gets beyond thinking about what one means by the *concept* of "value" so as to be free actively to engage in value thinking about *life* being shaped in educational experience. The concept of value is made so needlessly puzzling and complex, that all one's energies are used in trying to comprehend it. Little is left over for concretely examining values at work in every educational transaction–every moment of its flow. Indeed, "value" may be in danger of becoming an aversive word in education so long as this concept persists.

The present volume reverses this time-honored normative preference and procedure. It begins by placing the reader in the midst of the concrete valuing process in the classroom. No one will have the slightest doubts that values are being described and specified. No one will have the slightest doubts either that anything essential to the concept of value has been eradicated. What they will find–each and every one–is that the world of educational experience is rich in valuing, and there are simple ways to observe and record it in oneself and in others. The mind that experiences value in these ways is not sharply divorced from that experience by a set of over-formalized concerns that divert attention from the original purpose which often gets lost along the way.

In reversing the conventional treatment of values in relationship to education, it may well be that many of the favorite intellectual issues about the philosophy of values receive less than their usual accentation. The discussion, however, does move from concreteness toward generality so that just enough intellectual tools for value thinking are given so as to get ahead with the pragmatic task. The aim is to remain simple–and to keep our eyes open and our ears cocked for every refinement and expansion of consciousness needed so as to get at each subtlety and each large pattern that the facts of valuing in education demand from us. The aim is to contribute to educational practice–and not just another convoluted highbrow perspective whose significance for practice is moot and enigmatic.

The value thinking employed in this volume has been tried and tested. It works. It leads to discoveries of value excellence and uncovers needed improvement of valuing in the school. It has transformed the lives of those who have employed it, modifying both teachers and students alike. It is an American tradition that the final appeal is a pragmatic one. The reader is asked to do more than absorb the ideas in the volume—he or she is asked to apply them to education. The book bristles with concrete ways to make such applications. Still others will occur to the thoughtful reader. The worth of the book is to be discovered in such testing and not in some intellectual exercises apart from the experience. When such a test is made, the future direction of education will be found to reside in the value thinking elaborated in this volume.

Contents

Part I

•

DISCOVERY OF VALUING IN EDUCATION

CHAPTER 1

•

Classroom Practices For Maximizing Human Values

Why does everyone extoll the virtues of teaching? Teaching and teachers would appear to be the perennial solution to all social problems. To teachers, great men attribute their most sterling qualities of character or wisdom. The influence of the teacher is said to affect eternity. From the platforms of the land these potentials of a teacher are carried on the rhetoric of a thousand speakers—some close to teaching, many remote from its daily rewards and tribulations.

With such testimony to the promise of teaching, why are teachers not treated with greater respect on the job and in their communities? Why do many people question that teaching is a profession? Why are so many teachers so regimented, so filled with fear, and so discouraged with their unimaginative routine? Why are so many potentially good teachers alienated from teaching within the first five years?

Some high placed persons, both lay and academic, have attempted to limit the concept of teaching to that of a skill. Teaching, to them, often is a craft rather than a profession. Skill in teaching apparently is quite simple. It consists of the presentation of a subject. Understanding of the learner on the receiving end of the presentation apparently is not relatively important for secondary school teachers. Although most prospective teachers take courses in educational psychology and human development in their teacher education curricula, only elementary teachers, it is grudgingly thought, may profit by a minimum of preparation in such matters.

It is probably safe to speculate that the job of the teacher can be replaced by automation if teaching only consists of presentational skill. Programmed instruction, with or without teaching machines, and educational films and television already can do a better job of simple presentation of subject matter in the prescribed sequence than most teachers. If this definition of teaching gains wide acceptance, teachers will swell the ranks of unemployed due to the inevitable increase in educational automation.

Teachers and those who prepare teachers and many enlightened citizens know, however, that the performance of the teacher is far more complex and valuable to the society than the above naive generalization would indicate. Further, the new demands which will be placed on education to help promote desirable social change in areas of cultural lag should cast the teacher in an even more important and complex role than ever. Automation will be welcomed for the time it can save the teacher and learner in basic concept and skill areas in the new education. Automation will, in fact, give to the teacher that release from routine so badly needed if he is to attend to his principal humanizing task—the shaping and sharing of human values toward more mature personalities and a democratic society.

Skill is itself a value. Hence, the task of education is often taken to be that of producing children who can read, write, spell, memorize, and perform other basic skills of the same sort. Pride is often taken in the schools who turn out children with some excellence in the mastery of such skills. They enhance the literacy needed for both better citizenship and employable self-responsibility in American life.

The techniques of teaching and learning such skills are seldom considered as involving all other human values and, in turn, as leading to outcomes that touch upon all human values. For a long time, it appeared as though the schools could succeed in skill transmission without giving explicit concern to more than just the skill value for its own sake. All the rest seemed to take care of itself.

A time has come when the pursuit of skill for skill's sake alone no longer goes unchallenged. For a long time now, the question has been raised: How can so many children go for so many years to school and, yet, be so primitively advanced with regard to basic skills? One answer has been to merely find new techniques of, for instance, teaching reading. Another answer has been to make us aware of how mental and emotional disorder interferes with both teaching and learning skills. These and other solutions, however, bypass looking squarely at how all values shape skill acquisition, both as conditions and outcomes of it.

Value thinking is itself a skill. It can be and, in the future, will be added to the program of the schools as a skill, a skill as basic as reading or writing and one which begins as early as these. But it is a skill which both conditions and affects all other skills. One acquires a skill because it is a means (a base value) to an end (a scope value). Skill is seen to have significance beyond itself. Seldom will a skill be acquired if it is not seen to have some relevance for the future. Furthermore, practice at acquiring a skill is always going on in a human relationship. The values operating in that human relationship we characterize as that of teacher and learner *facilitate* excellence in skill mastery or produce, on the contrary, *indifference* or even *conflict*, leading to a wretched skill outcome.

We think of higher education as specialized to enlightenment. The value of enlightenment is present whenever we ask what the meaning or significance of what we are doing may be. To pursue enlightenment, we are required to place any detail in our lives within a large map of the whole so that we can see what importance it may have for the whole and how the whole allows us to see its importance as a detail. Value thinking is a skill (base value) specialized to enlightenment (scope value), hence, the skill of value thinking helps us to discover the true place of all other skills in our lives—it makes us see why reading and writing are significant for us as learners or as teachers attempting to "motivate" learners. Hence, as value thinking becomes more prominent in the schools, it will not compose "another area" of skill learning but will become part and parcel of all skill learning from the beginning of life. And as this happens, the interest in skill for *skill's* sake will be supplanted by the enlightenment skill of value thinking which allows no skill to be divorced from all of the value conditions and consequences to which in reality it is related. To put it more strongly: one cannot bring a concern with *both skill and* enlightenment closer together without raising all significant questions of value.

The new mathematics has already introduced advanced mathematical thinking into elementary education. It is only one sign of a whole new movement toward introducing concerns that were once exclusively part of the college and university into earlier education, often in simpler and clearer forms. The introduction of value thinking into pre-adult education is part of this new movement in educational reconstruction. Not only do children grasp the skill quickly, but they are transformed by it. The young are often bitter about their own early education for the gap it has left in their minds as to how *to think* about value questions intelligently. Just as one may know all the words in the dictionary and not be able to write or speak effectively, so one may have all the basic skills and yet not know how to live intelligently. Value thinking reduces the possibility of such "educated ignorance" as a product of a so-called "good education."

There is something wrong with an educational system that struggles to find some spot to introduce character education into its flow of legitimate activities. Concern with character never seems to be part of the "core" of education—and that will always be so when skill or skill's sake is taken as the normative view. Yet, in every school transaction, character is being formed. Even when all are focused on so "value-free" a skill as learning algebra, person is interacting with person to set value norms for that interaction in the classroom. Early value deprivations in the first exposure to skill learning have lasting damaging marks. It probably is a myth that the process of skill learning can ever be accurately described without considering how all values enter into it. The present volume is meant to provide a simple introduction toward how to promote the skill of value thinking in our schools. It comes out of several prototype projects in the schools which have already done just that, and with results so promising that the time is ripe—even overripe—for sharing these with the profession in as nontechnical a form as possible. The skill specialized to enlightenment—the skill of value thinking—is made the "core" of education in these pages. If education looks different than more conventional treatments of teaching and learning paint it, the departure from convention is in the service of enlightenment—and the pursuit of truth—rather than cleverness.

Implied in the question, "Education for what?" is the hope that value-thinking will be clarified. What are the values (wants and needs) of man which must be fulfilled in order to increase the probability that he can achieve self-actualization and a relative status of worth and dignity? What is man's responsibility for helping others to become self-actualized and achieve human dignity? An effort is made in this volume to suggest answers to these fundamental questions in terms of a value-oriented framework which undertakes to specify the conditions under which the realization of human dignity can be facilitated both within the self and in the social context.

Professor Harold D. Lasswell of Yale University in his work over some thirty years as a political scientist and psychologist made an extended analysis of the institutional practices and personal strategies of men throughout history and in a variety of primitive and modern cultures. Through this analysis he derived the eight major categories of valuing listed on the following pages under which he assumed could be classified the goals of man, his needs and wants, his preferred events. The categories derived from this empirical examination of the history of man's efforts to achieve his goals are employed here to clarify institutional practices and personal strategies within education and the other behavioral sciences in order to facilitate release of all participants to realize fully their potentials as human beings.

The authors have enlisted the aid of many teachers to develop a descriptive science of values for identifying actual classroom techniques and procedures that contribute to the process of wide value-sharing among all those involved in the educative process. This systematic effort to create such practices to validate theoretical constructs and to throw light on additional concepts in the continuing development of both theory and practice is open-ended. This pattern of innovation thus has infinite possibilities for the utilization of creative talents in Education and the other Behavioral Sciences. Whereas Lasswell facilitated generic beginnings by categorizing human valuing and employing them to create an intellectual framework for political inquiry, the authors, and many others to come, hope to introduce students of education and the other behavioral sciences to the inherent possibilities of this global discipline to influence human transformation in the direction of the realization of human worth and dignity.

VALUE INDICES IN TERMS OF CLASSROOM PRACTICES

Innovations in the classroom are to be encouraged of every teacher in order that the best practices may be discovered as indices of major value categories. These indices refer to events which indicate the degree to which values are made available and distributed among the students. As teachers cooperate in using such practices, we are able to appraise the curriculum in terms of its effect upon students in their search for the things they need and want.

The definitions of democratic and despotic classrooms will be found to be useful in the systematic creation of techniques and methods that contribute to the construction of classrooms that are prototypes of democracy. A classroom may be said to be moving toward democracy to the degree to which the institutional practices and personal strategies employed increase the probability that more and more human values are shared on the basis of merit, by more and more students and teachers.

Conversely, a classroom may be said to be moving toward despotism to the degree to which its institutional practices and personal strategies contribute toward concentrating the control of the values in the teacher or a small group, whose autocratic behavior prevents access of large numbers of students to the values they seek.

A sample but incomplete set of classroom practices as indices of values are presented below as a "pump primer." By describing classrooms this way, we are able to determine systematically the degree of value distribution actually existing in them. This list suggests to the teacher clues to other practices both time-honored and new which may be added to the list. One of the most important functions of a classroom teacher or school officer is assuming responsibility for creating many other appropriate indices which will build a value-sharing school and a value-sharing society.

Affection

1. Students are encouraged to promote congenial human relationships.
2. The teacher makes concerted efforts to establish congenial relationships with his students.
3. Hostilities which arise are overcome by deliberate efforts to restore friendly attitudes.
4. Definite efforts are made to reduce adverse and unnecessary criticism of individuals and groups among the members of the class.

Respect

1. Respect is accorded every member of the class on the basis of merit.[1]
2. All students are given positive help in overcoming handicaps that might otherwise prevent their achieving high respect status.
3. The good work of students is recognized before the entire class in ways that enhance their feelings of confidence (self respect).
4. Many opportunities are provided students for the employment of their individual talents.
5. Freedom of choice is made available to all individuals so long as democratic standards or the rights of others are not violated.
6. Wherever possible the privacy of individuals is insured.

Skill

1. Students are encouraged to develop their own talents to the limits of their capacities. In this connection the teacher is alert to opportunities to develop latent talents. Such talents may include the motor skills, the skills of thinking, communication skills, the social skills, and aesthetic skills. The teacher searches for hidden talents among his students. He develops these by providing innumerable opportunities to exercise these talents.
2. Students are encouraged to use all the skills they have developed.
3. Situations are provided which lead to extensive practice in the development of specific skills of handling interpersonal relationships. These may involve role playing, actual playground, classroom or home-centered situations.

---

[1] The term merit in this connection refers to the status of the person who merits access to human values to the degree to which he in turn accords these values to others.

Enlightenment

1. All available lines of communication are kept open for all students in their search for enlightenment.
2. The teacher establishes himself as an observer, learner, and guide with his classes. He does not attempt to become the "infallible oracle of all knowledge."
3. All reasonable effort is made to establish the authenticity of subject matter presented to or by the class.
4. Teacher and students have high respect for scholarship.
5. The teacher makes every effort to disclose pertinent facts on both sides of every issue under discussion.
6. Students are encouraged to solve many of their own problems by themselves.
7. Reality is faced in the search for knowledge, in the revelation of pertinent incidents involving interpersonal relationships which have deteriorated, or in all other goal-seeking activities.

Power

1. Students are encouraged to participate in the making of important decisions with respect to the establishment of many classroom practices.
2. Numerous opportunities are given members of the class to vote on important issues with which the class is concerned.
3. Students are encouraged constructively to discuss any classroom practices.
4. Students can take an unpopular side in arguments involving issues without fear of reprisals of any kind.
5. The attitudes of teachers and students are definitely against the concentration of decision making in only a few members of the class.
6. Students are encouraged to challenge the decisions which may have been made by the majority of the class but which the minority may feel requires further reconsideration in the interest of democratic justice.

Wealth (Goods and Services)

1. Students are encouraged to think of the work they may wish to do in making a living and to study the requirements of getting and keeping a job.
2. Students are encouraged to produce wealth in the form of learning materials or handicraft.
3. Students and teachers are encouraged to become of service to others.
4. Students and teachers are encouraged to conserve their own material resources as well as those provided them by the school. This definitely assumes a presumption by teachers and pupils against the needless destruction of property.

Well-Being

1. Safeguards of the physical health of students are provided by the teacher and by the school.
2. Teachers do all in their power to contribute to the mental health of students. (This is the value that depends greatly upon the degree of access young people have to the other values.) Efforts made to enhance status in respect and affection will usually be found to contribute effectively to the achievement of high status in well-being. The assistance of students in the promotion of these efforts is to be solicited by the teacher who reminds students on a continuous basis of everyone's responsibility for helping to conserve mental health in one and all.
3. Teachers recognize the serious problem of the quiet, obedient child who tends to be unusually submissive and withdrawn, and make every effort to lead this child into productive creativity.
4. Teachers recognize common symptoms of tension due to fears and anxieties that inhibit the creativity of pupils and take effective measures to reduce or relieve these tensions by getting at the deprivations which caused them and dealing realistically with them.
5. Teachers and students are provided with appropriate techniques which introduce them to the objective appraisal of their own statuses with respect to such values as respect, affection, well-being, wealth, and the other values. Practice in the use of such tools of analysis is expected to increase the teacher's self-knowledge, so important in his own avoidance of unrealistic behavior. Increasing the teacher's sophistication in this area can be expected to result in his giving more adequate attention to the mental health of students.

Rectitude

1. Students are encouraged to accept personal and collective responsibility for the sharing of values in the classroom.
2. Students are encouraged to set up their own moral standards above the minimum levels of "good behavior."
3. Students are taught that the moral person in a democracy is one who demands that other citizens have access to the values which he demands for himself.
4. Students are disciplined for antisocial behavior on the basis of factual evidence that can be substantiated without reasonable doubt.
5. Teachers clearly understand the difference between the democratic ideal which places a high premium upon the establishment by students of high standards of rectitude and the goal of the authoritarian school which demands that its citizens live according to externally prescribed "modes of behavior" which are enforced through coercion and fear.

6. The sense of responsibility and standards of ethical conduct are applied to problems of human interrelationships at the group level as well as at the interpersonal level.
7. Students are encouraged to take responsibility for and to practice skills of according values to others.

SUMMARY

Teachers really begin to teach when they identify and relate to the valuing concerns of individual pupils. The routine of mass instruction, typical in the American school, diverts and enslaves the teacher as well as the student. He cannot find the time to really know his students and to help each one move forward in development at a pace and with a quality commensurate with individual potential. He yearns for release from this trap which forces him to teach far below his own potential as a professional facilitator of learning. His release and that of his students await the application of a science of value shaping and sharing to the process of education.

The next two chapters present a galaxy of classroom practices reported by teachers which were either invented or identified among those already in use when the value framework was the catalyst for analyses of educational activities.

A discussion of the more technical details of a descriptive science of values will follow in Chapter 4.

CHAPTER 2

•

Creating Classroom Practices Compatible with a Value Framework (Power, Respect, Affection, Well-being)

Indices of the values have been proposed as measures of the degree to which values are shaped and shared in the classroom. Using a similar list of these indices specialized to each of the value categories, a number of experienced classroom teachers undertook to create classroom practices designed to improve the wide sharing of these values in their own classrooms. Several such groups, for example, participated in Value-Sharing Projects, which had as a major goal the maximization of human values in the classroom.[1] The justification for this goal was based upon its compatibility with the democratic demand for the realization of human worth and dignity through widely rather than narrowly shared values sought by man. The first group of participants were teachers of the Doolittle school of the Chicago Public School System. Their analyses of past events and current conditions relative to the degree of value sharing and the achievement of value status of pupils, teachers, administrators, and parents of the school were unusually realistic and factual. These analyses and appraisals of trends and conditions indicated that without intervention, the future seemed to hold little hope for significant permanent improvement in the value statuses of the participants in the operation of the school.

It has been shown that as a major consequence of low status or deprivation in any of the human values, mental, and often, physical health is impaired (low well-being status). It has also been shown that the tension of this frustration (symptomatic of low well-being status), is a significant deterrent to creative and productive activity. The tension of frustration accompanies a state of fear and/or anxiety which is the response of the individual to actual or threatened deprivation in any or all of the social values. Therefore, the teachers very early in their seminar sessions decided that in order to be able to provide an environment most conducive to the educative process, their most important instrumental goal should be to achieve high status of well-being among their pupils through the creation of school practices that contribute most effectively to the enhancement of their value assets.

[1]One such project, supported by a grant from the Wieboldt Foundation to the National College of Education was conducted in cooperation with the Chicago Public Schools from 1959 to 1964. The authors participated in this project as consultants.

As a matter of fact, this goal was proposed as the aim of Value-Sharing Projects at the beginning, but the realistic personal involvement of seminar participants, so essential to intellectual creativity and productive action, came only after they had individually directed their own thinking toward the realization of the postulated objective of democracy (human worth and dignity) and the consideration of the significance of the value demands, expectations, and identifications of human beings who aspire toward freedom.

The participants in these seminars contributed scores of alternative practices specialized to each of the eight value categories of the school process. Additional seminars made up of groups of teachers from other schools, as well as college students enrolled in graduate classes in education, analyzed and tentatively appraised the suggested alternatives and created still other classroom practices and strategies designed to achieve this goal.

The practices specified by these several groups were classified under each of the value categories. It can be seen that the systematic thinking of these teachers after several years, has gone far beyond the original proposals of criteria set at the beginning. The aspirations of those engaged in the conduct of the Value-Sharing Projects envisioned through this procedure, the creation of classrooms which were prototypes of the democratic community. Observational indices employed by teachers, administrators, and consultants have resulted in tentative appraisals of the proposed alternatives which are quite promising in terms of the goal of the project.

It must not be assumed that any final answer to all the ways and means of maximizing values in the classroom will be reached. Continuing systematic appraisal techniques are being employed and revisions and elaborations of classroom procedures are being made in terms of these findings. The dialogue of decision seminars indicates the continuing need for revision and refinement of classroom practices in line with the emerging instrumental goals of democracy and with consequent modifications of the value demands, expectations and identifications of people on the road toward the realization of human dignity.

We should, therefore, plan for a continuing systematic process of enlightenment and skill development by teachers whose activities are self-directed toward the solution of problems, and the realization of goals which are compatible with the ideals of democracy. The list included in this volume must, therefore, be considered as an interim statement of *classroom techniques and procedures* which are in the process of continuing refinement and elaboration. It is hoped this process will continue as educational practices emerge which are expected to lead to the provision of increasing numbers of opportunities for human beings to realize their full potentials in the preferred goals of man.

The eight value categories with alternative practices specialized to each follow.

POWER

A person's status of power may be said to be measured by the degree to which he participates in the making of important decisions. These are decisions which are sanctioned by the society or group of which he is a member. That is, they are expected to be lived up to by the people and are enforced against those who would violate them.

We refer also in this category to choice, which is an unsanctioned decision. We make thousands of choices during our lifetime which have important bearing upon our future personal lives but which may be of little consequence to others. For example, the choice between whether to vacation in the mountains or at the seashore is not a sanctioned choice. The important point to be remembered is that many people expect to take part freely in the power process and their well-being status suffers if they do not.

It is of great importance that our children be led to see the importance of decision making and are given wide opportunities actually to participate in the making of such decisions. It must be emphasized that the decisions in which class members participate are those which are expected to be enforced. Otherwise, the children will come to see that power and respect are being withheld from them and their well-being statuses will be consequently damaged.

This damage may be ignored by the teacher and the child may leave the classroom with the feeling that he does not measure up to what the teacher (and society) expects of him and may thus carry feelings of guilt which may permanently distort and restrict his relationships with other people.

Let us examine the alternative practices specialized to power proposed by the several seminars.

I. POWER

A. Pupils are encouraged to participate in the making of important decisions with respect to the establishment of many classroom practices.

1. Class members choose line captains and specify responsibilities of each. They also elect pencil sharpeners, milk distributors, cleanup monitors, and others.
2. Class sets up routine for use of school instructional materials.
3. Class sets up routine for use of toilets.
4. Class sets up routine for keeping room orderly by specifying places where wraps, books, collection of papers, and other items are kept.
5. Class discusses type of program schedule preferred.
6. Class discusses and helps teacher establish codes of courtesy and conduct.
7. Class discusses types of disciplinary action.
8. Class discusses and helps plan objectives of trips to be taken in connection with classroom activities.
9. Class participates in choice of social studies approach.
10. Class helps choose auxiliary books and required reading. They discuss extra credit reports to be made.
11. Class discusses approach to units, for example, in science class.
12. Class discusses whether their conduct and effort is up to standards they have helped create.

13. Pupils choose what to do after completion of assigned work while teacher is busy with another group (such as library, reading, creative art, etc.).
14. They choose a song to be sung in each assembly program.
15. They make a list of events in classroom behavior and classify such events as desirable or undesirable. They chart behavior that will make for a democratic room.
16. Pupils discuss and set up objectives for unit or subject area as standards by which to judge their own work.

B. Numerous opportunities are given members of the class to vote on important issues with which the class is concerned.
1. Pupils learn ways of voting and why voting is necessary.
2. Pupils actively seek enlightenment from both sides of issues to enhance the validity of their vote.
3. Elections are held by secret ballot to encourage everyone to vote as he thinks best and not as everyone else does.
4. Elections are held only for issues which are sufficiently important to warrant an election.
5. All pupils vote when they are given a chance.
6. Class votes for classroom officers, for citizen of the week or of the year.
7. Class votes on certain matters of discipline.
8. Class votes assessments, if any, for collections or means of raising money.
9. Class votes classroom routine practices as indicated under "A."
10. Class votes on certain prerequisites for office holders.
11. Consensus of class is sought regarding the excellence of pupils' work on notebooks, reports, or other available evidence of creative work by members of the class.
12. Class votes on activities they are to undertake during parent visitation.
13. Individuals or small groups within the class may be given responsibility for making decisions on their own. For example, the bulletin board committee may decide on materials and arrangement, the game committee on what to play and what supplies are needed; the special day (such as Washington's or Lincoln's birthday) committee on appropriate memorial activities.

C. Pupils are convicted and punished for antisocial behavior only on the basis of factual evidence that can be substantiated without reasonable doubt.
1. Guilt determined by:
   a. Sight.
   b. Confession.
   c. Witnesses (reliable, in number).
2. Value deprivations include:
   a. Withdrawal of power (office, assignment).

   b. Withdrawal of respect through withholding library, recess, or gym privileges.
   c. Withdrawal of rewards (nonparticipation in class awards–party, trip, etc.). There are a number of values included here.
3. Punishment rendered:
   a. Under standardization of penalties for same violation where possible.
   b. Objectively–never in anger.
   c. With antisocial act condemned rather than child.
4. Pupils are encouraged to refrain from accusing another until they have heard both sides of the story.
5. Pupils discourage classmates who constantly report the misdeeds of others.
6. Pupils are allowed to explain, as calmly as possible, their side of the case when they are accused of an antisocial act.
7. Every pupil is considered to be truthful until proved otherwise, but statements are double-checked when possible.
8. When there is doubt that all the facts of the case are known, no conviction is made and no punishment set.
9. The use of scapegoats is understood and deliberately avoided.
10. No child is convicted by classmates or teacher of an antisocial act solely on the basis that he has been known to commit such acts before and might possibly have committed this one.
11. Older pupils learn to look for the reasons and causes behind actions before they judge and punish the actions of another.
12. Older pupils try to help the person who committed the antisocial act to understand why he did it rather than to loudly declaim against him.
13. Children understand that punishments are not set up to hurt any particular pupil, but they are necessary to maintain order in society or in the classroom.
14. Children try to make the degree of the punishment or temporary deprivation of a value or values match the degree of seriousness of the act.
15. Pupils realize the importance of the power they exercise over their classmates in the matter of punishment for antisocial actions and they handle it carefully and wisely.

D. Pupils are encouraged constructively to discuss and suggest improvements in any classroom practices.
   1. Children discuss any discipline the teacher feels is needed (how and why).
   2. Children discuss methods of clearing the building during regular and emergency dismissals; sequence of events established (removal of coats, etc.)
   3. "Hands to ourselves" rule.
   4. "No running, sliding down bannister" rule.

5. All general school rules.
6. Courtesy toward others.
7. Previously made class decisions where:
   a. Modifications are needed or,
   b. New officers are to be elected.
8. Bulletin boards, room maintenance, decorations, placement of furniture, etc.

E. The attitudes of teachers and pupils are definitely against the concentration of power in the hands of only a few members of the group.
1. Show examples of poor results of activity planned by small group without taking others into account. This is a typical example of despotic or antidemocratic behavior.
2. Elected leaders should be rotated among members of the class who are able and willing to serve.
3. Give children the jobs which they are capable of fulfilling and fix responsibility for their completion.
4. Show consequences of pupils' apathy at every opportunity which illustrates failure to show interest in the affairs of the group.
5. Give opportunity for the total group to override decisions of a small pressure group made without reference to the majority.
6. In the primary grades, let each child trace his hand on a piece of construction paper, then cut out and print his own name on it. Place each cut-out hand into a box. Each week let one child draw from this box the number of hands needed for duties in the classroom. The names of the children who have performed duties are not put back into the box until all names have been drawn. This helps each child to realize his importance as a person of responsibility in society.

High school teachers participating in some of the seminars contributed the following:

1. If the teacher is to become a scientist in the class, then the class, itself, must be operated as a laboratory in which democratic techniques and practices are created, tried out, and if effective become part of accepted procedure.
2. Since a democracy is government by the people collectively through their elected representatives, we should begin by giving power to students elected to the student council, presidents of clubs, home room representatives, to make their own rules under the guidance of a sponsor, principal, or other faculty members. This guidance, of course, must never become dictatorial or coercive. This is a phony situation which pupils can recognize immediately and is a dangerous step toward developing a cynical disregard for democratic institutions and strategies.
3. We may begin the year with a student assembly before election, with candidates giving their qualifications, platforms or goals, and how they intend to meet these goals. The school may have a handbook, written by student council members of the previous year stating school policies, rules and philosophy. This should be given to every student and faculty member at the beginning of school.
4. The teacher is alert to every opportunity for pupil-participation in the clarification, identification, amplification, and implementation of goals of

the group. This cannot be done by an uninterested teacher or by a teacher whose power status has been restricted or damaged. When pupils take part in class planning, they have a sense of power in doing what they planned. Power status for each pupil is not instantly created; it must be developed through his personal involvement in the decision-making process.

5. Invest pupils with responsibility to act in such ways as they can to help other pupils achieve value assets. The pupils will be encouraged to unite forces with others to meet this responsibility.
6. Provide opportunities for pupils to act as leaders or participants in functional "buzz-sessions." In such activities, pupils develop the power of communication which would never be recognized in activities of the class as a whole.
7. Encourage pupils to clarify goals in terms of democratic ideals, justifying this further by appraisal of feasibility and realism in terms of pupils' capabilities. If the goals are realistic and attainable, the pupil will direct his efforts toward them, without being thwarted by unrealistic fears and tensions which may come from anticipated consequences of failure.
8. Provide all opportunities for pupils to appraise self-progress and develop abilities in this appraisal. With this information available, the pupil can set his own pace without floundering; he is strengthened by knowing his rate of progress and develops the skill of assessing his efforts and achievements.
9. Class meetings or Student Association meetings hold many opportunities for power sharing through parliamentary procedures and democratic decisions.
10. The high school teacher should take advantage of many opportunities to share power in working with different committees. A program committee, for example, may have the task of turning in copy to the printer, collecting the printed programs, and distributing them when necessary.

RESPECT

One of the most important needs of the human being is that he be respected by his fellowman. This applies to the child in school at all age and grade levels as well as to the adult throughout his life. One of the most important contributions to man's mental health is the knowledge that he is accorded recognition based upon the merit of his accomplishments. On the other hand, the feeling that one is discriminated against, especially without merit, is a major cause of mental ill-health.

Another point to be made in considering this value category is the significance for the individual of respect for himself. An important index of self-respect is the degree to which the individual has confidence in himself. It may well be said that in order to respect others a person must respect himself. This points to the great need the free society has for teachers who have respect for themselves, for only such teachers can be expected to promote the realistic enhancement of respect among his pupils. Such teachers tend to face their problems realistically with a minimum of substitution, self-deception, and retreat. The consequences of respect deprivation are most serious in terms of personality damage, not only to the individual from whom respect has been withheld, but also to those who are the victims of this person's unrealistic efforts to restore his respect status through such mechanisms as displaced hostility, guilt transference, and others. Let us examine the alternative practices and strategies which seminar participants decided were specialized to the production and wide distribution of respect.

II. RESPECT

A. Respect is accorded every member of the class on the basis of merit.

1. Give child opportunity to explain problems he faces in his living not only in the classroom but in his outside relationships.
2. Clarify uncertainty and lack of understanding for each child.
3. Allow child to practice self-discipline where possible.
4. Rotate positions of leadership.
5. Give each child time to participate in class activity.
6. Encourage courteous behavior among children. "Thank you," "please" and other such widely accepted amenities are highly effective in according respect.
7. Teacher in referring to the child always uses the name or nickname the child prefers.
8. Teacher never employs sarcasm as an instrument of classroom management.
9. Teacher speaks to children in a dignified and courteous way and does not shout at them.
10. Teacher and pupils respect each other's property rights.
    a. Children take books and materials only with the teacher's permission.
    b. Teacher refrains from borrowing paper, workbooks, etc. from children without their permission.
    c. Children refrain from borrowing excessively in the classroom.
    d. Borrowed property is carefully handled.
11. Each member of the class is allowed to answer questions and offer other contributions to group discussions.
12. A presumption is made in favor of the speaker's veracity until proven wrong.
13. Each child who is interested in doing so may try out for the class play, program, or athletic team.
14. Each person is allowed to have his turn to swing, to bat, to draw or to get a drink of water so long as his behavior merits it.
15. Those members of the class who have special talents are recognized for the exercise of these talents.
    a. They are asked to coach other students in areas of their special competence.
    b. They are asked to present demonstrations or performances.
    c. They are complimented verbally.
16. Children listen intently to a classmate who is speaking.
17. Teacher refrains from striking pupils or shaking them.
18. Honors based on popularity are given to the children who are courteous and most respectful of others.
19. Children are asked to stand and be recognized for honors received.
20. Children are recognized in all-school honors assemblies.
21. Honors won outside school by class members are brought to the class's attention by the teacher or another classmate at a regular specified time.

22. Children who have contributed much to a committee's work are allowed to present that committee's report to the class or the school.
23. Children are selected on the basis of merit to represent the class on errands, in activities, or in pictures.
24. Elections are held to recognize those who merit respect in one or more specific areas. Every class member is considered carefully as a prospective candidate for these honors.
    a. "Good Citizen of the Week" is elected.
    b. "Friendliest Boy and Girl" are elected.
    c. "Sportsmanship Award" is given.

B. No discrimination against pupils is imposed which is not compatible with the merit of the individual as a human being.
   1. Teacher does not discriminate against children in any way because of conditions beyond their control.
      a. Grades are given on the basis of merit alone.
      b. Public recognition and honors are given on the basis of merit.
      c. Jobs are assigned on the basis of merit.
   2. Children are not discriminated against because of socioeconomic background.
      a. Children accord respect to a classmate if he merits it as an individual, in spite of the fact that he speaks with an unusual accent.
      b. Children do not discriminate against classmates whose clothes are not as good as theirs.
      c. Children of differing socioeconomic backgrounds invite each other to take part in play activities.
      d. The parents of children of lower economic status are shown as much courtesy and respect by the teacher and children when they visit the school as are the parents of children of high economic status.
   3. Children of lower economic status are chosen as officers of the class, as captains of the athletic teams, or as class representatives to other functions or organizations. The only requirement for this selection is that the person individually deserves it.
   4. When children of higher economic status are in the minority, they are not discriminated against by the other children because of their better clothes or closer attention to manners.
   5. Each child is accorded respect for the unique contributions which only he, because of his socioeconomic background, can make to the class.
      a. Information about a variety of occupations may be gathered by a class which is composed of children of many backgrounds.
      b. Experiences of travel and work each child has will result in a unique background; so plan to use these resources.

C. No discrimination is practiced in the classroom because of religious or racial background.

1. Children learn about other groups in an effort to overcome false generalizations.
   a. They study the customs and holidays which people from other lands have brought to America.
   b. They learn about the distinctive and colorful costumes which other people have contributed to our heritage.
   c. They sample food from other lands.
   d. They learn why some children go to other schools because of their religion.
   e. They learn about the religious holidays which some children miss school to attend.
2. Children follow nondiscriminatory practices in their relations with their classmates of other racial and religious backgrounds.
   a. They choose friends from this group because of personal compatibility.
   b. They distribute classroom honors to this group on the basis of personal merit.
   c. Remarks of a cruel and unjust nature are never directed toward this group or groups by any member of the class.

D. All pupils are given positive help in overcoming handicaps that might otherwise prevent their achieving high respect status.
1. See that each child is given a task he can perform successfully.
2. Teach each child to do something well.
3. Give opportunity to display examples of meritorious work.
4. Devote any time possible for individual attention to the needs of the child which have been revealed by observation.
5. Refer special personality problems that demand professional attention to the proper agency.
6. Aid child to accept handicaps of all kinds and help him in trying to overcome their ill-efects.
7. Children who are physically handicapped do not have remarks directed at them because of these handicaps.
8. Children who are unusually small are encouraged to take part in all group activities, and they are encouraged to feel that they are making a unique contribution.
   a. They are allowed to participate in playground activities in some capacity. If they actually take part in the games, they are given special advantages, if necessary, but never pity.
   b. Activities where smallness is an asset are planned at times for their benefit.
   c. Any mental or motor skill which they have is stressed and used to the fullest.
9. Children who are unusually large or tall are encouraged to use their abnormality in doing things which no one else in the class can do.
   a. They reach for things on the tallest shelves.
   b. They lift and move objects which no one else can move.

c. They take part in playground activities where height or size is of importance.

10. Children who have a physical deficiency which keeps them from participating in almost any physical activity are given opportunities to achieve respect status in other ways.
    a. Their ability as scorekeeper for games is respected and utilized.
    b. Their ability to tell or write stories, draw pictures, sing, etc. is recognized and used for the benefit of the class and school.
    c. When they exhibit unusual helpfulness or cooperation, it is recognized in a favorable way, thus encouraging them to develop personality traits which will help them to be respected by their classmates.
11. Mentally handicapped children are assisted by teacher and classmates in developing traits and skills which will enable them to gain respect.
    a. Any achievement in scholastic areas is recognized and encouraged, but pressure is not put on these children to achieve beyond their own predispositions.
    b. Assistance is given in developing motor skills.
        (1) Children are recognized for their athletic skills.
        (2) If these children have abilities which enable them to get along with their classmates, they are given many opportunities to work with others and develop these social skills.
        (3) Outlets are provided for exercising any special skill such as woodworking, drawing, etc.
    c. Children with emotional handicaps are assisted in overcoming them.
        (1) Teacher searches for children in the class who are emotionally unstable and tries to help them.
            (a) He plots out a definite plan of action for assistance.
            (b) He tries to help these children avoid emotional situations for which they are unprepared.
            (c) He offers advice to children who are becoming conscious themselves of their handicap.
            (d) He offers encouragement to these children at every opportunity and makes certain that he recognizes and compliments each sign of progress made by the children.
        (2) Older children recognize their own and their classmates fears and tensions.
            (a) With their teacher's help, they try to plan their own program to recover their well-being statuses.
            (b) They try to be patient with each other and offer any assistance possible in order to achieve this progress.

(c) They recognize and encourage each other's progress toward more realistic behavior.

(d) They discuss together how much they have accomplished and what new steps they need to take.

E. The good work of pupils is recognized before the entire class in ways that enhance their feelings of self-respect.

1. Give praise whenever possible, especially to the discouraged child.
2. Give recognition to democratic behavior and desirable social attitudes.
3. Give praise at moment a meritorious act is performed.
4. Send note home occasionally about good work of pupils.
5. Encourage pupils to assume responsibility for self-direction in all appropriate areas.
6. Give time for pupils to practice skills they have been developing.
7. Display outstanding work, making sure that some work of all children is included.
8. Invite parents to come to school for the purpose of seeing the examples of good work by their children. This is very important in that respect is accorded the parent and the child.
9. High achievement in academic areas is recognized.
   a. An honor roll is kept of students who show greatest improvement over their own achievement records in each subject.
   b. At frequent intervals children have their names called or put on the board because of high achievement in some subject.
   c. Children who make unusually high grades on papers turned in are recognized before the class. However, the recognition is given without reference to any of their previous low grades.
   d. Unusually good papers are put on the bulletin board.
   e. Outstanding work by pupils is combined to form exhibits for the school display case.
   f. Children are encouraged to take examples of their good work home.
   g. Children's work is put on display at fairs and exhibitions.
   h. Each child is allowed to put examples of his best work on display when visitation is observed.
   i. Teacher makes personal, spontaneous comments to children on work as it shows favorable progress.
   j. Children who do outstanding research work on some subject the class is studying are allowed to make reports to the class on their findings.
   k. Children who pursue outside interests with some difficult study and work and who produce something which would be of interest and benefit to the class are allowed to bring it and present it.

10. High achievement in social areas is recognized.
    a. Children are publicly complimented for courteous and thoughtful actions on the playground, in the cafeteria, the auditorium, or the halls.
    b. Children who make introductions, greet visitors, and do other things of this nature in a competent way are congratulated.
    c. Children who take part in a program or perform in some other manner are complimented individually by classmates and teachers. Those who do an unusually good job of this are given opportunities to perform again.
    d. Pupils who serve conscientiously, showing interest and responsibility, on the student council, safety patrol, or in the choir are given recognition.
    e. A pupil who sincerely attempts to do something and then fails is given recognition by the teacher and his classmates for having tried.
11. Courtesy is widely shared among teachers and pupils.
    a. The teacher is courteous to the pupils.
        (1) He greets them whenever meeting them.
        (2) He answers their sincere questions in the best way possible.
        (3) He always speaks to them in a courteous manner.
        (4) He graciously and courteously accepts gifts from them in private.
        (5) He performs little courteous acts for them, such as picking up something they drop while they are working.
        (6) He apologizes after bumping into them or doing them an injustice.
        (7) He considers their invitations to various affairs, and if he cannot go, courteously explains why, if possible.
        (8) He does not hesitate to say "thank you" and "pardon me" when the occasion arises.
        (9) He listens courteously when others speak with permission in the classroom.
    b. The pupils are courteous to the teacher.
        (1) They speak courteously to the teacher and return his greeting.
        (2) They open the door for the teacher at appropriate times.
        (3) They help the teacher move objects in the classroom, carry things from room to room in the school.
        (4) They offer to run errands for the teacher.
        (5) They assist the teacher in the cafeteria.
        (6) They offer to give up their chairs to the teacher when there are not enough to go around.
        (7) They introduce parents and friends to the teacher.
        (8) They ask advice of the teacher about many matters.

(9) They follow advice which the teacher gives them concerning classroom or playground activities.
(10) They listen attentively to the teacher when he speaks.

c. The pupils are courteous to each other.
(1) They call each other by their preferred names.
(2) They do not interrupt each other unnecessarily when carrying on a discussion.
(3) They take turns in participating in all routine events.
(4) They refrain from pushing and shoving in line.
(5) Older pupils learn to tell each other the truth without hurting each other's feelings.
(6) They lend each other small items in emergencies.
(7) They use "thank you" and "pardon me" in talking to each other when the occasion arises.
(8) They perform small, courteous acts for each other, such as opening the door, picking up pencils, etc. as a routine thing.
(9) They assist each other in gathering materials for classroom projects.

OTHER ALTERNATIVE PRACTICES SPECIALIZED TO RESPECT

It is interesting to note several additional alternatives suggested by seminar participants who teach at various school levels. These were thought to have special validity for pupils at these levels. For example, participants who teach in the primary grades suggested the following practices specialized to respect.

1. Very often children are allowed to talk about their best friend (classmate) and tell the class what trait or skill they admire most about him or her. The teacher should be sure that no one is left out. Something positive would be said about each child such as "John can hit the ball best"; "Mary can print very well"; "I like the way Bobby can draw a horse," etc. This leads to self-respect and at the same time each child learns that he contributes something worthwhile to the group.

2. Having a few minutes each morning for the children to participate in what we call our "Sharing Time" will build respect among the children. For example, each morning a few children may tell something that happened to them which they think is interesting; what he saw on the way to school or what he did the afternoon before. This furnishes an opportunity for the practice of communication skill as well as achieving respect for self and sharing this value with others.

3. On Wednesday afternoon before Thanksgiving, a program is given in the school auditorium by the primary department. It is not possible for each child to be in the program. Those that are chosen often need costumes. They may choose someone to help them in dressing for the occasion. In this way the employment of the special talents of each child will enable him to gain respect.

4. During Public School Week, the children may serve as receptionists. Each day a different child is elected by the group. Their duties are to have the parents register and then "show and tell" the guests about the room. They also see that the guests are properly seated. Here the child shows respect to the parents and at the same time is accorded respect by his classmates.

5. The teacher should provide opportunities for recognition of good points of pupil's work. A child may have a poorly drawn picture, but has used good harmonizing colors. The teacher will lead the children to see and tell what they like about the picture. This should enhance the child's feeling of self-respect.

Seminar members who teach at grades four to eight suggested the following as especially pertinent to respect at this level.

1. Allowing children to help others is a great respect builder. Incredible blossoming on the part of the helper often results. Unexpected learning may also result. One teacher was amused and a bit startled when one pupil said to another, "What the teacher means is. . ." and proceeded in a few well-chosen words to make quite clear what teacher had not clarified.

2. If a teacher really respects human personality, it seems to follow that she will expect performance commensurate with individual ability. It is withholding respect from a highly intelligent pupil to accept mediocrity from him. Conversely, it is unfair to set unrealistic goals for pupils of lower capabilities. The effort which each individual is capable of making should be respected.

3. Criticism should be constructive and impersonal. The teacher might build up the idea that the work, not the person, is being appraised. Proofreading for one's own mistakes should increase self-respect through pride in good work.

4. Asking for a child's opinion on *anything* that he feels is important enhances his respect status.

5. Listening to children, really listening, is a very effective technique of according them respect.

6. Be courteous even in disciplinary situations. "Sit down, please" rather than "SIT DOWN"!

7. Allow a child to exploit his strong points. Ronnie reads poorly, but draws beautifully. He shculd be encouraged to contribute to committee efforts through his art, thus enhancing his respect status with the group as well as confidence in himself (self-respect).

8. A child has the right to privacy. His possessions and confidences should be respected.

9. A teacher should be careful to show respect for a child's parents and their opinions.

High school teachers who participated in these seminars made special reference to the following practices.

1. Courtesy is the rule for all occasions and activities; it should be found in all of the pupils' and teacher's words, tones, gestures, and actions.

2. Pupils should plan and arrange classroom displays, regardless of any preconceived mode of decor. The display will be varied, interesting, and attractive to the class, and the pupils doing the work will be granted due respect.

3. Recognition should be given for good work or a good part in a not-so-good whole. This recognition can be accorded by comments, display, or even applause.

4. The teacher will open all channels of communication with his pupils. They should have access to him when necessary.

5. Pupils' questions and interests should be given serious consideration. This practice may open entirely new vistas of learning.

6. Respect for pupil's choice of seating or grouping should be observed when this is possible.

7. If a student is tardy and his excuse seems unreasonable, don't deprive him of respect before the class. Question him about it after class.

8. Show respect for the beliefs of pupils.

9. Encourage good students to help less able students.

10. Never laugh at or ridicule a student or his work.

AFFECTION

Our society encourages the ideal of congenial human relations in ever enlarging circles until the world community is itself included. The term affection refers to the degree of love and friendship of persons in their primary as well as in their secondary relationships. This includes love for and loyalty toward groups, ranging from fraternal organizations of various types to the nation itself. For the person whose behavior is conditioned by hatred and fear of other human beings, life holds little promise for development as a mature personality. Therefore, one of the truly important goals of the classroom is to supplant fear and hatred of people, which can lead to extreme personality damage, with affection and kindly regard as a motivating value goal in interpersonal relationships.

Many thousands of our children have little opportunity to be accorded affection to any great degree except at school, yet it is one of the most important of all the values which contribute to the well-being of the individual. We consequently must direct all possible efforts toward the widespread sharing of affection in the classroom. If we can achieve this goal, not only in our classrooms but in our other school practices, then we can quite confidently assume that one important instrumental goal of our society has been achieved which will contribute to consistent progress toward democracy.

Some of the alternative practices specialized to the wider sharing of affection are listed below. They have been created and suggested by participants in various decision seminar groups who had for their goal the building of the democratic classroom.

III. AFFECTION

A. The teacher makes concerted efforts to establish congenial relationships with his pupils.

1. Teacher consistently treats pupils in a friendly manner.
   a. Teacher smiles and calls each child by name when greeting him in the morning.
   b. Teacher waves and speaks to pupils when he meets them anywhere in the community.
   c. Teacher talks informally with the children when he sees them on the playground or in the halls.
   d. Teacher eats with the class as a group in the cafeteria when the opportunity arises.
   e. Teacher's behavior is consistent. He avoids being very friendly one moment and ignoring the child the next, without cause.
   f. Teacher speaks in a calm and friendly manner when the child requests help.
   g. Teacher shares jokes and tricks with the children occasionally.
   h. Teacher bids children good-bye at the end of the day in a manner that will lead them to look eagerly to their return to the friendly environment of the school the next day.
2. Teacher takes an individual interest in each child.
   a. The teacher talks privately and informally with each child about his current hobby or interest.
   b. Each child is encouraged to chat with the teacher on the playground or during other free times about his latest trip or other activity.
   c. Arrange a once-weekly private "time-to-talk" with teacher. During room library period while class is busy, any child is made welcome to come and sit by teacher's desk and talk about anything he wishes (this is not an academic conference).
   d. Teacher makes a special point of scanning the local newspaper for mention of any pupil and brings the clipping to class for all to see.
   e. Teacher notices and comments on pupils who are doing well in the playground activities and offers those who need it a little extra encouragement.
   f. Teacher attends activities outside the school where a large portion of the class is participating.
   g. Teacher tries to take individual notice of each pupil as often as possible.
   h. Teacher shows concern over children who are away from school because of illness by sending a card and inquiring about their health when they return to school.
   i. Teacher makes a special effort to meet parents of his pupils.
   j. Teacher takes a little extra interest in those children in his class who are particularly shy or affection-starved.

k. Teacher becomes familiar enough with pupils to detect and interpret actions that reflect unusual tensions. Sometimes a child is troubled, but does not seek out the teacher. It then becomes the teacher's responsibility to seek him out and offer help.
l. Teacher lightly teases children who appear to be downhearted when they arrive at school and tries to find out the reasons for their unhappiness.

3. Teacher encourages children to be friendly with him.
a. Teacher graciously accepts the little tokens and gifts which children bring him. He does not make a show over them or encourage the pupils to continue this practice.
b. Teacher is always careful to return a child's friendly greeting.
c. Teacher accepts children's teasing in a friendly way although he does not encourage it.
d. Teacher is especially cordial to parents when the child introduces them on his own initiative.
e. Teacher writes "thank-you" notes for Christmas presents or birthday gifts.
f. Teacher commends children who are friendly to classmates and to other teachers.

B. Hostilities which arise are overcome by deliberate efforts to restore friendly attitudes.

1. Teacher tries to overcome hostilities by attitude and action.
a. Teacher does not place children in a position where they will openly have to oppose each other.
b. Teacher recognizes hostilities which arise and does not try to suppress them by ignoring them but rather tries to deal realistically with them. For example, to the angry child the teacher may ask "Johnny, what happened to your pretty smile?' This may be followed with a private conference with Johnny where he is encouraged to tell his side of the story, thus relieving some of his tension.
c. Teacher makes light of embarrassing situations and jokes about them to relieve tension when this is desirable.
d. Teacher separates the participants in hostile acts from each other until they can gain their equilibrium.
e. Teacher promotes resumption of friendly relations between participants as the "natural" thing to do but does not try to force them.
f. If possible, children who have had a misunderstanding are put together in a situation where there is no inherent tension and where it will be easy for friendly relations to be resumed.

2. Children try to overcome hostilities among their classmates.
a. Children tend to discourage hostile actions by their friendly attitudes towards all competing participants.

b. Children talk to each participant in an effort to get him to reconsider the unreality of his aggressive behavior.
c. Pupils actually separate classmates who are about to get into an action which might cause them to harm each other.
d. Following disagreements, children offer each other opportunities to get together again under favorable circumstances.
e. Pupils make an attempt to understand the causes of some of the hostile acts of their classmates and often allow their classmates to get tensions out of their systems by allowing them to express feelings orally without taking offense.
f. Children show respect for classmates who actively try to avoid conflicts with others.
g. Children's attitudes are definitely favorable to those classmates who do not hold grudges but who attempt to be friends again after an argument.

C. Definite efforts are made to reduce adverse and unnecessary criticism of individuals and groups in the class.

1. Criticism of individuals should be constructive.
   a. Children do not criticize just by saying that a conclusion is wrong. They give reasons why they disagree with it.
   b. Children offer suggestions on how a classmate can perform more effectively when this advice is requested.
   c. Children do not make it a practice to offer criticism unless it is requested.
   d. Even when criticism is requested, negative criticisms are not offered unless there is some suggestion as to how the condition or conditions could be improved.
   e. Teacher does not severely criticize any child's behavior before the class.
   f. On some occasions all children are given an opportunity to make remarks about the others' performances so that all will get accustomed to accepting suggestions without tension and resentment.
2. Criticism of groups is always made in an effort to improve the product of the group.
   a. Criticism of groups is offered in a helpful spirit.
   b. Minority groups in the class are not criticized as such.
   c. Criticism is given and received in a friendly spirit.
   d. When criticism is offered to a group, positive comments should be given first and if possible stated again after the criticisms are offered.
   e. Attention is focused always on the positive contributions a group has to make.
   f. An informal agreement is made among the children and teacher to try to find enough good points about the work of pupils to match or exceed the bad points they see.

g. Disapproval of undemocratic practices is shown by absence of smile. Frequently, teacher can simply praise the child who is acting in ways opposite to the offender, thus pointing up the offense. Example: "Johnny, I *like* the way you stand in line—so tall and straight, with your hands to yourself."

D. Any denial or affection is directed only against conduct which is incompatible with democratic goals.

1. The overt denial of affection is practiced only in serious cases of antisocial conduct and then only on a temporary bases.
   a. Children who do not follow practices of fair play on the playground are asked to play alone for awhile.
   b. Children who disturb their neighbors in the classroom are asked to sit by themselves.
   c. Children who refuse to cooperate on committees are temporarily not chosen for committees.
   d. Children who try to do bodily injury to other children are asked to remain by themselves for awhile.
   e. Children who consistently rebel against the actions of their classmates or their teacher are not included in some of the projects which are planned, and are given realistic reasons why this action has been taken.
   f. Children who have demonstrated antisocial behavior may be temporarily excluded from the elected honors and offices by group.
2. Children and teacher restore the affection status of a child who has committed an antisocial act when that child again practices conduct which recognizes the rights of others.
   a. Children who are taken from playground activities temporarily because of their conduct are given another chance to share in the activities of the group as soon as they express the desire to do so.
   b. When children who have been isolated because of disturbance in the classroom calm down, they are allowed to return to their places, and again take part in the activities of the group.
   c. Committee work of a pleasant nature is assigned children who have been barred from it, when they feel that they are ready to make a contribution and ask to be placed on a committee again.
   d. After an appropriate length of time, the teacher encourages children to resume friendly advances toward classmates who have been temporarily withdrawn from the activities of the group for disciplinary reasons.
   e. Efforts are made to bring children who consistently rebel into congenial relationship with the class.
      (1) Specific classmates take it upon themselves to encourage these children to join in projects.

(2) Opportunities are offered to these children to take part in pleasant tasks for the benefit of the classroom.

(3) The special talents of these children are sought out, recognized, and encouraged.

f. When children who have acted in antisocial ways again adjust themselves to acting in an acceptable manner, they are casually included in all honors and offices of the class, as well as projects. No publicity or big show is attached to this "returning to the fold" of these children.

E. The teacher undertakes to accord recognition and respect to students who try to establish and maintain congenial relations within the classroom.

1. Teacher makes casual comments which call attention in an inconspicuous way to the congenial actions of children.
   a. "How happy Joe looks this morning."
   b. "Suzie looks very bright and cheerful on this rainy morning."
   c. "I know this is going to be a nice day by the way Bill said that cheerful, 'good morning.'"
   d. "Sally, that was nice of you to help Jane pick up her books."
   e. "Dan, you're really a good sport for letting Mike have your turn at bat."
   f. "Jim and Bob work together so quietly that I hardly realized they were there."
2. Teacher offers recognition for friendly actions which are outstanding or are shared by a group.
   a. Children who have worked quietly, quickly, and happily on a project are asked to stand for recognition.
   b. The teacher tells the child privately how pleased he is with the child's efforts.
   c. Teacher personally congratulates children who, at inconvenience to themselves, offer assistance to a classmate.
   d. Teacher, by his example, causes children to be conscious of congenial behavior and to offer recognition for such.
   e. Teacher reports efforts of child to promote friendly relations in classroom to parents. Too frequently parents are asked to visit the school only when child's conduct is not up to par.

Primary grade teachers who participated in seminar groups offered the following alternatives in the affection category which they decided were of special significance to children at these grade levels.

1. A pat on the back for a good piece of work; a word of comfort to the child who may have been hurt mentally or physically, may mean more to him than anything else because he believes that someone cares about him.

2. Even six-year olds have problems which are big to them. If the teacher will only take time to listen to them and offer suggestions, it will lighten their

burdens. An example of this, "Jane is mad at me because I know how to jump the rope and she doesn't." Here the teacher asks the child to show Jane how she learned.

3. The above examples are primary relationships. In the first grade we also should encourage the development of secondary relations. An example of this is learning and repeating the Pledge of Allegiance to the flag and the singing of "America."

4. The child must be helped to know and like other children. Occasionally the teacher should provide an opportunity for a child to work with someone he seems to dislike. This method may result in the two becoming good friends. Assign them together on special work or running errands; or permit them to leave the regular group and make something that will add to the class project. A good way of choosing partners when there are isolates in the class is to cut pictures from two identical picture books, paste them on cards and pass them out indiscriminately. Pupils are then asked to find their partners by matching the pictures. Words or numbers can be used the same way.

Elementary grade teachers suggested the following practices in this category.

1. A child in the group may be assigned to a new pupil for a few days to help him in friendly ways to learn the "ropes" and to give the newcomer a feeling of security.

2. Pupils may be assigned to welcome visitors and offer chairs.

3. The teacher should be on the alert for opportunities to accord affection to children. Listening to them, laughing at their jokes, complimenting new clothes or hair cuts, sympathizing with real or imaginary aches or pains can help a child feel loved.

4. The teacher should show that she values any thoughtfulness or consideration shown her. Tangible offerings such as sticky apples, mashed layer cake, or slightly crumpled flowers should evoke a gracious response. One teacher keeps a special spot on the blackboard for writing little personal notes, sometimes in colored chalk: "Thank you, Carol, for the lovely flowers." "Thanks to Someone whose father came early this morning and set up an aquarium for us." A little boy may slip up later, grinning, and whisper that he is Someone. The teacher is properly surprised.

The following practices were suggested as particularly appropriate with high school pupils by seminar participants who teach at this level.

1. The teacher greets the pupil cordially and calls him by his name as soon as he can. This makes the pupil aware of the teacher's concern for him as an individual.

2. The pupil should be made welcome in the classroom. The classroom climate, created by teacher and pupils, should be such that each pupil finds it attractive and acceptable to him as a member of the group.

3. The teacher must be concerned with each pupil's interests and show him that other pupils recognize him as one of them and that they wish him to contribute to the activities of the group.

4. If the classroom is such that the pupil feels that it is his home-away-from-home," the pupil will cherish it. Each individual knows that such a classroom climate can be established only through pupils' and teacher's cooperative activities in an atmosphere of friendship and freedom.

5. Teachers discuss pupil's personal problems privately if asked to do so.

WELL-BEING

The general enhancement of well-being (mental and physical health) is especially important in a free society which depends for its growth and maintenance upon a continuing process of creative and productive activity. The validity of this statement becomes obvious when we recall that a lowered status of well-being which usually reflects serious value deprivation with its accompanying fear and tension offers the greatest block to creative and productive activity. Therefore, one instrumental goal of education that is of great relative importance is the achievement and maintenance of mental and physical health among school pupils.

The scientist teacher, who will have become quite familiar with the most important factors in the dynamics of personality, will be able to trace the consequences for the individual of value deprivations. The discussion in Chapter 7 indicates that this inevitable consequence is tension which is reflected both in psychic and bodily symptoms that indicate a low status of well-being. The scientist teacher therefore, will realize that his most important duty as an appointed officer of a free society is to direct his efforts toward the creation of a classroom environment which is most conducive to the maximization of human values. This provides a necessary foundation for the achievement of mental and physical health. Following is a list of practices and strategies specialized to the well-being category that evolved from the deliberations of decision seminars.

IV. WELL BEING
- A. Safeguards of the physical health of pupils are provided by the teacher and by the school.
  1. The classroom is made as conducive to good health as possible.
     - a. Proper ventilation and lighting are provided at all times.
     - b. Desks and other equipment are of the proper size and therefore contribute to normal posture (exaggerated posture is uncomfortable and unhealthful).
     - c. Proper heating is provided throughout the year. Care is taken that the classroom does not become too hot and stuffy.
     - d. Fire drills are a part of the school program.
  2. The playground is arranged in such manner as to insure maximum safety.
     - a. If possible, the playground is laid out away from busy streets.

b. The playground is separated from any streets by a fence, to discourage the headlong pursuit of balls into the street by children.
c. The playground is large enough to provide separate areas for the younger and the older children.
d. Baseball diamonds and other regulation areas are situated so that children playing on other parts of the playground are not likely to be hit by stray balls.

3. Pupils are given periodic and special care throughout their elementary school years by the school health officers.
   a. Children are checked regularly for adequate hearing.
   b. Children are given vision tests, and their parents are informed if there is need for correction.
   c. Children receive dental checkups regularly and are notified of any cavities.
   d. Children are regularly checked for growth in height and weight, and the causes of any deficiencies are investigated.
   e. Children receive special emergency care when they are injured or become ill while at school.
   f. Children receive all of these medical services free and also receive all corrective assistance, such as glasses and hearing aids free if their parents cannot afford it.
4. Pupils are given instruction which will tend to safeguard their physical health.
   a. Children learn the proper care of their teeth.
   b. Children learn ways of conserving their eyes and ears.
   c. Children learn something of the common diseases caused by germs and viruses and how to combat them.
   d. Children learn simple health precautions.
      (1) They learn to use handkerchiefs and turn their heads when sneezing.
      (2) They learn to avoid close contacts with other children when they or other children have colds or other symptoms of contagious diseases.
      (3) They learn to refrain from exercising or getting hot when they have a cold.
      (4) They learn to wash their hands before eating.
      (5) They learn to avoid using cups or towels of other persons.
      (6) Specific instruction is offered in safety habits and practice.

B. The teacher does all in his power to contribute to the mental health of pupils. This is the value that depends greatly upon the degree of access pupils have to the other values. Efforts made to enhance pupil status in respect and affection will be found to contribute effectively to the achievement of high status of well-being.

1. Teacher undertakes to accord values to every child in the classroom. Systematic attention by the teacher to the suggested practices specific to each of the value categories will enable her more effectively to perform this function.
2. Pupils' assistance in the promotion of these efforts is solicited.
   a. Pupils receive explanations appropriate to their maturity level on the things that affect mental health and how they influence them.
      (1) Children are made acquainted with the value categories in a simple way.
      (2) Children are taught that well-being status is lowered when values are withheld. Illustrations appropriate to the maturity level of children are used to demonstrate this effect.
   b. Pupils are given opportunities to appraise the value statuses of themselves and their classmates.
      (1) Children identify the values which they think they are sharing adequately with others.
      (2) Children identify values which they think their classmates are sharing adequately with others.
      (3) Children consider which value deprivations they have suffered.
      (4) Children consider which value deprivations their classmates have suffered.
   c. Pupils take definite steps to share values with classmates. Special attention is given to the enhancement of specific values of pupils who give evidence of needing this help.
      (1) When pupils discover that a classmate is suffering from a lack of well-being because of respect deprivation, they attempt to accord him respect by choosing him first for a team, by complimenting an unusual piece of work that he does, or by asking his opinion on various matters.
      (2) If a classmate seems to lack well-being because of economic reasons, children are careful to refrain from calling attention to his state of poverty and in little unobtrusive ways they see that he always has a pencil and paper or a choice bite of food at lunch.
      (3) When a classmate is in need of affection, children provide it by inviting that classmate to sit by them in the cafeteria, to play with them during recess, or to walk home with them.
      (4) If a child suffers from a lack of skill in an area where this lack of skill is a detriment to well-being, classmates make an effort to help him gain this skill by giving him a chance to practice it outside of school and by unobtrusively coaching him, if he desires it, while in school.

(5) If a child lacks well-being because of confusion over a conflict of standards between his home and school, classmates are understanding and accord him affection and respect.

(6) When deprivation of enlightenment is the cause of a low well-being status of a child, classmates share information and give assistance in locating data for further enlightenment.

(7) If a need for greater share in making decisions seems to be the cause of a classmate's loss of well-being, children encourage him to take a more active part in class discussions and research. They also elect him to committees in which he is required to participate in making decisions.

(8) When a child's poor health or physical handicap cause him to feel rejected, classmates attempt to help him gain self-confidence by guiding him to positions where he can make contributions to the class for which he will be respected.

C. Teacher recognizes the serious problem of the quiet, obedient pupil who tends to be unusually submissive and withdrawn. Realistic measures are taken with such pupils.

1. Teacher attempts to identify children who are too submissive.
   a. He watches for the children who never talk to their neighbors in class, and systematically brings them into active discussion of matters in which he finds they are interested.
   b. He is alert to those who seldom answer a question in class or take part in class discussions and leads them into active participation.
   c. He is alert to children who withdraw themselves from activities on the playground or from contacts with their classmates, and helps them to overcome these withdrawal practices.
2. Teacher creates measures designed to bring children out of their quiet, withdrawn ways.
   a. The shy child is given a small, but important, task to perform regularly.
   b. The child is given opportunities to take part in class discussions for which he is well prepared.
   c. The child is given more work of a pleasant nature which draws him into contact with other children.
   d. The child is given respect for his worthwhile contributions to the classroom.
   e. Teacher sees through the pretense of shyness used by some children as a way of getting attention, and tries to involve the child in activities where he can more realistically achieve respect and thus restore his well-being.

D. Teacher recognizes other symptoms of tension due to value deprivations that inhibit the creativity of pupils and takes effective measures to reduce or relieve those tensions by restoring their statuses in these values.

1. Teacher recognizes attention-getting mechanisms as symptoms of tension and undertakes to provide opportunities for these children to achieve respect in realistic ways.
    a. Teacher is alert to children who made abnormal efforts to excel and to gain respect through approval, admiration, and praise. He looks for goal deprivations which led to this unrealistic behavior and tries to provide opportunities for these children to achieve realistic goals which will enhance their respect statuses.
    b. Teacher is alert to children who try to become the teacher's pet through doing exactly as they are told and provides opportunities for these children to engage in more creative activities with other children.
    c. Teacher observes children who are noisy, restless, and constantly talking out of turn as evidence of value deprivations which can be restored by appropriate measures.
    d. Teacher assists children who are untidy, clumsy and helpless to enhance their status of self-respect by providing opportunities for them to participate in important classroom activities.
    e. Teacher encourages children who have little or no confidence in their own abilities by assigning them jobs they can do.
2. Teacher recognizes unusual efforts to secure power as a symptom of tension and refuses to be drawn into the power struggle.
    a. Teacher sees in children who refuse to follow directions in any of their school work evidence of value deprivations and takes realistic measures to restore status in the values deprived.
    b. Teacher observes children who do not respect order and discipline and defy authority, as evidence of personality damage requiring careful observation and study.
    c. Teacher attempts to develop an understanding attitude, free of inferiority feelings and concern for his personal prestige.
    d. Teacher encourages children who seek power to help other children and offer them protection. Teacher shows such children that he is their friend and attempts to make them feel that it is in their power to help him.
3. Teacher recognizes revenge seeking as a symptom of tension and takes measures to reduce the tension.
    a. Teacher is alert to children who show signs of violence and brutality, or are sullen and defiant, and make continuous efforts to convince these children that they are liked and

respected. These children are likely exhibiting symptoms of displaced hostility and will probably require much patience in leading them toward realistic behavior. The teacher avoids lining the class up on his side in opposition to these children except when such actions will lead the child realistically to see that he has acted undemocratically.

b. Teacher privately asks the cooperation of other children in the room in taking a special interest in the revengeful child, drawing him into the group, showing him respect and affection.

4. Teacher recognizes displays of inadequacy as symptoms of tension and takes measures to alleviate this condition.
   a. Teacher watches for children who have no belief in their own ability to accomplish anything and leads them to undertake important assignments.
   b. Teacher helps children who are having difficulty and are becoming discouraged in academic areas.
   c. Teacher is alert to children who display inability to draw or exhibit lack of musical talent. He refrains from giving more poor grades, more corrections and criticisms of these children. He convinces these children of his friendship and interest, and takes notice of and comments on each improvement made, no matter how small.
   d. Teacher works slowly convincing these children that their belief in their inability is unfounded.

E. Teachers are provided with appropriate techniques which introduce them to the objective appraisal of their own statuses with reference to such values as respect, affection, well-being, economic security, and the other values. Practice in the use of such tools of analysis is expected to increase the teacher's self-knowledge—so important in his own avoidance of neurotic behavior. Increasing the teacher's sophistication in this area can be expected to increase the effectiveness with which he can contribute to the goal of maximizing human values among his pupils.

1. Teachers are provided with the framework of the social process, value categories, indices of values, specific definitions, value-oriented rationale and the component operations of problem solving to use in appraising their own value statuses and in solving other problems and achieving other important goals.[2]
   a. Teachers discuss these tools of analysis in meetings.
   b. Teachers practice these skills in groups.
   c. Teachers appraise important events in their own lives by use of the tools.

---

[2]See *Personality in Social Process,* Arnspiger, V. Clyde, et al., Wm. C. Brown Publishing Company, Dubuque, Iowa, 1969, Chapter 4.

d. Teachers study their interactions with children and each other by the use of these tools.[3]

e. Teachers begin to look for indices of values being given or withheld in every situation involving two or more persons.

2. Teachers make plans to improve their own value statuses and face up to them realistically as problems to be solved.

a. Teachers identify and appraise the effects of their own value deprivations (actual or threatened).

b. Teachers outline specific plans for self-improvement designed to achieve these value goals. They carry out these plans in a systematic manner.

Primary grade teachers who participated in the seminars decided that the following suggestions were especially pertinent to the production and sharing of well-being at these levels.

1. There is need in the first grade for acquainting the children with safety rules, both in the home and elsewhere. The doll house of one of the children may be used in safety training. It may be placed on a table in front of the chalkboard, and, using lengths of narrow red ribbon, the pupils may indicate where and what kinds of accidents occur most frequently in the home. Pupils then may make a poster list of "do's and don'ts" to prevent these accidents.

2. The children may actually construct safety rules in the community by building a toy village. This is done by using a cardboard layout with painted streets; stop signs, and traffic lights painted red, yellow, and green; buildings made of various size boxes and labeled such as post office, school, etc. Through group discussion, safety rules are formulated and recorded on the experience charts. While this practice is specialized to well-being, it may be used to promote creative and productive effort which could be classified under the skill category. It would involve all five of the major skills.

3. Provide opportunities for activities that increase enlightenment with respect to physical health. Living things in the classroom can be used to generate student interest and to motivate learning. It is suggested, therefore, that the teacher use living plants and animals, which require food, water, air, and other favorable environmental conditions. This leads the children to a better understanding of their own daily health needs. Health posters, notebooks and units on health may be made by pupils to create interest in physical health.

4. Health clubs may be formed. Reports, dramatizations, and games may be utilized in achieving goals of health clubs. Parents may be requested to cooperate with health rules at home.

5. In every child there are undiscovered aptitudes. The teacher can keep a record with the childrens' names and the one or more activities in which each child is successful. Participation in these activities, of course, leads children to an

[3] *Ibid.*, Chapter 4.

enhanced status of well-being. Sometimes teachers think they are aware of each student's talents but if he writes these out on paper he may be surprised to find that he really does not know what a particular student does best. Writing it down will lead him to search for this characteristic capacity.

Elementary grade teacher-participants offered the following list which they decided were valid for the sharing of well-being at grade levels four to eight.

1. The statement by the child that he is sick should be taken seriously. He may not be seriously ill physically, but this way of seeking relief indicates a low status of well-being.

2. Children should be given practice in applying that they have learned about health practices in their daily living. One might ask pupils to keep a time log for a week or so. Use these figures to record hours slept. Raise such questions as "Can one stay up to see the late, late show and get the proper amount of sleep?"

3. During a study of nutrition, plan and bring sack lunches to share in the room. This often provides an enjoyable experience.

4. Role playing is a valuable technique not only for its therapeutic effect but also for the insight it may give the teacher into the conditions favorable to well-being. A language arts class offers many opportunities for using this procedure.

5. Most children like for the teacher to read to them. If the teacher will occasionally gather a group about her, perhaps at the free-reading center, and read to them, the experience will be rewarding. A sense of sharing which takes place in such a situation contributes to well-being.

6. A calm teacher and a well-planned but flexible learning situation are necessary to the well-being of the students.

7. Music therapy in such simple form as playing soothing music at low volume can have a magical effect on well-being.

8. Search for opportunities to let under-achievers do something worthwhile. See that their efforts are recognized and appreciated.

9. Give every child a responsibility. A job to do helps develop a feeling of being respected and wanted. This enhances well-being. In addition, this practice also promotes a high status of rectitude (responsibility for personal behavior).

10. Make an opportunity early in the year to let each child know you like and respect him.

11. Make friends with the child's parents if at all possible. A feeling of hostility between parents and teacher is extremely deprivational to all persons involved and can seriously impair the child's well-being.

12. Linger a bit after school instead of rushing off or shooing the children out. Fifteen minutes or so after school, when everyone is free from the demands of the day, may prove a most important period which the teacher can use in promoting congenial relations with his pupils with consequent well-being effects.

13. Encourage strenuous physical activity as a release for pent-up emotions in appropriate cases.

14. Encourage a balanced "diet" of work and play.

15. During a study of nutrition, a meaningful experience might be to try a simple breakfast experiment. Many children come to school without breakfast. Let volunteers, whose parents consent, set up two groups. One group will eat an inadequate breakfast; the other group, one that is nutritionally sound for a definite period, perhaps a week, and record carefully how each group feels, acts, and reacts. Have the groups change practices, still recording the results. After the results have been organized and discussed, the groups may present their findings and try to reach conclusions.

High school teacher participants offered the following list which they decided were essential to the promotion and maintenance of well-being at these levels.

1. The teacher must ascertain the physical and emotional status of each pupil, insofar as he is able. He should also recognize that this status is not static, but ever-changing, and that it requires constant and consistent attention.

2. Pupils should be encouraged to make every effort to achieve physical improvement, and these efforts should be acknowledged.

3. The teacher, though not a physician, may release pupils from tensions which hinder their progress toward maturity by providing opportunities for these pupils to restore their status in values of which they have been deprived. When the mental health of a child is good, his physical health will likely be improved.

4. Teachers should show pupils that "learning can be enjoyable.' This can be done through games, programs, dramatizations, and other interesting activities. When pupils realize this truth their well-being is enhanced.

5. The teacher should strive to achieve amicable relationships between pupils, teachers, administrators, and parents. These relationships contribute to the goal of mental and physical health.

6. Teachers and pupils must do all they can to make the classroom physically attractive and suited to individual and group needs. The classroom should not be a static but a moving and developing environment in which the well-being of pupils is more important than an artistically designed setting of an "institution."

CHAPTER 3

•

Creating Classroom Practices — Continued (Skill, Enlightenment, Wealth, Rectitude)

SKILL

The provision by the school of an environment which offers many opportunities for pupils to achieve their full potentials, demands that systematic attention be given to the development of latent talents in a number of categories. These include motor skills, skills of thinking, communication skills, social skills and aesthetic skills. High status in these skills is demanded of those who would participate as mature citizens in a free society. Specific attention has been directed to the skills of communication. In addition to these the teacher must be alert to the creation of practices and strategies designed to discover their latent talents among pupils and to promote the development, also, of important motor skills, social skills and aesthetic skills.

The teacher seminars previously described yielded the following list of practices in the specified value categories.

I. SKILL

A. All pupils are encouraged to develop their own talents and skills to the limits of their capacities.

1. Motor skills.

a. Children are encouraged to try various playground activities such as skipping, jumping, running, and other forms of basic exercise.

(1) An amount of class time is devoted to discussing the enjoyment gained from these activities.

(2) Children tell about times they have found these particular skills useful, such as jumping across a ditch, running to catch up with friends, and so on.

(3) Children are allowed to take a few minutes before recess period to choose sides, appoint leaders, and so on.

(4) Teacher takes some part in the activity by throwing the rope for jumping or being the starter for races.

(5) Children who do not normally take part are encouraged personally by the teacher and by other classmates to do so.

(6) Children who are particularly good at skipping, jumping, running, etc. are asked to train others who are not so proficient in these skills.

(7) Children are urged to judge themselves on progress against their own individual standards, rather than against each other.

(8) Meets are held in which children may participate in various simple events with recognition being given to those who have most improved their own records.

b. Equipment, time and instruction are made available for older children to play organized team sports.

(1) If boys and girls do not each have their own sets of equipment, some arrangements are made to share.

(2) Special instruction is given in some of the basic skills needed for each sport.

(3) Children are allowed to spend enough time on each sport so as to develop some degree of skill.

(4) They are encouraged to move on and try new skills before their interest in the old ones has completely dissipated.

(5) New teams are chosen regularly so that all may have an opportunity to experience being teammates with the others.

(6) Children are encouraged to practice skills at times other than in school.

c. The development of the formal skills of writing sentences and drawing are encouraged in the classroom.

(1) Specific instruction is given in writing in each class.

(2) Incidental instruction is given whenever the opportunity presents itself to write for special purposes such as in the preparation of plans for classroom work.

(3) Children write invitations to other classes or to special guests to visit their classroom.

(4) Children write announcements which are placed on the bulletin board.

(5) Children write notes which are carried home to parents.

(6) Children are encouraged to practice writing skills and have their work evaluated by the teacher during any free period.

(7) Opportunity is given in class for children to draw pictures of things that interest them.

(8) All children are shown how to draw simple figures and designs for their own enjoyment.

(9) Children who show special talent in drawing are encouraged to make posters and charts for classroom use.

(10) Children are allowed to draw illustrations for class projects.
(11) Children draw picture stories of class excursions.
(12) Opportunity is given for the class to work together on murals and other joint projects.
(13) Children design and build exhibits and displays for the entire school.
(14) Children illustrate their own special assignments.

d. Children are given opportunities to explore potential skills in music.
(1) All children are encouraged to sing for their own enjoyment.
(2) Children take turns teaching songs and singing games to the other members of the class.
(3) Children are encouraged to sing alone, with groups, and in harmony.
(4) Those who have special talents in singing are encouraged to find a group with which they can practice and sing regularly.
(5) Children plan and practice musical numbers to present to their class or other classes.
(6) Those who have special talent take the lead in planning musical entertainment for classroom parties or programs.
(7) Children are encouraged to look for and suggest appropriate music for special occasions.
(8) Children are encouraged to write their own songs and musical numbers.
(9) Children who show no special talent in music are not told to quit singing or playing, but are led to take this only as a hobby and to concentrate more on something at which they show more talent.

e. Children are introduced to tools and machines used in everyday life.
(1) Common tools are provided and used in the classroom.
(a) Children use hammers, saws, and nails in classroom projects.
(b) Screwdrivers, pliers, and wrenches are used to make simple repairs in the classroom.
(2) Professional and occupational tools are introduced in the classroom.
(a) Children interview doctor, dentist, or nurse about their tools and the importance of being skilled in using them.
(b) Children make trips to see garagemen, farmers, or construction workers using their tools.

(3) Energy-saving equipment is studied.
   (a) Children learn how to operate gas and electric stoves safely.
   (b) Children use can opener and similar utensils in class projects.
   (c) Children study other household appliances.
   (d) Children type and run the mimeograph machine.
(4) Pupils learn about mechanical tools of communication.
   (a) Children use the telephone.
   (b) They use small telegraph sets.
   (c) They speak over the school amplifying system.
   (d) They present programs on local radio and television stations.

f. Teacher attempts to recognize other potential talents among children and to give personal help and encouragement to the child who needs it.
(1) A kind word at the right time may wipe away much discouragement.
(2) Teacher finds opportunity to display any worthwhile motor skill exhibited by any child, such as woodcarving, basket weaving, pottery making, and the like.

2. Thinking skills.
a. Children learn methods of solving problems.
(1) Children learn to state problems and to justify trying to solve them by answering the question–will solving this problem help me or other people achieve any of the values? (Here the teacher takes the first step in teaching children to think systematically in solving problems. He uses verbal equivalents which are appropriate to the maturity levels of his pupils in introducing them to goal thinking and the other component operations of problem solving which follow.)
(2) Children search for accurate information relative to what has happened in the past which has to do with their problems (trend thinking).
(3) Children gather information about what is happening at the present time which is pertinent to their problems (condition thinking).
(4) Children make estimates or predict what is likely to happen in the future with reference to their problems unless they "do something about solving it" (projective thinking).
(5) Children think about and suggest ways of solving their problems, making a complete list of all the solutions suggested by each child. (This is the first step in alternative thinking and provides the teacher with a

priceless opportunity to lead his pupils into the exciting experience of creative thinking about how their problems may be solved, how their goals may be reached.)

(6) Children select which of the solutions suggested *seem* to be the most promising for solving their problems and try them out in order to determine which *are most effective* in reaching their goal. If none of the alternative solutions suggested proves to be effective in solving their problems, the pupils create and appraise other possible ways to achieve their goal. (This is the final step in alternative thinking and if they have succeeded in solving their problems, they have made most important and significant use of their minds.) The foregoing set of practices in problem solving represents what is probably the most seriously neglected responsibility of educational institutions at all levels of instruction from the primary grades to the graduate school. Much lip service is given to the goal of teaching pupils to think but there has been no clear record of any school, college, or university that has undertaken to achieve this objective on an institution-wide scale.

b. Children are given many opportunities to practice the use of the component operations in solving problems of the classroom and playground.

(1) Problems which affect the class as a group are studied.

(a) Problems arising in the course of studying hygiene, or any of the other natural sciences, history or citizenship courses.

(b) Problems which are related to activities on the playground are studied by the class.

(c) Problems affecting practices and procedures in the classroom are considered.

(d) Problems affecting the use of all-school areas are discussed by the class, and ways in which the class can help solve the problems are proposed and studied.

(e) Many members of the class may have problems outside of school, the solutions of which can be approached systematically by the class using the technique described above.

(2) Pupils are encouraged to solve their own individual problems.

(a) Teacher does not tell children what to do each time they come to a roadblock.

(b) Teacher offers suggestions as a guide to solutions rather than as solutions to children who are having difficulty on subject matter assignments.

(c) Pupils are encouraged to undertake the systematic solution of their own personal problems which they face on the playground, at home, or elsewhere. Most of these problems will involve the breakdown of interpersonal relations. The teacher may suggest a simplified categorical framework such as the one given in Arnspiger, et al.[1]

c. Situations are provided which lead to extensive practice in developing the skills of handling interpersonal relationships.

(1) Opportunities are given for role-playing.

(a) Teacher presents situations and asks for volunteers to play the roles.

(b) Children are also allowed to suggest situations to be acted out.

(2) Classroom situations are developed to give practice in handling interpersonal relationships.

(a) Teacher suggests that several children work together on a project which gives them a chance to experience a rewarding interpersonal relationship.

(b) Better adjusted children are casually and privately asked to choose some of the more withdrawn ones for partners in various activities.

(c) Each child in the classroom is given an opportunity to work in a group with each other child during the term.

(3) The playground is used as a field for practicing the effective management of interpersonal relationships.

(a) Teacher observes children at play to determine those needing therapeutic help.

(b) Children of varying academic achievement levels are put together in games so that they may have an opportunity to associate with each other on more nearly equal terms.

(4) Home-centered situations are provided for children.

(a) Domestic scenes are acted out in connection with a classroom play in the intermediate grades.

(b) Children assume family roles for the purpose of play activities.

3. Communication skills.

The teacher may introduce the "formula" of communication in simple terms which include the following categories; the communicator, the message, the audience, and the effect. He explains the meaning of each of these terms and

---

[1] The teacher may wish to refer to the more complete framework of analysis used in the study of interpersonal conflicts as given in *Personality in Social Process,* Arnspiger, V. Clyde, et al., Wm. C. Brown Publishing Company, Dubuque, Iowa, 1969, Chapter 9.

explains to pupils how these categories are used in preparing to make a talk or to write. The teacher may give the class the following framework of analysis and point out some of the questions which should be asked under each of the categories in preparing to create a message which pupils are to present orally or in writing.

I.	II.	III.	IV.
My audience	The effect I want my message to have on my audience	As communicator, am I sufficiently prepared to speak or to write to my audience	My message

Under Category I, the pupils ask just who is my audience, whom do I want to receive my message? In order to prepare myself to create a good message I must not only know who my audience is, I must know all I can about them. What they are interested in learning, what they enjoy doing when they are not working? Are they adults or children? What age levels? (The teacher should ask many more questions which would reflect the probable value preferences of the children's audiences.)

Under Category II, questions to be asked may include: Do I wish to entertain my audience? Do I wish to enlighten them in some way? Do I wish to lead my audience to support a movement, issue, or policy that I believe in, such as better playgrounds or public swimming pools for the community? Will the effect I hope my message will have on my audience lead to the wide sharing of one or more values among my fellow citizens or to less sharing of these values? If the answer to this question is positive, the goal can be said to be democratic and the teacher can lead the child to see that in stating his goal (the effect upon his audience he hopes to create with his message) and in justifying it in terms of democratic ideals, he has performed the first important step in creative writing for a purpose. At this point, it may be well to call the teacher's attention to the great amount of writing without clear purpose that goes on in the educational system from the primary grades to the graduate school. Many sophisticated teachers of English refer to such purposeless instruction as "teaching pupils to write writing."

The teacher can easily lead pupils to see the close relationship between the skills of thinking and the skills of communication. In reality, any pupil who would hope to become an effective and responsible communicator must state and justify the effect upon his audience he hopes his message will have, as a problem to be solved (goal thinking) and the message he is to design and write to produce this effect, as the creation of alternative ways of solving the problem, and the selection of those he decides will be most effective in reaching the goal he stated before he began the construction of his message as the appraisal of alternatives (alternative thinking).

Again under Category II, the pupil may employ the other component operations (or intellectual tasks) of problem solving; trend, condition and projective thinking, when he considers the past experiences of his audience, their present goals and actions and their probable behavior in the future if he does not construct the message which he hopes will produce the effect he desires (his goal).

Under Category III, the pupil must assume responsibility for studying himself as a communicator. Here he may ask such questions as: What is my role in preparing this message? Am I a friend and supporter of my audience, or do I oppose on moral grounds many of the things they believe or think? Am I a relative? Am I a pupil who needs the support of my audience? Am I a prospective employee of my audience? Do I feel that I am capable of preparing the message for my audience? How do I proceed to increase my competence for doing this job? Whom shall I consult in getting much of the information I need to write this message? What books shall I read? Am I acting and thinking democratically in trying to produce the effect I want upon my audience or am I acting selfishly and undemocratically in trying to reach this goal even though I deny others (without merit) of some of the things they need or want (values)?

Under Category IV, some of the questions the pupil may ask in preparing to create his message will include: In preparing my message are my purposes clear? Just what do I want to say to my audience? What shall I refer to in my message which will lead my audience to be sympathetic with me. (What symbols shall I use such as references to the good things the audience has done or to things they believe in and want.) Am I justified in promising my audience that they will profit by doing what I want them to do in terms of more money to spend, better health, more understanding, more congenial relations with other people, higher moral standards, more respect from their fellowmen or what? Am I justified in warning my audience that they are likely to lose these things if they ignore my message? In either case, if the answer is negative, then if I make these promises I am acting immorally in violating the standards of rectitude which are established for democratic citizens.

Is what I say in my message *true* and have I presented both sides of the issue in my message? If the answer is positive, I have lived up to high moral standards. If not, I have violated these standards and my rectitude status is lowered.

USING THE COMMUNICATION "FORMULA" AS A CONSUMER OF COMMUNICATION

It is suggested that one of the outstanding responsibilities of the scientist teacher is to lead his pupils in the systematic approach to the study of communication. The foregoing analysis of the process of preparing to write or to speak to an audience deals with an important part of this process, the creation of communication.

In addition, the teacher can introduce his pupils at an early level to the roles they are to play as consumers of communication either as readers or listeners. Here the teacher may construct a framework which includes the important categories for analyzing the communication process somewhat as follows.

I.	II.	III.	IV.
Effect desired by the communicator upon what audience	Characteristics of the communicator	The message (what was said and how)	Appraisal of effect of message upon the intended audience

The teacher may lead his pupils in the study of any written or spoken message by leading them to ask appropriate questions under each of these categories. For example, the following under Category I. To what audience did the author speak or write? Give their outstanding characteristics. What effect did the author wish to have upon his audience? Did he wish to entertain them, or to instruct them or get them to support a point of view? and so on.

Under Category II: Who is the communicator? From what he has written do you think he is democratic in his belief and actions or not? Why? Is he enlightened? What are his other value statuses?

Under Category III, the questions leading to the analysis of the message are asked. Does the message present its purpose clearly? Are both sides of any issue presented fairly? Are all the facts presented in the message true? What does the author promise the audience in this message? Is he justified in making these promises? Does the communicator use terms which his audience is likely to understand? How did the author try to get the sympathy of the audience? Do you think the message meets the standards of rectitude or do you think the effect will be to deny certain people the things they need and want? In other words, did the message tend to promote democratic ideals or not?

Under Category IV, the teacher leads his pupils to evaluate the probable effects of the message by asking: Do you think the message achieved the effect the author sought to create upon his audience? Why? Did the message contain anything that would likely antagonize the audience? If so, what? Do you think of other things the message could have presented which would have done more to enlist the sympathy of the audience? Do you think the failure to establish the truth of anything presented in the message tended to lead the audience to reject the message?[2]

Obviously the teacher will base his presentation of the systematic use of the "formula" of communication upon the maturity levels of the pupils. He will use this approach where appropriate in offering the following opportunities given pupils to practice the skills of speaking, writing, listening and reading.

a. Children are given opportunities to develop their skills in oral communication.
   (1) Children take part in class discussions.
      (a) They decide when and what to contribute to the discussion.
      (b) They decide how far to pursue their argument.
      (c) They make a contribution that is worthwhile.

---

[2]A more complete analysis of the process of communication and techniques of transmitting skills in this area will be found in *Personality in Social Process,* Arnspiger, V. Clyde, et al., Chapter 11.

(2) Children are given instruction in ways to make simple talks.

(3) Children are allowed to bring simple articles from home and tell about them.

(4) Children are given a period once or twice a week when they can talk about events which have happened to them.

(5) Pupils give directions to the class on how to perform a given task.

(6) Pupils make reports on a favorite story or book.

(7) Pupils explain the procedures and results of a science experiment.

(8) Children read minutes of a meeting to the class.

(9) Teacher makes his spoken instructions to the class clear and concise, thereby setting a good pattern for the pupils.

b. The value of good listening to oral communication is stressed.

(1) Each child is given an opportunity to practice listening and reporting what he has heard. The other pupils judge how well he has been listening.

(2) Games are played which show the need for careful listening.

(3) Children interpret the suggestions and reports of classmates.

(4) The teacher sets the example by listening carefully to each pupil.

(5) Children practice following teacher's comments, stories, poems, films, and radio programs to see if they can understand them clearly.

(6) Children are encouraged to participate in plays and other dramatic activities.

c. Effective written communication skills are stressed.

(1) Children are requested to write a description of an event and read it to the class. The class is asked to report how much they have learned about the event from the description.

(2) Children are given specific instructions how to write simple descriptions, reports, requests, and announcements.

(3) Pupils are introduced to punctuation, paragraphing, and other forms appropriate to making ideas clear.

(4) Teacher makes sure his written instructions are always carefully worded and clearly written.

(5) Children are given opportunities frequently to write reports of things they have done.

(6) Practice is offered in writing invitations, announcements, and other communications for classmates and other classrooms.
(7) Children make notes on material read.
(8) Children write about their own lives.
(9) Children write directions for a game or science experiment.
(10) A classroom diary is kept with each child making a contribution to it.
(11) Children write letters to friends.
(12) Children write poems, plays and skits.
(13) Children read and criticize each other's reports in a constructive manner.
(14) Children write reports on books and stories.

d. All modern methods are employed in the effort to teach children to read with appropriate speed and comprehension. One of the most significant conclusions from research in the field of reading has been that reading mastery develops most efficiently in situations that proceed from experience to reading. One of the most effective ways to provide common experiences for children is through the medium of the films which presents a significant experience from which to proceed to reading. The teacher will make use of this medium in his reading instruction.

e. Pupils are given opportunities to practice the skills of analysis using the framework given on page 50 in the study and appraisal of what they read in their reading and English classes. This is undertaken, of course, with classes whose members are sufficiently mature to profit from this practice.

f. Pupils learn to communicate with quantitative symbols. They are taught to look upon mathematics as a form of communication to be employed in the transmission of precise quantitative concepts and relationships.

(1) Children are introduced to quantitative symbols and relationships.
  (a) They interpret numbers used in daily activities.
  (b) They read price tags.
  (c) They use the values of money in their classroom activities.
  (d) They interpret distance, weights, amounts of objects of interest.
  (e) They interpret simple graphs and charts.
(2) Children are given opportunities to estimate amounts.
  (a) They estimate the amount of change to expect after a purchase.

(b) They estimate distance in moving classroom furniture.
(c) They estimate paper and pencils needed for the class.
(d) They estimate the number of cookies required for a party.
(e) They estimate space required for books or water for an aquarium.

(3) Children perform operations which require exact computations.
(a) They keep accounts in the school store.
(b) They decide on the amount of wood needed to make bookshelves.
(c) They draw simple maps to scale.
(d) They keep score in games.

(4) Opportunity is given to use measuring instruments.
(a) They use yardstick and rule.
(b) They use pints, quarts, gallons.
(c) They use scales to weigh themselves.
(d) They read the speedometer.
(e) They read thermometers.

4. Social skills.[3]
a. Children are introduced to basic social skills in the classroom which can be used also away from school.
(1) Children learn the acceptable way to make simple introductions.
(2) Children learn suggested way to answer the telephone.
(3) They learn how to await their turns in activities where this is appropriate.
(4) Table manners, to be used particularly in the cafeteria, are discussed in the classroom.
(5) Children learn to receive visitors in the classroom courteously.

b. Practice is given in basic social skills.
(1) Children divide into groups and present demonstrations of introductions.
(2) Pupils make a special effort to see that each member of the class practices good table manners in the cafeteria.
(3) Children are given opportunities to practice the use of the telephone.
(4) Children may be allowed to assist in the principal's office by answering the phone and receiving visitors.

c. Children learn the skills of informal social situations.
(1) They are given opportunities to be courteous to each other.

[3] Social skills are those involved in sharing human values.

(2) They have opportunities to make requests of other people.

(3) They learn that friendliness and helpfulness beget friendliness and helpfulness.

(4) They learn to accept gracefully the decisions of the majority.

(5) Children discuss how more cooperation and better feelings might be developed between individuals and groups in specific interpersonal relationships.

(6) Teacher and pupils take time to point out to each other when an individual or group acts in a democratic way toward others.

(7) Teacher sets the example by demonstrating these skills in ordinary classroom procedures.

5. Aesthetic skills.

Aesthetic skill may be defined as the ability to enjoy or to create well-arranged patterns of form, color, and sound. This group of skills involve the shaping (as with the artist) and the sharing (as with the consumer of art) of beauty in the environment. This ability to create beauty or to abstract sensuous pleasure from the beauty of his environment is a value goal highly prized by the mature person.

a. Children are introduced to art.

(1) Reproductions of great works are brought to the school and children are encouraged to look at them during free time. The teacher will select pictures of particular interest to children.

(2) Children are taken as a group to art exhibits, and are encouraged to look at and to discuss the works in which they are interested.

(3) They are encouraged to discuss works of art, such as paintings, which they have seen or which have been brought to the room and to tell what they like or dislike about them and why.

(4) Children are given opportunities to make their own evaluations of works of art which they see although they should also be exposed to a little of the background of the artist and his work and of what other people think about it.

(5) Pupils should never be forced to accept without question a certain opinion about what they see. They should be exposed to what others say, but allowed to practice skills they may have in any of the creative arts. Systematic instruction should be offered all children who display latent talents in graphic skills.

(6) Children help plan what materials will be required for art work in the classroom.
(7) Children organize hobby clubs to exercise their skills and to pursue their interests in art.
(8) Children are encouraged to develop their abilities to get pleasure from the beauty of their environment as reflected in plants, animals, clouds, sunsets, storms, natural and man-made designs, and other aspects of their environment.

b. Children are introduced to music.
(1) Records of great works are played in the classroom during rest periods.
(2) Children are encouraged to sing.
(3) When possible, children are taken to band, choir, or orchestra concerts.
(4) Children tell what they hear in certain musical productions including movements and instruments.
(5) They create rhythmic motions of their own choosing to records.
(6) Those who choose are encouraged to act out music, but no one is forced to do this.
(7) Children tell what they like or dislike about music they hear.
(8) Children are allowed to select from records available, those which they like to hear.
(9) Children are invited to join the school choir or orchestra.
(10) Children select radio and television programs which present music they enjoy.

c. Children are introduced to literature.
(1) Teacher reads excerpts from children's classics to the class.
(2) Simplified versions are made available for the children to read themselves.
(3) Children read and act out appropriate plays.
(4) Trips to the library are made to select books.
(5) Pupils may have a day when they come dressed as their favorite characters from stories they have read.
(6) Children make reports on favorite stories they have read.
(7) Children are encouraged to tell what they liked about a certain story or book and why.
(8) They are given interesting background material on the authors and on the stories they read.

ENLIGHTENMENT

The term enlightenment refers not to knowledge per se, but rather to knowledge about the past and estimates of the future relative to important decisions. It will be recalled that important decisions in this context refers to the decisions sanctioned by society.

One of the persisting dilemmas of the school has been the question of what content shall be presented in courses of study. Without an overriding objective and a set of implementing goals, the curriculum maker has difficulty in validating or justifying the inclusion of specific subject matter. For example, the history teacher will agree that since the course of study cannot encompass all the events of history, he must of necessity make a selection. But upon what is he to base his selections? His answer to this will make sense if he replies that the events he selects are pertinent events. But the next obvious question is "pertinent to what"? The answer to this question in a society that aspires toward freedom is that the subject matter offering of the school shall be pertinent to the ideals and objectives of such a society. As we have seen, the overriding objective which has been postulated for the free society is the realization of the worth and dignity of the individual. We have seen, also, that such a society favors the wide rather than the narrow sharing of social values. The answer then to the question–what events of history are pertinent?–can be provided by referring to those events of the past which are relevant to the construction and maintenance of institutions, and institutional practices which determine the degree to which human values are shared among the people, for upon the wide availability of social values the realization of human dignity depends.

The study of pertinent events of history, therefore, consists of the analysis and appraisal of institutions which have contributed to the sharing or to the deprivation of social values among the people, and the social consequences thereof. This approach provides enlightenment in the field of history. The technique of validating subject matter suggested here may be employed in other areas of the curriculum which make up much of the content of courses of study throughout the schools. One of the most important purposes of the school is to lead pupils from erudition, the possession of sheer knowledge, to maturity and wisdom in which the individual can analyze, select and manipulate knowledge to assist him in the achievement of his clarified goals.

Let us examine some of the proposed alternatives of practice which have emerged from the seminars designed to promote the enhancement of enlightenment among the pupils of the school.

I. ENLIGHTENMENT
   A. All available lines of communication which are appropriate to the maturity levels of the class are kept open for all pupils in their search for enlightenment.
      1. Children are given access to a variety of books on a variety of subjects.
         a. A basic book collection is provided in each classroom.

   b. A collection of books for sharing among many rooms is provided in the schools.
   c. Children are given opportunities to take field trips to the public library, in order to check out books and to secure library cards.
   d. Children are encouraged to secure and take care of books of their own.
2. Magazines are provided in each classroom for the use of the children.
   a. The school subscribes to magazines for each grade, if possible.
   b. The teacher brings magazines from home.
   c. Children are encouraged to bring magazines from their homes.
   d. Especially worthwhile magazines are kept on file and are available to members of the class.
3. Reference books and reports on pertinent subjects appropriate to the grade level are made available in the classroom.
   a. Each classroom has its own set of up-to-date encyclopedias, if possible.
   b. Each classroom has a good dictionary.
   c. Gazateers, atlases, and maps are available in each classroom.
   d. Almanacs and other yearbooks appropriate to the grade level are provided in each classroom.
4. Films are provided for the classroom.
   a. Films are used which contribute in a unique manner to the instructional program. (Many biological and physical phenomena, for example, can be shown clearly by means of the film which cannot be presented graphically through any other medium.)
   b. They are clearly integrated with the units of instruction.
   c. Films are used which are of sufficient technical quality to be easy to watch and to hear.
   d. The teacher employs effective techniques in the use of films and other audiovisual materials. For example, he always introduces the material by specifying the purposes for presenting it in class.
      (1) He presents the material immediately after specifying these purposes.
      (2) He leads a discussion by the pupils immediately after the showing in which:
         (a) They determine whether the purposes for seeing the material have been achieved.
         (b) They decide what steps should be taken to integrate what they have learned from the audiovisual material with their own learning experiences.
5. Newspapers are used as a line of communication with the outside world.

a. Children are encouraged to read the newspaper and to bring interesting articles related to classroom activities.
b. Newspapers are provided daily in classrooms for older children.
c. Older children are given specific instruction in how to read the newspaper.

6. Radio and television programs are studied as a means of enlightenment.
a. Children are encouraged to listen to or to watch specific programs which are related to classwork.
b. Programs which are related to classwork are discussed in class.
c. Radio and television programs in general are discussed by older children and an attempt is made to set up standards for evaluating the worth of these programs.

B. Teacher establishes himself as an observer, learner, and guide with his classes. He does not attempt to become the "infallible oracle of all knowledge."

1. The teacher continues his own education.
a. He keeps up-to-date with new developments in his field through extensive reading.
(1) He subscribes to and reads professional magazines.
(2) He establishes and adds systematically to his own library.
(3) He keeps himself familiar with what is available in the library and with recent additions.
b. The teacher learns through the analysis and appraisal of his own experiences, in the classroom and in his other community relationships.
(1) He listens to worthwhile radio programs.
(2) He watches selected television programs.
(3) He makes trips to industries or places of historical interest in the vicinity of his town.
(4) He makes longer trips, when possible, and tries to visit the places that he teaches about.
(5) He attends concerts, lectures, art shows, and other events which will help him to become a more enlightened person.

2. Teacher tries to guide his pupils in their continued learning.
a. Teacher attempts to arouse children's interest in the subject matter which is required of them in school.
(1) He learns as much as possible about the background and current developments in the areas studied.
(2) He points out to individual children specific parts of the whole area which might be of interest to them.
(3) He shows interest in the children's questions, and does not hesitate to suggest that they search for the answer together when he does not know it or is not sure of it.

(4) He does not try to furnish an answer to every question asked, many times at the risk of spreading the wrong information.

b. Teacher attempts to instill in the child a continuing interest in many broad subjects.

(1) He encourages the children to be selective in their choices, but also to take advantage of many good movies, radio programs, television programs, books and magazines.

(2) He tries to give each child a mental picture of the library as a place where both information and pleasure are available.

(3) He introduces children to concerts, plays, art shows, and other worthwhile activities.

(4) He tries to leave the child with an attitude that it is better to be interested in experiencing new things, in learning new things, and in searching for answers than to refuse to admit lack of knowledge in any area.

C. All reasonable efforts are made to establish the authenticity of subject matter presented to or by the class.

1. Teacher checks his own material before presenting it to the class.
   a. He checks material with the textbooks being used.
   b. He checks material from the textbooks with other sources.
   c. He checks information presented in some areas personally with people who know the facts.
   d. When presenting unfamiliar subjects, he also offers his source of reference.
   e. If his subject matter material is questioned, he must approach the validation of his conclusions in the spirit of inquiry rather than advocacy.
2. Pupils are encouraged to establish the authenticity of any material they present to the class.
   a. Children are asked to give the names and pages of any sources consulted for a report.
   b. Children are encouraged to check facts found in books, magazines, or newspapers with other sources and with people who actually witnessed or experienced the event.
   c. Children are allowed and encouraged to courteously request proof from each other of statements made in class.
   d. Children are encouraged to give the source of their information any time they make a contribution in class discussions.
   e. Older children are led to evaluate the various sources of material which are used in the classroom.

(1) They check information found in magazines and newspapers with the encyclopedia, textbook, or other books.

(2) They check information found in one encyclopedia with that found in another, or one textbook with another, when that is possible.

(3) They check information found in textbooks and encyclopedias with what they know from experience to be true, such as information on their hometown or events in their area.

(4) They check newspaper accounts of events they actually saw to find how much discrepancy there is between the report and their own impression of the event.

f. Children are encouraged to establish the authenticity of their material only by use of sources which have themselves been proved authentic.

g. Children are given opportunities to recognize and reject false attempts at establishing authenticity.

(1) They study examples of information that was not true even though printed in books or reported in newspapers.

(2) They study examples where an authority is reported to have said something which he did not say.

D. Teacher and pupils have high respect for scholarship.

1. Teacher has respect for scholarship and shows it by his attitude and actions.

a. He refuses to accept haphazard reports or research.

b. He refuses to accept reports of questionable authenticity.

c. He encourages the children to do thorough and complete work on projects.

d. He presents only complete, thorough and properly authenticated material to the class.

e. He offers recognition and respect to the children who do a thorough job on any assignment which they have.

(1) These children are allowed to present their research and other work to the entire class.

(2) They are given opportunities to do more work on projects which are of special interest to the class.

(3) They have their work put on display for other teachers and other classes to see.

f. Teacher stresses what is learned more than the grade or rating obtained.

2. Pupils show respect for scholarship through their attitudes and actions.

a. Children are encouraged to respect their classmates who do outstanding work in subject matter areas.

(1) They show genuine interest in what is being done or has been done.

(2) They are encouraged to tell their friends in other classrooms what is being done in their room.

(3) They report to their parents what they and their classmates are studying and accomplishing.

b. Children do their best on assignments which are given them.

c. Children do not attempt to hand in half-finished or slipshod work.

d. Children tend to pay more attention to what is learned and how it can be used than to the grade or rating it is given.

e. Children work as hard on projects or reports for which they will receive no grade as they do on those which will be graded.

f. Children demonstrate eagerness to move on to more advanced work when they have successfully completed their present work.

E. Pupils are encouraged whenever possible to set their own standards of achievement.

1. Older children are given opportunities to set their own standards of achievement in academic areas. Of course, they are encouraged to set their standards high enough to be challenging.
   a. They are allowed to decide, at times, how many spelling words they think they can spell for the next test.
   b. Occasionally, they are asked to predict the number of pages that they think they will be able to read in a period.
   c. They sometimes decide on the length and form of their reports and themes.
   d. Many times they are asked to evaluate their own papers on the basis of how well the papers reflect their ability.
   e. They are given opportunities to record their progress in a school subject, such as spelling, and to predict their future achievement.
   f. They are allowed to keep files on their themes, reports, and written work so that they may recognize the improvement which they have made and how much more progress they should be able to make in the future.
2. Children are encouraged to set their own standards for the activities in which they participate outside of class.
   a. Teacher individually encourages each child to evaluate his progress in skills on the playground and to plan for future proficiency.
   b. Children are encouraged to consider the ranks which they should be able to pass in the near future in Cub Scouts, Boy Scouts, or Camp Fire Girls.
   c. Children are encouraged to consider what they do to help with the work in their home at the present and to set up some standards for further achievement in this area.
   d. Children are encouraged to set up standards for their own achievement in the area of interpersonal relationships.

e. Children are given assistance in setting up standards concerning their hobbies and other interests and are encouraged to do worthwhile work in these areas.

F. Analytical thinking is promoted by encouraging pupils at various maturity levels to make value analyses of important events, of books read, or art work studied, of music heard, of radio and television programs studied.[4]

1. Children are encouraged to make analyses of important events.
   a. Children discuss things that happen in the classroom which are important to them.
      (1) They write a short report of certain events in their lives. This may be a diary of one morning.
      (2) They attempt to identify the social values which are involved in these events.
   b. Children discuss events which take place in their community in terms of what values are involved.
   c. Older children discuss and analyze events which take place outside of their community in terms of what values are involved.
2. Children are encouraged to analyze books read.[5]
   a. Children are asked to give reports of books they have read.
   b. Children discuss books which they have read and attempt to analyze them.
      (1) They discuss the author.
      (2) They discuss the characters and movement of the plot.
      (3) They try to identify which values are involved in the interaction among the characters.
      (4) They discuss the values which the author of the book is sharing with the reader.
      (5) They discuss the characteristics of the people who are likely to read the book and what the effect on them will probably be.
3. Children talk about art work they have studied.
   a. They talk about the artist and his characteristics.
   b. They discuss the medium which the artist used.
   c. They explain what the work of art means to them.
   d. They discuss whether they think the artist achieved the goal for which he was striving in his work.
4. Children analyse music they have heard.
   a. They form a common background by listening to some music together in class.

---

[4]*Ibid.*, Chapter 4, "Identifying Value Goals in Human Behavior." In this chapter the teacher will find a framework which will suggest how the value content of human behavior can be analyzed.

[5]The Human Value Series, Teachers Editions, present methods of analysis, Steck-Vaughn Co., Austin, 1967-69.

b. They discuss the accomplishments and characteristics of the composer.
c. They explain to their classmates their own feeling about the music.
d. They try to determine whether the composer is really reaching his audience through his composition as he intended.

5. Children discuss and analyze radio and television programs they see and hear.
   a. They attempt to determine the message that the program was trying to present.
   b. They discuss the manner by which the producers attempted to present their message.
   c. They analyze how well the message is presented.
   d. They suggest cirteria to be used in selecting worthwhile radio and television programs.

G. Teacher provides intellectual tools which pupils can use in critical analysis to extend their enlightenment. These may include appropriate definitional tools that are clear-cut and specific in character. For example, definitions of democracy, of despotism, definitions of social values, indices of the values, a "formula" for analyzing communication and the like.[6]

1. Teacher introduces intellectual tools to the children.
   a. Definition of democracy: A society may be said to be moving toward democracy to the degree to which its institutions or practices are so constituted as to increase the probability that more and more of the social values are shared by more and more of the people on the basis of merit.
   b. Definition of despotism: A society may be said to be moving toward despotism to the degree to which its institutions contribute toward the concentrating of control of the social values in the hands of a relatively small group not responsible to the people, and these are withheld from large portions of the population on bases other than merit.
   c. Definitions of social values: Values refer to the things people need and want.
      (1) Power refers to the degree to which people take part in the making of important decisions. The act of voting is an act of power.
      (2) Respect refers to the degree of discrimination against people or recognition of them in their capacity as human beings.
      (3) Wealth refers to the goods and services people need and want.

---

[6] A more comprehensive statement of the tools of thinking and their use will be found in *Personality in Social Process*, Arnspiger, V. Clyde, et al., Chapter 4. The teacher will be guided by the maturity of his pupils in the selection of these tools for actual use.

(4) Enlightenment refers to the information one needs to make important decisions.
(5) Skill implies the full development of one's native talents.
(6) Well-being refers to good mental and physical health.
(7) Rectitude refers to moral practices and ethical standards.
(8) Affection means a warm, friendly relationship with people.

2. Teacher gives children opportunities to practice the use of these intellectual tools.
   a. Children use the tools to analyze classroom situations.
   b. Children use the tools in connection with their study of subject matter.
   c. Children attempt to analyze situations outside of school by use of intellectual tools.

H. Many situations are created which provide motivation for learning and thus tend to promote the inner desire to learn. Such situations may be classified as appeals to pupil's interests in terms of value goals, such as the need to be respected, to be enlightened, to acquire certain skills, to be loved, to earn money, to be healthy, to help make decisions, or to be considered a "moral" person. Any one or more of these feelings of need or want may be used to motivate pupils to seek understanding in all areas of instruction. It would be difficult to justify instruction to all pupils in any subject in which such motivation could not thus be provided.

1. Motivation for learning is provided by appeals to children's need to be respected.
   a. Teacher shows respect to those who demonstrate achievement in their studies.
   b. Children who do extensive research outside of class are given opportunities to present their findings to their classmates and thereby gain respect.
   c. Outstanding handwork or projects are put on display in order that the child who produced it may gain respect.
2. Motivation for learning is provided by appeals to children's need to be enlightened.
   a. Children are shown how to use resource materials in order to find the answers to their own questions.
   b. Children are urged to consider what additional enlightenment they need in order to solve problems which present themselves, and they are shown how to reach this stage of enlightenment.
   c. Children are given interesting samples of areas in which they need further study and are urged to search for this enlightenment through assigned readings, field trips, radio, television or films available to the school.

3. Motivation for learning is provided by appeals to children's need to acquire certain skills.
   a. Children are encouraged to learn how to read in order to read information about things of interest to themselves–sports, hobbies, animals, etc.
   b. Children learn how to write in order to be able to communicate with friends over long distances.
   c. Children learn how to manipulate numbers in order to keep scores and records of games.
   d. Children are urged to gain enlightenment concerning social skills because they will feel a need to be competent in them.
4. Motivation for learning is provided by appeals to children's need to be loved.
   a. Children are urged to gain enlightenment concerning the handling of interpersonal relations in order to live effectively with other people who cooperate with them in the wide sharing of human values.
   b. Children are motivated in some cases to gain enlightenment in certain areas in order to gain more respect and love from their parents.
5. Motivation for learning is provided by appeals to children's need to earn money.
   a. Children are encouraged to learn to change money and to keep records of expenditures and receipts.
   b. Children learn that the ability to write neat, concise, clear letters will help them get and keep jobs.
   c. Children are encouraged to enlighten themselves concerning personal traits which will enable them to make better employees.
6. Motivation for learning is provided by appeals to children's need to be healthy.
   a. Children seek to gain enlightenment concerning the causes and cures of diseases.
   b. Children learn safety rules which will help them preserve their health.
   c. Children learn about community health measures, about water purification, etc.
7. Motivation for learning is provided by appeals to children's need to help make decisions.
   a. Children are led to study how the governments of our city, state and county work.
   b. Children learn about the ways in which adults make decisions.
   c. Children are motivated to gain enlightenment in many differing areas in order to be able to make decisions in those areas.

8. Motivation for learning is provided by appeals to children's need to be considered a "moral" person.
    a. Children are urged to gain enlightenment concerning the moral and ethical standards of other peoples.
    b. Children study the differences between various sets of standards and attempt to formulate their own.
    c. Children seek enlightenment in order to be able to gain their achievements honestly.

WEALTH

As we have seen, wealth refers to goods and services people need and want in their everyday lives. The term economic security is a relative term referring to the degree of goods and services required by an individual to maintain a desirable standard of living and to prepare for the future.

An important concept in this value category to be transmitted to the school pupil is that wealth is sought as an instrumental goal, or as a *base* value, from which other *scope* values can be gained, for with increase in the status of wealth, the accessability of many other value goals which depend upon the expenditure of wealth increases. This principle applies to paying the costs of tuition to educational institutions, money for the purchase of books and other materials designed to enhance the enlightenment and skill categories. Better health services also become more accessible with increasing wealth. Wealth is often used also as a base value to secure certain scope value effects as power and respect.

Money itself should be thought of as wealth only in that it represents a claim against society, a claim upon the goods and services of that society.

While it may be said that economic security is a value goal toward the achievement of which few children at the elementary grade levels can be expected to participate, it is a highly important deferred goal which every child will inevitably be seeking during most of his lifetime. It is in this area that we should undertake to provide the experiences and practices with the tools of thinking that will lead the child to important predispositions which are favorable to the achievement of economic security with all due regard, of course, for the freedom of choice and the value assets of others. Many of the practices already proposed in other value categories should contribute to the future enhancement of the individual's status of economic security. For example, about eighty per cent of the jobs that are lost by people in industry have resulted from their not being able to get along amicably with others. That is, they have not mastered the important techniques involved in the effective management of their interpersonal relationships. Many of these practices were presented under the categories respect, affection, skill and well-being.

Following are the alternative practices suggested by teacher-participants in the decision seminars which are specialized to the value wealth.

I. WEALTH
    A. Pupils are introduced to many of the occupations followed by people in making a living.

1. Pupils interview their parents on the jobs they have, what they do on the job, what skills are required, and to what other opportunities they might eventually lead.
2. Pupils report to the class on what they have learned about their parent's occupations so that all may share the knowledge.
3. Pupils investigate the jobs their neighbors have and report on them.

B. Pupils explore other jobs available in the community.
1. The types of industries in the community are explored and discussed. If possible, trips may be taken to some of them to see people actually at work. Special studies of industries in the community should be conducted by the pupils under the direction of the teacher who will base his planning of the nature and scope of these studies upon the maturity levels of his pupils. Such studies could involve the types of goods and services made available to the community, the number of people working in the industry, the number of children having parents working in the industry, basic resources needed in the industry, etc.
2. Representatives of various occupations may be asked to speak to the class. Each representative of these occupational groups should be requested also to discuss other occupations with which he is associated in his work. For example, if the production is interrupted, or the construction industry slows down, many workers may be unemployed. The teacher might thus begin to establish the concept of interdependence existing in the industrialized society of today; how workers in one occupation depend upon workers of other occupations for the continuance of their jobs.

C. Occupations in cities outside the local community are discussed.
1. Occupations not represented in the immediate community are explored through books and other reference materials.
2. Films and pictures are used to show how people throughout the world earn their livings.
2. People who have lived in other parts of the United States or in other parts of the world may be invited to discuss the various occupations with which they have become acquainted in their travels.

D. Pupils are encouraged to think of the kinds of work they may want to do.
1. The requirements for specific occupations are compiled and studied.
   a. A committee is appointed to study all the related occupations in a general area.
   b. The committee compiles its report in the form of a notebook for permanent reference.

c. A listing is made of the books available to the class which portray the lives of workers in various occupations.
d. Children are asked to read books, fiction or nonfiction, related to occupations which they think they might like to follow.

2. Children are asked to choose one occupation in which they think they would be interested.
   a. Each child makes a short talk to the class on this occupation, telling why he chose it and any particularly interesting thing about it.
   b. Each child analyzes his abilities in relation to the job requirements in the occupation which he prefers.
   c. Each child makes out a plan of what he will need to do in the near future to help prepare himself for that occupation.

E. Pupils are encouraged to study the requirements of getting and keeping a job.
   1. Pupils study how to get and keep a part-time job when they become old enough to fulfill its requirements.
      a. Through talking to older brothers, sisters, and friends, as well as adults, they learn what part-time jobs are available in their community.
      b. These and other advisors are also questioned about the probable value of a part-time job to a young citizen.
      c. The important steps in applying for a job are carefully analyzed.
      d. Role situations are acted out in which a pupil applies for a job.
      e. Ideas relating to the proper dress and behavior are compiled and listed for future use.
      f. A list is made of things to avoid when applying for a job and they are discussed.
      g. Employers of pupils are interviewed to determine what they expect of their employees.
      h. A list is made of the qualities which are expected of a worker, such as promptness and courtesy.
      i. Specific instances when these qualities are shown are listed and demonstrated in role playing by pupils.
   2. Pupils study the requirements for getting and keeping a permanent job.
      a. The procedures for making application and having an interview are studied.
      b. The above procedures may also be acted out in role playing.
      c. The qualities which a permanent employee should have in addition to those of a part-time employee are discussed.
      d. Professional and occupational representatives are invited to make speeches before the children in which they outline the

personality characteristics which contribute to getting and keeping a job and those characteristics which are undesirable on the job. Reasons for losing jobs are analyzed.

F. Pupils learn how to secure goods and services for themselves.
   1. They investigate how goods are distributed.
      a. Children find out why certain things are produced in their community.
      b. Children find out who handles products that they use.
      c. Children learn how goods are distributed through warehouses, stores, and other commercial institutions.
   2. Children study buying and selling in relation to quality and prices.
      a. They learn why stores ask different prices for similar materials.
      b. They learn why certain materials are warmer than others.
      c. They learn what labels mean.
      d. They study advertisements.
      e. They make their own choices when buying similar items of different quality.
   3. Children practice managing money.
      a. Children pay for lunches and keep account of money.
      b. Children put money in school bank.
      c. Children help plan the spending of class funds.
      d. Children analyze and make use of saving and budgeting system.

G. Pupils are encouraged to oppose all kinds of job discrimination for reasons other than merit. Obviously, the employment of practices involving the study of job discrimination will depend upon the maturity levels of pupils.
   1. Instances from history are studied involving job discrimination for reasons other than merit.
      a. One child or a small group takes each instance of discrimination and does research on the historical facts and reasons underlying the situation.
      b. The researchers make reports to the entire class.
      c. Children discuss the situations and try to determine what led to discrimination and why. If possible, they use the value categories of the social process in determining the value deprivations suffered.
   2. Current examples of job discrimination are studied.
      a. Newspaper and magazine reports of instances are brought to class and discussed.

H. Pupils are not discriminated against in the classroom because of their wealth or lack of it.
   1. Children are not selected for honors and offices in the classroom on the basis of their economic status.

2. The children whose families are wealthier than others do not receive high grades on any basis other than high achievement.
3. Children are not asked to bring money for drives, donations, etc. that can possibly be avoided.
4. Purchase of workbooks and other class materials is reduced to a minimum. When such are necessary, special provision is made to get these materials for those who cannot afford to buy them.
5. All children are provided with hot lunches, medical and dental care while at school whether they can afford to pay for it or not.
6. Children are not condemned for their failure to bring the proper amount of money for drives, nor are others publicly praised for having brought an unusually large amount.
7. Pupils are not required to buy expensive costumes or materials for class plays and projects. Special arrangements are made to secure the necessary costumes for such affairs for children who cannot afford to buy them.
8. A premium is placed upon originality shown in adapting old clothes and objects to new purposes. Children are complimented for their ingenuity rather than the elaborateness of their costume or project.
9. Cleanliness, neatness and simplicity in appearance are stressed more than the quality or quantity of clothes owned.

It has been suggested that among the most important goals to be achieved by our public schools is the realization by the pupil that the major function of the individual engaged in an occupation or profession is to provide the goods and/or services required by his society in promoting the wider distribution of human values. The teacher will implement this goal by leading his pupils to see that the creation of wealth is not an end in itself but rather a means to the realization of human potentials in all the value assets.

RECTITUDE

The term rectitude refers to the degree of moral practices and ethical standards. The question of what practices are moral and what standards are ethical has long challenged the semantic virtuosity of many amateur and professional philosophers accustomed to the circuitous manipulation of linguistic ambiguities. However, the answer to this question involves the perspectives of the society of which the individual is a citizen. A society that aspires toward freedom holds as an ideal, the wide sharing of human values. Therefore, in such a society, moral practices "doing the right thing," observing ethical standards; all these denote the employment of institutional practices and personal strategies which contribute to the achievement of this ideal. Thus it may be said that an individual's status of rectitude depends upon the degree to which he assumes personal responsibility for and in fact contributes to the wide shaping and sharing of human values.

The free society, because of the freedom of action it accords its citizens, can maintain itself only if these citizens assume responsibility for the creation of institutional practices and personal strategies which promote high standards of rectitude in their day to day living. Therefore, in a free society, high status in this value among its citizens is of prime importance. This is emphasized in the final statement of the value-oriented rationale which specifies that the perspectives and strategies (of citizens) should be so integrated with one another through appropriate institutions that minimum damage is done to the freedom of choice and to the (value) assets of all members of society. In other words, this means that such people in seeking their own values will in fact accept responsibility for seeing that other citizens have equal access to the values.

This places direct responsibility upon the educational system for the creation and employment of instructional techniques designed to maximize the value rectitude among all the participants in the work of the schools. Following are the alternative practices proposed by the various seminars to fulfill this responsibility.

I. RECTITUDE

A. Pupils are encouraged to set their own moral standards above the minimum levels of prescribed rules and regulations.

1. Pupils consider obligations to constituted authority.
   a. Children learn in which situations parents, teachers or other adults expect obedience.
   b. Children learn in which areas older people have better judgment than they can be expected to have.
   c. Children learn in which situations they can rely on personal judgment in making up their own minds.
   d. Children learn what school regulations must be met and why.
      (1) They practice fire drills.
      (2) They observe opening and closing hours of school.
      (3) They observe hall regulations.
   e. Children learn what leadership responsibilities are carried by various members of the school personnel.
   f. Children learn what authority is vested in the owner of a store, of property near which they play, in parents of other children, and why.
2. Pupils react to group mores, customs, and traditions.
   a. Children are assisted in resolving conflicts between home standards and community and school standards.
      (1) When they act according to unacceptable standards, children are taken aside and are given sympathetic understanding and patient explanation.
      (2) Children discuss why these standards differ.
      (3) Through mutual discussion and encouragement children help each other to set their own high standards of behavior.

b. Children react to conflicts between the gang's standards and those of their school or church.
   (1) They attempt to be members of the gang while still maintaining the standards which their conscience tells them they should.
   (2) Children attempt to analyze the parts of their gang's code of conduct which differs from the school's.
   (3) They try to determine why the difference exists.

3. Pupils set their own guides to action.
   a. Pupils are given opportunities to set their own standards of behavior.
      (1) Children are given responsibility for handling money and property belonging to other people.
      (2) Through private conversations the teacher attempts to help children reconcile conflicts in their standards.
      (3) Children have chances to make promises and keep them.
      (4) Children get experience in changing plans to meet the needs of others.
      (5) Children learn to analyze situations which require the making of choices in order to discover what values are involved.
      (6) Through role playing of critical situations, children are confronted with problems of the kind that will enable the teacher to lead the class in the appraisal of behavior in the situation. The questions include what would have been right? Would you want to have such a thing done to you?

         Children who propose ways of acting that seem to conform with the law or the rules of the school are asked whether such solutions really take into account the full responsibility the moral person must assume in sharing values with others. An example of such a situation follows.

         George borrowed $2.50 from Edward and gave him his baseball glove as security until the following Saturday. He also agreed to pay twenty-five cents interest. George collected from his paper route customers more than enough to repay Edward, but before he could redeem his glove on Saturday, he lost his wallet and all his money. He needed his glove to play his regular position at second base with the little league team on Saturday. He asked Edward to take his watch as security instead of his baseball glove. He had paid $7.50 only a month before for his watch, which was in excellent condition. Edward refused, saying that if he failed to pay the debt on Saturday he intended to keep the glove and also refused to extend the loan another week for an additional fifty cents interest which George also promised him. Edward said, "business is business" and that if George didn't repay the loan on the date agreed upon, the glove would become Edward's property.

The teacher should have members of the class play out the roles of George and Edward and lead the children in full discussion of right and wrong behavior in the situation. He should ask specific questions pertinent to the moral positions of each of the participants. He will remind the class of their responsibilities as democratic citizens to set moral standards for themselves which are higher than those which are generally regarded as legal requirements in business transactions. He will remind them that these standards should be based upon their commitments to accord values on the basis of merit and lead them in the analysis of the values involved for each of the participants in the controversy. What values did each stand to lose or gain? The decision relative to the various problems raised should be reached by secret ballots in which the entire class and the teacher vote as members of the community. The votes are counted by a committee selected by the class and the results of each ballot reported by the chairman of the committee.

The teacher asks members of the class to submit other situations which involve similar moral questions that provide practice in the analysis and appraisal of behavior on the basis of its conformance with democratic ideals.

(7) In the study of the critical situations presented by the children, the following questions are asked and comments made both about theoretical problems and practical problems as they arise.

(a) What would have been the fair thing to do? What actions taken in this situation were "good"? What actions were bad?

(b) Would you want to be treated as the participants were in this situation?

(c) Was courtesy shown in this situation? Who acted as gentlemen? Who acted as ladies?

(d) What would you have done in the situation? Why?

(e) Pupils are led to realize through instruction and example that most of their actions affect others. For example, talking aloud when the class is studying prevents others from concentrating. Values are withheld from the other members of the class. What are they?

(f) Children are taught that in order to gain respect they must show respect to others.

(g) A "Boy of the Week" and a "Girl of the Week" are chosen from their good conduct.

(h) Children are given numerous opportunities to exercise self-discipline. Example: The teacher steps next door on an errand, leaving no monitor in charge. Each child is responsible for his own conduct. The teacher will vary this approach by naming "monitors" at times, thus providing individual students with the opportunity to lead the class by giving an example of proper conduct.

B. Teacher clearly understands the difference between the democratic ideal which places a high premium upon the establishment of personal standards of rectitude and the goal of the dictatorship which demands that its citizens live according to externally prescribed "modes of behavior" which are enforced through coercion and fear.

1. The teacher creates a classroom atmosphere in which it is easy to establish and maintain personal standards of rectitude.

a. Specific acts by a pupil, which show evidence of personal standards, are recognized by the other pupils.

(1) Children are given favorable consideration for telling the truth about something they have done, even though it was against the rules.

(2) Children are complimented for keeping their promises even when some sacrifice or work was demanded.

(3) Children are recognized for consistently being on time and accepting and carrying responsibility for the good of the group.

(4) Outstanding examples of honesty, such as when the child found money, pencils, erasers, etc. that he could have kept, but returned, are personally commented upon by the teacher.

(5) Children are offered respect and affection when they make changes in their plans in order to help the group.

b. Guidance is offered children in developing their standards.

(1) Teacher gives many opportunities for children to discuss the "right" and "wrong" in many actual situations which arise in the classroom.

(2) Children are encouraged to present examples of difficult situations and then to act out desirable solutions.

(3) Teacher sets example of sharing rectitude by his own actions.

(4) Any question proposed by a child concerning standards and conduct is given careful consideration by the class and the teacher.

2. Teacher refrains from using fear to secure actions consistent with externally prescribed "modes of behavior." (Rules of the School.)
    a. Teacher attempts to use reason rather than force in securing adherence to necessary rules of the school.
        (1) Children discuss how these rules help everyone in sharing specific values.
        (2) Children discuss the reasons for these rules and suggest new ones and changes in old ones when the need for change is obvious.
        (3) Children discuss how cooperation may be obtained from everyone in observing these rules.
        (4) External control is used only as a last resort to gain adherence to the rules which are absolutely necessary for safety.
    b. Teacher refrains from setting up a series of concrete rules to be followed year after year in his room.
        (1) Rules which must be set up are made flexible to coordinate with the various levels of maturity and experience of each year's class.
        (2) Teacher attempts to present the "regulations" as guides for pleasant relations with each other rather than as iron rules to be observed "because I said so."
        (3) Children who demonstrate competence in creating codes of conduct help set up some of the regulations or group standards.

C. Teacher and pupils assume personal responsibility for their own behavior.
1. Teacher and pupils determine their responsibility in carrying out commitments.
    a. Children find what it means to make and keep promises to parents or friends.
    b. Children are recognized for carrying out committee assignments.
    c. Children meet other school obligations such as returning questionnaires on time.
    d. Children decide what obligations must be fulfilled if one is given special class responsibilities.
    e. Children set up their own standards for a job which no one is going to inspect.
    f. Children have opportunities to decide whether or not to try to "get out of bargains."
    g. Children discuss and decide how important it is to be on time in running errands or in meeting time obligations when other people are involved.

h. Children discuss the importance of meeting obligations on a part-time job.
i. Teacher makes promises to the class carefully and always keeps them if at all possible.
j. Teacher is on time for meetings and other appointments and carries out all obligations which he has assumed.

2. Teacher and pupils respect each other's property rights.
a. Children learn when other people's property should not be disturbed.
b. Children return things they have borrowed.
c. Children take care of classmate's books, toys, etc.
d. Children find why flowers should not be picked from other people's gardens.
e. Children help care for school buildings.
f. Children help protect neighborhood trees, flowers, shrubs, etc.
g. Children discuss the importance of respecting property rights.
h. Children help to repair or replace property they have damaged.
i. Children learn the importance of keeping accurate accounts of class or committee funds.
j. Teacher is careful with all property borrowed from children or others.
k. Teacher borrows child's property only with his permission.
l. Teacher sets good example in taking care of the school building and grounds.

3. Teachers and pupils assume responsibility for being truthful, honest and considerate of others.
a. Children learn when it is important to tell what actually happened.
b. Children learn to distinguish occasions when truth is needed from those when imagination can be used in the interest of maintaining the well-being of others.
c. Children are given opportunities to learn that by taking the blame for something they have done, they have not only increased their status of rectitude, but also of respect.
d. Children decide whether or not to report another child for antisocial behavior.
e. Children learn to report the facts accurately when asked to help settle an argument.
f. Children decide how much credit to give others who have helped them complete tasks they have performed.
g. Children report the facts of a situation accurately.
h. Children decide when to offer and when to withhold comments.
i. Children distinguish between fact and unsupported opinion.

j. Teacher tells the truth to pupils, but always in a tactful way.
k. Teacher openly admits his mistakes.
l. Teacher gives credit to the children when credit is due them. This is especially important in the presence of the principal or other visitors.

D. The sense of responsibility and standards of right conduct are applied to problems of human relationships at the group level as well as at the interpersonal level.

1. Groups within the classroom apply standards of conduct consistent with human dignity in all their relationships with others.
    a. Committees needing the same resource materials work out a plan to share it.
    b. Teams within the classroom who compete against each other on the playground observe standards of good sportsmanship.
        (1) They jointly decide on the rules.
        (2) They share the equipment they have.
        (3) If the sides are uneven, they work out a plan to make the competition more even.
        (4) They offer to compromise on their side of an argument in the interest of fair play and harmony.
        (5) They live up to their agreements on when, where, and how long to play and how to keep score.
        (6) The attention of the teacher is called to the democratic handling of interpersonal relationships. This was discussed in the skill category. In dealing with the development of these skills, the teacher has a good opportunity to point out to his students the close interrelationships between the values rectitude and skill. In other words, the exercise of any of the skills should be carried on in full recognition of the responsibility the democratic citizen has for living up to high standards of rectitude. Again, it should be pointed out that an outstanding index of high rectitude status is the degree to which the individual contributes to the wider sharing of values based on merit.
    c. Groups who are doing research share any material they find on another's subject.
    d. When several groups make class presentations at the same time, all groups make positive rather than negative comments on the others performance.
    e. Groups within the classroom fulfill the obligation of keeping the work area straight and of putting away used materials for the benefit of the next group to use the area.
2. The classroom as a group attempts to maintain congenial relationships with other groups in the school.

a. Children share playground equipment and area with other classrooms of the same grade level.
b. Children use only honest and fair methods when engaged in athletic or other competitions against another classroom in the school.
c. Teacher refrains from praising his class by the method of degrading another class in the school.
d. Children leave all-school areas such as the cafeteria, auditorium, or music room in clean and orderly condition for the next group who uses it.
e. Class as a group or as individuals offer congratulations to other classroom groups on outstanding achievements.

E. Pupils are encouraged to learn and to practice skills of according respect and affection to others.

1. Pupils learn and practice formal skills.
   a. Children learn how to write congratulatory notes.
   b. Children write these notes to other classes and members of other classes in the school congratulating them on their accomplishments.
   c. Children learn and practice correct ways of greeting, introducing, taking leave of others.
   d. Children learn and practice appropriate skills to be used on social occasions.
      (1) They learn how to answer an invitation.
      (2) They learn how to ask for and accept or refuse a dance.
      (3) They learn how to express appreciation to the hostess at a party.
2. Pupils learn and practice informal skills of according respect and affection.
   a. Children learn to be respectful to adults.
      (1) They greet them in a friendly, but respectful way.
      (2) They allow adults to be seated first or to go through a door first.
      (3) They serve them first at parties.
   b. Children accord respect and affection to their peers.
      (1) They allow them to be first at least part of the time.
      (2) They help others carry heavy loads.
      (3) They allow others to take their fair share of turns at play or on other occasions.
      (4) They occasionally allow another to have the best book or the biggest piece of candy.
      (5) They compliment others on any outstanding achievement.

SPECIAL COMMENTS BY PRIMARY GRADE TEACHERS

Following are some of the comments and suggestions which grew out of seminars made up of primary grade teachers. While some of these practices may seem to be somewhat repetitive in character, primary grade teachers decided that they were sufficiently appropriate to this level of the school to be listed for special consideration.

The teacher encourages children to learn and practice skills of according values to others. A pupil will seek and enjoy the success of others if he is permitted to help others master a skill. For example, if he can help another child with his spelling list or word recognition practice, he will gain real pleasure from the progress of the other child. It is highly important that he experience this enhancement of his feeling of well-being that comes with sharing values with others.

The playground can provide experiences for developing democratic habits and attitudes that may carry over into all phases of child society. Fairness on the playground may be promoted by writing experience stories about incidents of fair play.

When a child is found guilty of some misdemeanor, he must experience being deprived of something important to him, but punishment should never be inflicted in anger or in a spirit of revenge.

The child likes to be called on to perform errands. This may be to pick up or deliver something to the principal or another teacher. Many youngsters enter school with the idea that the principal is someone to fear. The habitually disobedient child can be sent to the principal's office on an errand so that he will understand and know the principal as a friend.

Let the children dramatize the rules played by the officers who enforce the laws which help to protect them as well as adults. This helps transmit to children the need for laws and law enforcement.

SPECIAL COMMENTS BY ELEMENTARY GRADE TEACHERS

Elementary grade teacher-participants in the seminars felt that the following special alternatives deserved attention at these levels.

Discussion of school citizenship can aid in developing standards of conduct compatible with democratic ideals. As the year progresses, discussions may center about evaluations of progress being made and needed additions or modifications of the children's "code of behavior." Suggestions may be charted and displayed in the classroom.

Develop clear understandings of acceptable behavior patterns and their justifications. Discuss in the group or individually as seems indicated where progress is being made and where more effort or better understanding is needed. Stick-figure drawings can help dramatize desirable social traits on posters or blackboard.

A mock court trial in which "for" and "against" arguments covering ways of acting are presented will help children form judgments about democratic behavior.

Children might make a mural, posters, or a diorama depicting "Things for Which We are Responsible in Our Room."

A teacher should ask a child what he is capable of doing. If a child is constantly asked to undertake tasks which he cannot perform, he may conclude that he is unworthy and inadequate. To borrow a phrase from Lewin, the child might feel he does not justify the "Life Space" he occupies. Teachers should be realistic in setting tasks and goals for children.

The teacher should analyze and appraise himself and his methods periodically. He should ask, "To what extent do I contribute to the wide sharing of values among the children of my classes, my colleagues, and other people with whom I come in contact?"

DEMOCRACY DEMANDS CONTROLS OF HUMAN BEHAVIOR

Many unenlightened people seem to be of the opinion that the democratic school is a school that approaches the laissez faire in its operation and management. This is not true. Neither is the democratic classroom an autocratic classroom. The approach to instruction outlined in this volume is not "permissive" to the point of the laissez faire. Just as the democratic society demands controls of human behavior, so does the promotion and maintenance of the democratic classroom.

The controls employed in the democratic society, however, differ from those of the autocratic society in their origin and enforcement. The autocratic society depends upon externally applied coercive techniques and the employment of fear-inducing methods in controlling the behavior of its citizens. The aspiration of the democratic society, and of course, of the democratic classroom, is that the all-important control of human behavior shall have its origin and shall be internally applied within the personalities of its citizens. Such a society, of course, depends upon the formation of personalities who as they achieve mental and physical maturity are moving toward increasing controls over their own behavior. Democratic societies, however, demand that until the individual can assume personal responsibility for controlling his own behavior, the community must employ external controls over his actions. In the free society these necessary external techniques of control are created by elected representatives responsible to the people as a whole. This principle must be employed by the classroom teacher, who also is in reality a representative of the people and responsible to them for his actions.

VALUE OVERINDULGENCE LEADS TO DEPRIVATION OF RECTITUDE

In his creation of practices specialized to the enhancement of rectitude, the teacher will be alert to the detection of the child who has been overindulged in one or more of the social values. This happens often with children who come from homes at relatively high levels of wealth. Even in homes very low in economic scale we find children being overindulged in the amount of their weekly allowances, which are higher than those of children whose parents are far more economically secure. The child is thus encouraged to make material demands upon his family which deprive the other members of their rightful proportion of the family income. In this sense, the child's status of rectitude is lowered even though it may be said that "this is not his fault." The important point here is that the child who is overindulged beyond what he knows he deserves feels guilty (deprived of rectitude).

An analysis of this situation may lead to the conclusion that the parent in overindulging the child by giving him a large allowance is acting unrealistically. The parent may, in fact, be practicing a well-known defense mechanism in compensating for his own feeling of guilt (loss of rectitude) for having deprived the child of love earlier in his life. This may occur with mothers who resented having to care for their children while they were very young and demanded so much of their time which deprived them of many opportunities to indulge themselves in recreations afforded by the community. The fact that this behavior is unconscious does nothing to reduce its deprivational impact upon the overindulged child and the guilt-ridden parent.

The analyses of some cases have revealed mothers who did not want their children, and after discovering they were pregnant, made efforts to prevent impending birth. Others in this situation were rebellious and resentful for having to experience childbirth. Such mothers have in many instances, after their children reached school age, sought unrealistically to relieve their feelings of guilt for having thus deprived their child of love, by practicing the compensating mechanism of giving the child more than his share of the family's money and overindulging him in other ways such as showing inordinate concern for his welfare, by being unusually possessive, or showering him with simulated affection. This behavior, whether conscious or unconscious, is unrealistic in that it only temporarily relieves the tension of guilt (rectitude deprivation) but does nothing to restore the lowered value status (rectitude). The persisting fear and tension which follows this deprivation can be relieved only by facing up to the basic problem. Here again, we have an example of overindulgence leading to deprivation of rectitude with its accompanying feeling of guilt.

Still other examples of overindulgence often occur in wealthy families where children are deprived of love and respect because of the preoccupation of the father with the demands of business and of the mother with her social obligations. Such parents in their quieter moments, often realize with monstrous pangs of remorse, the degree to which they have deprived their helpless children of the loving care and attention which they have so eagerly sought. (It has been noted that deprivation of affection and respect often leads to disastrous effects upon the personalities of children.) These parents often try to "make it up" to their children when they are older, sometimes long after their tensions have reached dangerous levels, by overindulging them in various ways. They sometimes give them money far beyond their needs and to be spent as they wish. Sport cars as birthday presents are common among the wealthy as soon as the child reaches the legal driving age. These overindulgences frequently lead the child into behavior that is bewildering to parents who mistakenly believe they can overcome the damage of love and respect deprivation by material overindulgence. They cannot understand why their children are always "getting into scrapes" that embarrass and sadden them. It seems never to occur to many parents to consider the possibility that such actions may represent the child's need to gain attention (respect) which his world has denied him, or that he may be striking back at all symbols of authority in such a world. Juvenile authorities often hear parents claim that they cannot possibly be responsible for the delinquency of their children. "Don't we give our child everything?" "Haven't we always?" "This is how he repays us." "What shall I do?"

Too often the teacher is confronted with the problems of what to do with cases of overindulgence such as these long before they become actually delinquent. And to their great credit it can be said that through their sympathy, warm feeling for children, and the insight necessary to recognize the symptoms of this damage, they are able in many cases to lead the child to more realistic behavior before society has confirmed finally that he is a delinquent.

These examples of overindulgence have been in the wealth category, but it is obvious that this may occur in the case of other value categories. Take for instance the teacher who overindulges with power, the child to whom for one or another reason, he is sentimentally attracted. This child may be allowed to decide what the entire class will do time after time to the chagrin of the other pupils who have thus been deprived of their rightful share in the making of choices. This indulgence may be almost completely without merit, and often such teachers do not consciously recognize their predisposition in this direction. Nevertheless, this overindulgence with power of the child because she "likes him" is directly responsible for the power deprivation of the other pupils of the class without merit and is an obvious example of antidemocratic behavior (lowered standard of rectitude).

Any experienced teacher can cite many additional cases of value indulgence without merit which she has encountered in her work. This teacher will also recognize the validity of the conclusion that value overindulgence tends toward the lowering of standards of rectitude and will employ her ingenuity in creating classroom practices to overcome this antidemocratic tendency. Some teachers find it easier than others to employ the practices that have been proposed as alternative ways to maximize human values among children and thus enhance the status of their well-being. However, those who aspire to become scientist teachers will find this to be an extremely rewarding approach to democratic instruction and well worth all the time and effort required in the consistent employment of these practices.

CHAPTER 4

•

A Descriptive Science of Values

There is a difference between mere empiricism and science. While science maintains the same emphasis upon experience, it analyzes experience systematically. Experience does not come announcing its own meaning. We have to code, by the use of concepts and language, whatever flow of moods and images we undergo so as to extract what is contained within that flow. To be scientific, therefore, means to have a system, not merely to be empirical. Unfortunately, the language we bring to our analysis of interpersonal experience, and the concepts represented by our language, are usually much less systematic than that used for the natural sciences. Scientific analysis requires a systematic language that is economical yet comprehensive. An endless proliferation of terms, for instance, makes it difficult to be systematic, as contrasted with a short list of terms. A set of terms which leaves components of our experience unclassified makes our analysis biased and creates selective inattention and overattention to the multiple components of an experience. Needless to say, it is not easy to have a list of terms that is both comprehensive and economical. Some educators and social scientists have been working with such symbolic sets of terms that do neither violence to comprehensiveness nor to economy. Effective pooling of minds–of bringing the experience of all members together in integrated patterns–requires such symbolic sets of terms. We distinguish between method and technique in introducing such a procedure. The conceptual lists provide us with a method. There are numberless ways in which these may be technicalized by creative teachers using the method.

THE MEANING OF VALUE STUDY

Long ago Plato called to our attention that the most significant way to study was in terms of "choice making." Much of the categorization we have used to study human behavior does not call attention to this "choice making" character of behavior–or what we now call "decision making.' In order to highlight choice or decision making, we are required to have a system of categories that calls our attention to all the outcomes that might be sought by an individual in a situation and to show how one of these has been ' selected' from among all the other alternatives. This is the significance of the concept of "value." For, traditionally, the term has been employed to refer to "preferred events." When we say wealth is a highly preferred value for an individual, we have to demonstrate that the individual behaves in various situations in such a way that wealth outcomes are more likely to ensue than any "other" value outcomes. But, then, we must have terms for all of these other value outcomes that differentiate them from wealth pursuits. If we do not, we cannot say we have ourselves considered the "choice making" features of the pattern of behavior we are describing and interpreting. We have not "ruled out" alternatives to the one we feel governs the behavior sequence we are studying.

If we take competing concepts that could be considered vying with the value approach, such as that of "drive," we soon discover that we do not have a complete and economical list of drive terms that provide all possible purposes people seek in the social process that we can bring to bear upon any pattern of behavior to show that one "drive" is being more "preferred' to any of the others. Furthermore, if we were to take all the drive concepts put forward, we would find that they do not form a coherent system. This is primarily because each drive concept had grown up in relative isolation from the other to dominate (each in turn) the literature and research and practical thinking in the field. A whole set of drive terms were not originally put forward as a system so that by the use of them the "choice making" in any empirical act we wish to research or deal with practically could be clearly specified. Instead, we tend to deal with one drive at a time. Indeed, when we have gone over the various "fashions" in how one drive concept after another has appeared over time, we have discovered that each drive concept appeared when it did because it was the most pressing value concern in the world at the time, even though people, who did not consider themselves interested in "practice" but posed as "pure scientists," were devising the terms. In other words, the order in which these drive concepts appeared were themselves an example of choice-making behavior on the part of scientists that show a value process at work in them. For instance, during the depression, the hunger drive was widely fashionable; the aggressive drive came to prominence as the Fascist states grew and expanded; the anxiety drive took over as America was more and more touched by war; the dependency drive arose to prominence with prolonged separation of families during the war; the conformity drive appeared in response to the McCarthy movement; the achievement drive in response to the space race with Russia; and so on. Values operating in the social process were, therefore, impinging on the social scientist and creating successive waves or fashions of drive concept concentration which reflected choice behavior. Yet, at the same time, since there was no system of such concepts used by the social scientist, the drive concept could not be used to promote value studies of himself or his subjects as choice makers. (One doesn't have to use the word "value" in order to do value study of individual or collective decision making. Those who want to use "drive" for it can do so as long as they offer a system.)

Certainly, one consideration which has held back the development of such choice making study is that, if we take every possible goal people seek in the social process, we would find the list would fill several roomsful of files. To bring all of these categories to bear upon every response would simply be too demanding and unmanageable for us. Like all content analysis problems, it is possible to arrive at a few abstract categories that cover all of these specific details. They are abstract only in the interests of economy of thought, not because abstraction is preferred as an end. Yet, no specific goal can be left unclassified by the system of concepts, if it is to be comprehensive. Everyone who has done content analysis knows the difficulty of devising categories which are both economical and yet comprehensive. Value-institution analysis can provide a resolution of this difficulty, and in a way that provides categories of equal levels of abstraction, which are necessary to form a coherent set.

In any event, the introduction of the concept of "value" is meant to interest us more centrally in the choice making process, which begins in infancy and becomes progressively more complex with growth toward adult status. Since the process is sequential, we are interested in what transpires during the early phases of it as tending to shape what happens during later phases. At every phase, however, we are required to utilize the same system of terms, rather than invoking a new "drive" for each phase, so that each phase in the growth of the choice making process can be maximally related to other phases, whether earlier or later. Since adults are playing a role in the socialization (or educational) process during every phase, and since adults have already had exposure to all cultural values and developed preferences among them, their role in shaping the developing personality as decision makers can also be studied with the same set of categories. One of the difficulties of "drive" analysis, in fact, is that it tends to use different sets of drive concepts to handle different roles in the socialization process, so that the whole process of coming to share values in the education process often is lost to study. (The parent is "nurturant" while the child is "dependent" and the two sets of terms are devised and operationalized in a way so as not to be simultaneously applied to both participants.) This is especially noticeable–i.e., different drive concepts invoked for different roles in the attempt to analyze psychotherapy in motivational terms. There has been little effort to bring out the drama of value clashes and value sharing that goes on in psycotherapy. The same criticism has been valid for much of the motivational analysis of education.

Clarifying Value Preferences

There is a distinction between valuation and evaluation. Value patterns are facts. Culture X values *a* (for example, head shrinking), which Culture Y abhors, and the opposite arrangements hold for *b*. Such patterns of value can be described. Having described them, we can then evaluate them. To do so, we usually refer to the conditions and consequences in terms of all other values that have given rise to the descriptive patterning. People often confuse evaluation with valuation. What we hear described about ourselves or others so quickly leads to a negative or positive judgment, we take the description for an evaluation. Yet, if we look at the context of conditions and consequences that have produced and supported a particular pattern, our evaluation might be considerably weakened from what it first "intuitively" was.

Indeed, a more refined look at the conditions and consequences associated with a pattern of valuing may make us even describe it as a value pattern quite differently, since we become more aware of the context in which the pattern appears and "empathize" more with those engaged in practicing the pattern. What from our point of view first looks like hypocrisy, for instance, may turn out, when examined from the perspective of others, to be ignorance rather than willful irresponsibility about principles. Needless to say, evaluation patterns can also be described. In this sense, there is no dichotomy between fact and value. Values are a fact in the world of social process. It is this viewpoint which pervades the distinctive American philosophical system–i.e., pragmatism–and which makes it so similar, so we are told, to various forms of Eastern thought represented, for instance, by Buddhism.

There is often a strain to distinguish values from drives, needs, wants, attitudes, interests, etc. All of this proliferates technical distinctions which seem neither necessary nor valid, often confusing the whole field of the study of purpose more than clarifying it. *A value is simply a preferred event.* To describe a value, therefore, we have not only to say what is distinctive about the pattern that embodies it but, as part of that, what it is being preferred to in terms of alternatives. In short, if we are to describe a value pattern operation in any practice, we have systematically to utilize all the value categories to find which one or more of these is receiving high emphasis in the event being scrutinized. We are engaged in describing "preferences" and not mere "physical pushes and pulls" when dealing with values. If we try to utilize most of the existing language for drives and motives and other similar and related concepts, we discover they are not organized as a system to enable one to discover what the "preference" operating can be taken to be. They do not allow us clearly to envisage people as decision-makers engaged in considering alternative outcomes. The system of value analysis forces us to become aware of the decision process that goes on at both individual and collective levels.

Value Categories

The value categories employed are highly economical but contextual. They are wealth, well-being, enlightenment, skill, rectitude, respect, affection and power. Each of these values is institutionalized in some form in each society. Some form of concern with well-being by a system of medical practices is found in all societies. Each institution can be said to be relatively specialized to one value (or a few). Business and banking institutions are more or less specialized to wealth. Social class institutions, like country clubs and groups which confer recognition upon a person in his community, are specialized to respect. The family is specialized to affection. Religious institutions are specialized to rectitude–the sense of individual and collective responsibility. It is important, however, to distinguish between a conventional and a functional analysis of institutions. An institution may be set up for the pursuit of enlightenment, such as a research center. If we investigate by a careful value analysis the decisions that characterize the institution, however, we may find that enlightenment–the acquisition of new knowledge–may be much less important than power, respect, affection, or other values. We have mentioned before that the family is relatively specialized to affection–that is, among all institutions operating in any society, the family practices are more conventionally "suitable" to the pursuit of warmth and congenial interactions. However, there is no doubt that often the accumulation of wealth, the family as a power arm of the State, the limitation of respect and many other values have taken control of the family and have interfered with the pursuit of affection. There are many who believe that the family is slowly moving toward being what it was first designed to be–i e., an institution of relatively pure affection. Modernization has reduced the importance of the family for the pursuit of all other values. Furthermore, there are many who believe that modernization consists in each institution becoming "purer" with regard to the values it specializes in, rather than attempting to become a "whole society" in itself. This becomes possible, furthermore, only insofar as each institution faces and reduces its conflicts with all other institutions. There are many who believe the failure of any institution to do this leads to more and more need for governmental control of their activities. The point being pursued here, however, is that the value to which the institution "naturally" is specialized may be found not to be what it is actually pursuing primarily, when subjected to value analysis.

One of the rewarding ways to engage in value analysis is to take any one institutional context and examine how in the name of certain values to which that institution is naturally specialized, it nonetheless attempts to influence practices that relate to all the other values. For instance, certain religious groups in certain cultures may be engaged primarily in power, wealth, respect, medical, and other value pursuits under the guise of using religious symbols. This may retard the development of institutions devoted to the pursuit of these other values, or may assist them, as the case may be. Generally, each institution becomes "purer" insofar as its activities move toward assisting rather than hindering all other institutions from doing their jobs well–and do not swerve them too much from their specialization.

Values in the Social Process

How shall we identify the role of values in the social process? Society is not just a collection of individuals but also is a dynamic pattern of processes by which values are distributed among the people. The social process when observed at either the most primitive or the most complex level appears to operate as a process oriented to value goals. Arnspiger[1] using Lasswell's definition of the social process, *man* seeking *values* through *institutions* using *resources*, has made educational and psychological applications, especially in the area of personality development. An elaboration of the framework of the social process follows in chart form.

[1] V. Clyde Arnspiger, et al., *Personality in Social Process,* Wm. C. Brown Publishing Company, Dubuque, Iowa, 1969, Chapter 2.

THE SOCIAL PROCESS FRAMEWORK

MAN seeks (INTERACTING THROUGH CULTURE AND PERSONALITY)	VALUES through SUCH AS	INSTITUTIONS AND PERSONAL STRATEGIES SUCH AS	using RESOURCES SUCH AS
	POWER (MAKING SOCIETY'S DECISIONS)	GOVERNMENT POLITICAL PARTIES PRESSURE GROUPS	SOILS WATER
	RESPECT	SOCIAL CLASS PRACTICES CASTE SYSTEMS, HONORS	ENERGY PLANTS
	WEALTH	PRODUCTION, DISTRIBUTION INCOME, SAVINGS	MINERALS
	ENLIGHTENMENT	EDUCATION, DISCUSSION, COMMUNICATION CHANNELS RESEARCH	ANIMALS HUMAN
	SKILL	TRAINING, OCCUPATION, ART EXPRESSION, TASTE STANDARDS	
	WELL-BEING (MENTAL AND PHYSICAL HEALTH)	HEALTH, RECREATION, POLICE PROTECTION	
	RECTITUDE	MORAL PRACTICES, ETHICAL STANDARDS, CRIME PREVENTION, CHURCHES	
	AFFECTION	COURTSHIP, THE FAMILY, FRIENDSHIP, GROUP HERITAGE	

Value Definitions

In order that values not be merely designated in terms of conventional institutions, therefore, and so that they may be employed functionally and scientifically rather than in any one set of cultural conventional terms, it is necessary to give each of them definitions. It is the concept being evoked by the definition that is important and not the particular "word" used to speak of that concept. It is this process which is systematic, not the mere list of words, requiring us to ask when we examine any practice whether one value concept or the other is more appropriate to it, quite apart from which word is conventional to designate that practice.

Affection means the degree of love and friendship for persons in primary and secondary groups. Primary in this case refers to person-to-person relationships. In this connection it may be noted that one's actions may be motivated by affection and kindly regard for people or by hatred, often unconscious, which may stem from value deprivations suffered early in life in unfortunate conflicts with other people. One of the major purposes of education should be to supplant hatred and fears, which may lead to mental and even physical disintegration, by affection and kindly regard as a motivating value in human behavior. Affection among primary groups is expressed in terms of warm, friendly, and congenial feelings toward one another. Among secondary groups affection may be expressed as loyalty to country or state. The classroom offers many priceless opportunities for the teacher to provide leadership in the sharing of affection and in the promotion of congenial relationships among children.

Respect refers to the degree of discrimination against or recognition given to people in their capacity as human beings. This is one of the most important of all human needs. The withholding of respect is one of the most insidious weapons that can be used against any person or group of persons, whereas the wide sharing of respect is one of the most enriching and rewarding of all social practices. An individual may achieve only a low respect status in his community, as in the case of habitual criminals, or he may enjoy high status of respect, as in the case of a recipient of an award for good citizenship. High respect may be based upon any one or more of the values, such as enlightenment, skill, rectitude, wealth. The child in the classroom from whom respect is withheld can never be expected to participate creatively in the learning process.

Skill refers to the degree of development of potential talents. Human skills range from those involved in mental and manual manipulation, such as skills acquired in one's occupation, to the social skills involved in managing one's personal relationships. More specifically, the skills include motor, thinking, communication, social, and aesthetic skills. Obviously, a person's status may be high in one skill and low in another. He may be high in the skills of the drill press operator and low in that of communication. He may rank low in social skills, such as those of according respect or affection to others. Aesthetic skill refers to the capacity for sensuous enjoyment of the beauty in one's environment. An individual may rank low or high in this skill. The person who seeks maturity will strive to develop his talents in all of the areas named. Examples of serious erosion of human resources are children who have never been given the opportunity to develop and use their latent skills.

Enlightenment refers to information about the past and estimates of the future relative to important decisions. The formation of policy in a society should grow out of decisions based upon profound enlightenment. Enlightenment may be said to be the possession of the knowledge necessary to make important decisions. The significant point here is that enlightenment status depends upon the possession of knowledge of information relevant to the overriding objective, value goals, institutional practices, and resources of society.

Many children who have been deprived of this value have consequently fallen victims to superstitions and misinformation which have hampered their intellectual progress.

Power is a value concerned with decision making in the social context under consideration. We say that a man has achieved power in a society to the degree in which he participates in making important decisions. Important decisions are those that are sanctioned by society and that carry with them the expectation that they will be enforced against any challenger through the exercise of value deprivation. For example, the decision to enact a law forbidding public gambling may carry with it a fine of $500. Here the law exercises wealth deprivation as a penalty. However, if the penalty for violating this sanctioned decision is a term in jail, other value deprivations are effected, such as those of respect, power, and consequently well-being.

Another significant term in this connection is choice. For example, the decision as to whether one shall go to a private or public school is a choice, not an exercise of sanctioned power. The decision that affects wealth distribution may be a sanctioned decision (a tax law) or it may be an unsanctioned choice (a banker's choice in the approval of loans). A person's achievement of power may range from a very low status; as in the case of a convicted criminal, to a very high status, as in that of the Speaker of the House of Representatives in the United States, who participates directly in the decisions that lead to the making of laws. Absolute power does not exist in a free society. Institutions such as the judicial system curb the exercise of such power in a democracy. In a dictatorship, however, the judicial system, if there is such an institution, is ineffective in curbing the dictator's power. Such an institution can be described as having only formal authority. It carries little if any effective power, and cannot help extend power to any large group of ordinary citizens.

The child who has never been allowed any freedom of choice and who has never participated in decisions in the home or school has been deprived of the value power.

Wealth refers to goods and services. Most people seek incomes adequate to satisfy their needs and to provide for their future. A high standard of living is one index of the degree to which wealth is widely distributed among people. The status of wealth may range from no available goods or services to great available quantities of these. Wealth in the form of money is a claim against society for goods and services. To render service is to accord wealth. Obviously, therefore, wealth is relative. Economic security is relative to the needs and wants of individuals. Many children have lived all their lives in economically deprived homes. Others, while not members of wealthy families nevertheless have never known economic want.

Well-being refers to the degree of mental and physical health. One of the important achievements of students will be the mastery of some of the important techniques of self-study. Through knowledge of himself, gained by self-analysis, the student may overcome many frustrations and fears that threaten his status of well-being both mental and physical. Mental and physical health are interdependent. Research on the frontiers of psychosomatic medicine has broadened our understanding of the intensive interdependence of body and mind. We are beginning to recognize that mental health is greatly dependent upon the achievement of status in any of the preferred values, such as affection, respect or rectitude. In fact, serious deprivation in any of the values is likely to result in mental ill-health. One of the most critical problems of the school is the great number of pupils who suffer from this deprivation of well-being with its consequent distortion of their creative and productive capacities.

Rectitude refers to the degree of moral practices and standards of ethical conduct. This implies also the degree of responsibility for one's behavior. An educational objective in a free society is the development of citizens who can assume personal responsibility for implementing democratic goals. Here the aim is the citizen whose personal standards in his relationships with others extend beyond the minimum ethical and moral standards of his society. This responsibility expresses itself in concern for other people. We may say that a person has achieved a high status of rectitude in a free society to the degree that he contributes to the widespread sharing of values. The enhancement of the child's rectitude status is one of the most important concerns of the school.

Institutions Defined

The term institution refers to patterns of practice relatively specialized to the shaping and sharing of values. In other words, institutions are specific ways of doing things by which values are brought into existence and distributed among people. The institution may be constructed so as to increase value sharing, as does the 19th Amendment to our Constitution, granting women the right to vote. This amendment greatly increased the distribution of power among the people. The recent civil rights demonstrations were mounted against institutions which were thought to have effectively narrowed the distribution of respect and were clearly discriminatory. As we shall see, the appraisal of institutions will be based upon whether they contribute to value shaping and/or sharing or to value deprivation. The former are appraised as democratic, the latter as anti-democratic or despotic. This approach will thus enable us to make clear-cut distinctions between societies that aspire to freedom and those that maintain themselves by human control and exploitation.

Resources Defined

The term resources refers to man's biological heritage and to the physical setting in which he carries on his activities. The physical setting comprises the organic and inorganic processes of the earth, the solar and stellar systems that surround it. Included are energy, soil, water, mineral, plant, animal, and human resources. The people of a society are its most important resources, and it is well to remember that the greatest resources of man lie within himself.

The Nonnormative Character of the Social Process Framework

The categories of the framework of the social process presented and defined above provide for analyses of value facts, or the *what is*, and do not in any sense present conditions as they *ought to be*. This framework, therefore, provides an intellectual tool for analyzing any and all types of societies ranging from the most despotic to the most democratic. It thus provides for recording data regarding distinctions between societies in terms of the degree to which their institutional practices and personal strategies contribute to the distribution of values among people. It is a valid conclusion of history that while the personal strategies and the institutional practices of a despotic society tend to control the distribution of values and thus to withhold them from a great number of its members, those of a democratic society tend to be so constructed as to facilitate the wider sharing of values among participating members.

The non-axiological concepts presented above will always be needed as significant intellectual tools in both teaching and research when purely objective and scientific data about human values, institutions, and resources are required in social sciences, humanities, and education.

If, on the other hand, we prefer to promote a particularly desired pattern of value distribution (through personal strategies and institutional practices) over any other, we raise for the first time the axiological or "ought" question in value analysis. Such a preference is stated in proposing a value-oriented conceptual framework for education in a democracy—the principal purpose of this volume.

THE VALUE-ORIENTED RATIONALE OF DEMOCRACY

The Overriding Objective of a Free Society

The value-oriented conceptual framework was developed primarily to implement democracy in everyday living and to refine democratic institutions. It is *believed* that the potential in our society and in our educational system can be realized when our society becomes oriented with more precision toward democracy.

It is postulated that the overriding objective of a democracy is the realization of human worth and dignity in theory and in fact on a grand scale and on the basis of merit. Meritorious people are those who assume responsibility for participating in the process of value shaping and sharing. This overriding objective of democracy is used as an ultimate hypothesis in the process of inquiry. In a despotic society, we believe such an objective probably could not be implemented as the overriding goal even though it were stated for propaganda purposes. The overriding goal is an attempt to give direction to the growth of an entire society and all of its critical components. Intensive analysis suggests it is the central concern of people everywhere who strive for freedom.

Supporting Concepts of the Rationale for Education

The value-oriented rationale for the school includes not only the postulation of the overriding objective, it also suggests supporting concepts which may be used as criteria to determine progress made toward this objective. These criteria of the value-oriented rationale are:

(1) A school which is oriented toward human dignity is one in which values are widely rather than narrowly shaped and shared on the basis of merit. (The person who merits access to human values is one who in turn contributes to the wide shaping and sharing of these values among his fellow men.)

(2) Such a school should promote the formation of mature personalities whose value demands and capabilities are compatible with these goals.

(3) The long range goal to which we aspire for America's schools is to provide opportunities for as many human beings as possible to achieve the highest potentials of their inherent capacities as human beings.

(4) The perspectives and strategies of teachers and students who are seeking to achieve their value potentials are so integrated with one another that minimum damage is done to the freedom of choice and to the value assets of all members of society. (In other words, the school should lead individuals who seek to maximize their own values, to accept responsibility for seeing that other individuals have the same access as they to these values.)

HUMAN DIGNITY AND CHILD DEVELOPMENT

The concept of value is to be used descriptively. We scan facts (behavior) in order to describe value preferences at work in child-adult interactions. In this sense, the study of values is a study of facts, even though operations of child and teacher always have to be "interpreted" for the intentions and outcomes expressed by the operations. The same system of concepts can be used to evaluate these descriptive patterns.

In a democracy, we want to recognize and nourish individual differences. Yet, we want also to promote a community identity. The strain between both aims of a democracy appears within the childhood period of development. It is possible to introduce the concept of "human dignity" as a conceptual device to evaluate patterns that value analysis allows us to describe. Human dignity is defined as the pursuit of any value goal in such a way so as not to over-deprive or overindulge the values of others with whom one is interacting or other values of the self. Generally, the implication of this evaluation gives us a positive model for personality and character, a model long missing from our literature in any explicit form. We want the teacher and the developing personality to be multi-valued–i.e., to have whatever goals they please, but to pursue them in such a way as not to severely overlook and ignore every other value that can be a goal for others or for the self. Individuality which is merely based on selecting a single value goal can be most shallow. A deepening of individuality comes from finding how every other value can be taken into account. It is the removal of value overindulgence in the situations one passes through as teacher and promoting multi-valuedness that can be considered "democratic education" (or socialization). The institutions of our society at present fall far short of actualizing this democratic ideal of multi-valuedness among their leaders and within their established and ongoing patterns of practices. These adult flaws can be traced back in part to partial socialization failures, where opportunity was not provided to prepare to act in multi-valued ways. In any event, every teacher and every scientist of socialization can keep at the back of his mind this criterion when examining adult to pre-adult interactions, and especially the start of those in infancy, for the valve preference patterns within them. It is a holistic way of thinking that sharpens descriptive acumen rather than confuses description with evaluation. At present, we need to avoid the other following alternative extremes. One is to describe endlessly without ever evaluating, in which case what usually happens is that the descriptions begin to be formulated in such a way so that evaluations are smuggled in under the guise of being technical and factual. The other extreme is to never separate out a description from an evaluation when dealing with motivational patterns.

What constitutes an operation of the teacher or child that could be characterized as "overindulgence" or "overdeprivation" is not a routine matter. The indulgence and deprivation is not "in" the operation. It is "in" the experienced outcome of it—as well as in the experienced intention. Studies of delinquent personalities at various stages of personality growth suggest to us that much of what is called delinquency consists in experiencing severe deprivations where others would only experience very mild deprivations and experiencing mild indulgence where others would experience extreme indulgence. Furthermore, the stability of how any deprivation or indulgence is experienced is low, shifting from time to time in rather drastic ways.

When we consider that the concept of delinquency implies norm-violation, we become aware that this violation is at work at the bedrock level of how the value indulgence to deprivation is maintained when contrasted with most norms operating for similar youngsters. It seems reasonable that such "norm-violation" may start in the childhood period—on the part of the child in terms of reacting too strongly to mild operations and too weakly to strong ones and on the part of the teacher in terms of using operations too similar for strong and weak intentions of deprivation and indulgence so that a confused experience results for the child. The nonparticipant observer of child-adult interactions must constantly exercise caution in not "mistaking" his own standards of severity or mildness for what is being experienced by either infant or adult in their interacting participation in each other's life course. Delinquency need not only be applied to norm-violations of public behavior—like temper tantrums—for it can also be expressed in somatic norm-violations (cholic) or fantasy norm-violations (intense self-absorption) involving images and feelings (inappropriate moods). Above all, we would expect all delinquent patterns to be associated with a move away from multi-valuedness—and an educational program which made that outcome more attractive than its opposite.

It is useful to think of every response pattern as being chosen by either child or teacher in terms of being the best way to maximize all values in each situation—and when that response pattern takes on the character of not being multi-valued in relation to others, the preferential patterning demonstrates that either child or teacher expect to be better off in terms of all values by not behaving in a value-sharing way toward others.

One of the advantages of having a system of categories to deal comprehensively but economically with value meaning is that we can begin to characterize some teachers as highly multi-valued in their dealings with young children and others as rather mono-valued. The emerging personality of the child, especially with regard to norm-violations, can then be studied in relation to such types. The effect of much descriptive and evaluative (advice-giving) work among experts in the field of childhood may be to make teachers of the child more mono-valued than they should be. Hence, they may swerve the personality process from reaching maximal approximations of human dignity. The overemphasis on affection in child-adult relations could lead to such mono-valuedness, even forcing "a regression" of the teacher's personality from a prior milti-valued state. At present, we tend to assume by "postulate" what the "primary" needs of the child's personality are, often based on pseudo-physiological thinking. These postulated systems are value-laden and dogmatic, since postulates are not "proven" but only "assumed." The appeal to "physiological principles" often by loose use of biological metaphors, makes them take on some of the qualities we often associate with legal systems, since they cannot be contraverted. Psychologists of childhood who would rebel at Marxist dogmatism about the wealth value as "primary" to all other values in human relations often seem to experience no similar twinges of protest when they themselves select some one universal pivotal "drive" that explains everything else. Furthermore, there is no need to introduce such "postulates," since all such matters can and should remain empirical, and if they do remain empirical, it is likely that more creative and imaginative regimes of rearing children will be found to make each later phase and the ultimate adult socialization outcome move more easily and fully toward multi-valuedness and human dignity.

We may have discarded much of the thinking about "instincts" that suffused throughout America from Europe, but we did not entirely eliminate some of the dogmatism we wished to combat when we refused to give the "instinct" notion authoritative scientific support. Indeed, the instinct lists of William McDougal can be seen as very crude ways to provide a physiological basis for all eight values we have described. It is not necessary to provide that biological base, however, in order to utilize the categories for the study of choice making in socialization, any more than it would be for the study of any other arena of choice making. Sexual activity, for instance, is not fully described merely by the physiological and behavioral operations that compose it. The mood and images accompanying one sex act make it a "holy" or "deeply meaningful" interaction for the people involved, whereas in the second similar act, it is a matter of sheer lust and physiological comfort. Moods and images start in childhood. The act of an infant, like thumb-sucking, can have a wide variety of moods and images going along with it or none at all. We simply do not know the values entering into such acts without looking at the operations in terms of the possible accompanying moods and images. By refraining to consider such experimental factors, we too frequently begin to introduce value postulates into child psychology that may undermine both our scientific and our democratic purposes. What we are more likely to discover is that there is no "universal" key value biologically dictated.

BECOMING MORE CONTEXTUAL

The last point we have made regarding moods and images in childhood will provide some suggestions for a program of research that child psychologists need to conduct—and this program will be outlined throughout this volume. Before entering into that more technical direction, however, with regard to new regimes of child rearing, it seems useful first to look back over the ground we have covered to see if we cannot grasp it as a whole and take meaning from it in more than one point at a time.

If there is any one single theme that threads the previous discussion together, it is this demand: Experts on child development will have to become more contextual if they are not to irresponsibly pose at expertness. Many will quickly associate the idea of contextualism with the mathematical and systematic thinking introduced by A.N. Whitehead. Very briefly, the main idea is that every fact existing in the universe (down to the slightest detail of an individual child's movement) is conditioned by every other fact that surrounds it, whether from the past, present or (since we reprocess history continually) future. Therefore, the understanding of the meaning of any fact—converting facts into data—consists in finding the larger configuration of relations that this fact forms with its context. We all now accept the contextual theory of meaning and our social science theories are rich with it in principle. But our own procedures for observing and processing data do not yet insure that we ourselves operate in terms of it. In fact, the growth of the social sciences has resulted in a proliferation of specializations, many of which make no effort at all to relate the facts in their field to the larger configurations that would emerge if they spoke and thought across specializations. The growth of the field of child development as a specialization is, of course, a very rewarding development—but should it result in the emergence of overtechnicalized language and set of concepts peculiar to data about childhood, it will snuff out its own rewarding potential for growth. The child psychologist can do more to make configurational and contextual study a reality than perhaps any other field. Hence, what happens within it may mediate and symbolize what is going on within the whole family of social sciences. For, by tradition and convention, the child psychologist is thought to need to know "less" about adult institutional life than those who study the emerging personality at stages nearer to adult status. If the child psychologist can break this "dogma" with regard to what his training "should" be, he is likely to emerge with some highly revolutionary findings about the social process, both of a theoretical and practical policy-making nature. To become aware of value conflicts operating among institutions or within them at the adult levels by exposure to "experts" specialized to such inquiry may set off a train of inquiry about those same value conflicts in child-adult relations that would produce findings modifying all existing theories of personality development in fresh and more useful ways. As it is, we are now living off the assets that theories of personality development devised several decades ago. These assets are deteriorating. The theories proved to be less and less rewarding. New ones will come and there never was a time when better theory that would promote sounder practices for desired outcomes was needed. They will not come, however, until those least configurationally oriented by tradition reach out and provide the empirical contours of larger relations. The kind of value analysis we have been proposing gives us a realistic alternative to the non-configurational practices that now more frequently than not characterize our field.

VALUES IN EXPERIENCE

We have said that values are "in" experience and not "in" the operations teachers and children use to convey that experience to affect the experience of the others. But what is "experience"? It consists in the flow of moods and feelings and the flow of images (including memory and anticipatory images) that goes unremittingly throughout all continuing social interaction. We have become so operation-fixed that we forget operations only make sense when we know the images and feelings to which they refer.

Since values are "in" experience, they are present in both moods and images. One may have wealth moods and wealth images, deprivational or indulgent. One may have affection moods and affection images, negative or positive. There are many value-moods that would be difficult for us to associate with some images without experiencing an internal crisis that we usually call "emotion." By now, psychoanalysis has provided us with a battery of mood-image complexes that produce "emotion" and which are inhibited.

Consider, however, a regime of child training in which, through selecting stimuli carefully, one could evoke every value-mood and, independently, every value image. It would then be possible to pair each value-mood with every value-image—and each value-image with every value-mood. In short, the child would be able to experience under matter-of-fact conditions every possible value combination of mood and imagery. Preferences then could be adopted on the basis of experience itself, rather than being established on the basis of cultural convention that only allowed some combinations to be experienced. Such cultural conventions would not be ruled out but they would be one among a variety of not "imagined" but experienced alternatives.

At the present time, it seems likely that music represents a language that is specialized to the symbolization and evocation of every value mood and feeling. Recent research has demonstrated that musical stimuli function with this range of mood meaning. Additionally, it seems possible that every value could be presented by drawings of a quite simple nature that would reduce the value conception to a simple abstract image. We have made an attempt to set up such image material. With these, it then becomes possible to pair the music-mood values with the drawing-image values in any and all combinations. Some students have begun to unsystematically introduce such pairings into the lives of their young children with results that often seem to lead to early and surprising creativity. It suggests that creativity as a trait in children has been produced by an infant regime with such multiple exposures unwittingly present. With adults, we find meanings of music shift as the drawings they are combined with alter (and vice versa) and, hence, all kinds of unconventional value coalitions become possible. In short, although the technique is still crude, it appears it can ultimately be worked through for adoption toward promoting multi-valuedness at the very start of life.

There are many who believe man's potentiality for consciousness has only begun to be realized—and that the limiting factor thus far in allowing the full potential to develop has been the inadequate cultures he had devised. The anthropology of the future becomes, therefore, essential to anything we might call "progress" in man's evolution. The procedure for studying moods and images in childhood as value carriers takes on double significance in this context. It allows child specialists to investigate "consciousness" from the start of life, with special regard to raising the level of consciousness by early programming procedures that maximize alternative and configurative thinking, at a time when the elementary senses are first at work establishing routine habits that are likely to survive into later phases of the life span. It provides us with tools for building the anthropology of the future—and, hopefully, it makes less attractive the resort to biological dogmatism that stands in the way of imaginative and creative inquiry. It is on the promising note that we can do much more to maximize human dignity and multi-valuedness in our society than we usually do that the discussion can come to a conclusion. It is a pause—which may have touched off a spark somewhere to move us all into much more than words.

THE CHALLENGE TO EDUCATION

The western world is just beginning to realize that the future of free societies, and, perhaps, of the civilized world depends largely upon the creation of practices which contribute to the realization of the highest potentials of all men as human beings. The free world must "through precept and example" help all people to abolish social institutions designed to establish external controls over the behavior of men in ways that make them dependent upon the whims and the idiosyncracies of a self-elected elite who are not responsible to the people for its actions. Thus, to achieve freedom, more of the people of the world who would be free must undertake with redoubled vigor the creation of social institutions and personal strategies which will make possible the realization of human dignity on a grand scale. This struggle will be won or lost not in the degree of development of material resources alone but rather in the development and consistent employment of the full potentials of the minds of free men.

It is suggested that one of the institutions in which this great resource of the free world can be nourished and maintained with effectiveness is the public system of education. Here the true goals of freedom can be systematically implemented, not merely through sentimental and hopefully intuitive methods of instruction, but by the planned application of practices and strategies which have emerged from the findings of research in the behavioral sciences that have too long been the concern of only a relatively small group of specialists. These findings must forthwith be put to the service of education. They must provide the powerful intellectual tools by which can be re-created in each generation the means of sustaining and renewing man in his struggle to free himself and his fellows from the physical and intellectual bonds of dependency and slavery.

A democratic institution should contribute to the achievement of goals which promote the wide shaping and sharing of human values and thus the enhancement of human worth and dignity. Too often in the past it has been typical of democratic societies to "take for granted" that new institutional proposals and their ultimate construction have conformed with the ideals of democracy. However, in the absence of clearly stated goals implemented by appropriate practices, the resulting effect of many such institutions has been in fact to violate the very principles upon which they were supposed to have been built. Much of this can be laid to the fact that many institutions have been supported by citizens who, while in every statement of their faith contend that they are "in mind and deed" truly democratic citizens, are in fact inarticulate and confused when called upon to clarify the goals toward which their activities in the building of institutional practices are directed.

This has often proved disastrous in leading to the realization of outcomes which were never expected by those responsible for creating such institutions. Extensive observation of the operation of classrooms and intensive discussions with teachers directed at the actual determination of their goals have revealed the degree to which many teachers feel threatened and insecure because of their lack of understanding of why they are doing what they are doing, why they are teaching the subjects they are teaching, and why they are undertaking to develop the skills they are expected to promote among children.

An extension of this list of factors which threaten the teacher would include some of the following in varying degrees. Since the teacher is not at all clear about his goals, his self-image is correspondingly unclear. While he does not aspire to the position of policeman, in actuality he too often sees himself as the officer of society responsible for the correction "of the behavior of children" so that they will be truly acceptable as citizens who conform in all respects with the rules and regulations imposed upon them by society. Fortified by this self-picture, he often resents what he thinks are serious challenges to his authority. Any aggressive behavior of the child may become a threat to the teacher's respect status. Any show of opposition by the child may be seen as evidence that the child withholds power and affection from him and will encourage the withholding of these values by other children.

Still another consequence of the unclear conception of the function of the classroom has been the extreme preoccupation of teachers with the development of specific skills and the mastery of certain subjects at great expense to the statuses of children in other values such as respect, affection and well-being including both mental and physical health. This consequence loses nothing in its significance because of the fact that these value goals along with others have not been articulated as fundamental objectives of the educative process. For example, many of the aggressive actions and hostile attitudes of children can be traced directly to the setting up of unfair competitive situations "to motivate mastery of the tool subjects." Such children, because they tend to lose confidence (self respect) in themselves, acquire feelings of inadequacy and guilt, and in responding with antisocial behavior, tend to strike back at the institution which through its competitive arrangements has forced them into these unhappy situations. As a consequence of these deprivations children develop fears and anxieties often leading them to resort to the practice of defense mechanisms which serve as temporary releases from these tensions but which in themselves contribute to further deprivations, further fears, increased anxiety, and compounded unrealistic behavior in their interpersonal relations not only with other pupils but also with their teachers.

Many children will respond to the insistent demand that they conform with "rules" of the classroom by trying to be "good" children under all circumstances. They may very rarely require the teacher to "control" their behavior and conform strictly with what they consider to be the requirements of the teacher by unrealistically withdrawing from any active participation in the formation of their own personalities or in expressing themselves as human beings. Such children become docile, obedient, and apparently attentive. They read what they are told to read; they perform all the tasks which meet the demands of their teachers in their effort to be loved and respected. These internal needs lead them to try to seek affection of the teacher by doing precisely and only what they think the teacher wants them to do. In their pitiful efforts to conform so as to be loved and respected by teachers, they have become dependent and subdued personalities. Such impaired personalities fall far below the standards of young citizens whose actions should tend increasingly to become self-directed toward the realization of goals that are compatible with democracy's ideals.

Unfortunately too many teachers are unaware of the damaging consequences to personality development of such attitudes and consequent unrealistic practices. They see too often the quiet child never in need of disciplinary action as the "ideal child," the good citizen. To the competent observer, however, such children are actually in danger, for they may easily succumb to neurotic processes which may project them into extremely serious psychosomatic damage that may persist throughout their lives. Such children may grow up as citizens who would conform with the aspirations of despotic societies in which the centralization of total power depends upon the formation of just such conforming personalities. It is indeed ironical, however, that in a society that aspires toward freedom, too often educational institutions that have been created in the name of freedom contribute to the formation of such personalities. Damaged persons such as these cannot be expected to make the decisions which sustain the society that aspires toward freedom. The quiet docile child may never become an obvious object of disciplinary action, but neither will he create new and better ways of achieving the wide distribution of values among the people. Unless he overcomes the debilitating effect of controls that have forced him into mental subjection, he cannot be expected to challenge any of the practices which have kept the mind of man in subjection.

American society is facing an intellectual invasion of giant proportions from the communist dominated part of the globe. The sophisticated citizen will, of course, contend that institutions of education are not alone in the promotion of conditions which contribute to personality damage as broad in scope as has been outlined above and rightly so. If the free society is to face up realistically to the maintenance of its perspectives against this intellectual invasion, all of its institutions must be recruited in the grand task of contributing to a long-range goal which is compatible with these perspectives. This goal is embodied in the determination to provide as many opportunities as possible for all citizens to realize their full potential—their full dignity—as human beings. Such citizens can be expected to provide an impregnable defense against the spread of totalitarian forces dedicated to the subjection and exploitation of man.

Our classrooms should provide countless opportunities for our young citizens to master concepts and ideas which are pertinent to the realization of this goal. We should give our young citizens wide practice in systematic thinking which will enable them to analyze and appraise what is going on in the world. We should lead them to understand that external controls undertake to build submissive personalities who are essential to the maintenance of a self-elected irresponsible governing elite such as we have witnessed, for example, in the growth of the Communist Party in the Soviet Union and in China.

The authors suggest the creation of instructional techniques and methods designed to build in the classroom a prototype of a free society. In this environment constant attention can be given to the values sought, the strategies employed, and the resources made available to the participants in the operation of the classroom. This broad conception will facilitate the long-range goal of the school which is to provide as many opportunities as possible for students to achieve their full potentials as free and responsible citizens.

CONCLUSION

The purpose of this chapter has been to sketch for the teacher a descriptive science of values which can command greater respect from society for the role of the teachers. A new dignity for teaching probably cannot be achieved wholly by the "bootstrap" efforts of teachers, but a more effective professional rationale will furnish the substance with which all interested groups can boost the public image of teaching.

The significance of this new rationale for teaching goes far beyond the upgrading of the teaching profession, however. The stakes include the survival of free societies on this planet. There is no question but that democracy is under critical trial everywhere. The world revolution which has characterized the twentieth century will continue with acceleration. The sweep of change could bury many of our cherished democratic institutions if these are not dynamically related to the value goals of the earth's people. Time is of the essence. Who can say how much time democracy has left to demonstrate its effectiveness in meeting the needs and wants of man?

The descriptive science of values, if used in the enchancement of human dignity necessarily breeds democracy in institutional practices, in personal relationships, and in self images. It can become a powerful force in developing the democratic, the mature person. This new science, then, is our signpost in the advance toward humanity's moral evolution.

Part II of this volume deals with the release of learning potential in the individual—the next four chapters present techniques and strategies designed to promote order and discipline in the classroom, the enhancement of the self-image of teachers and pupils, self-study through memory analysis, and the appraisal of mood and feeling in the classroom.

Part II

•

THE RELEASE OF LEARNING POTENTIAL

CHAPTER 5

•

Order and Discipline in the Classroom

Teachers in every society are delegated a considerable amount of power to be both the architects and the supervisors of a process of living and learning for students. In autocratic societies the teacher is considered a dictator over the children in all respects with power to indulge or deprive them of the values which they seek. Teachers in a democracy, on the other hand, are concerned with the fair distribution of values for all students, and hold out positive expectations for performance of children in value distribution activities. Democratic teachers, then, are interested in the process by which children learn how to live in a democracy—how to share values. In this sense the teacher is the director (in reality, an enlightened guide) of a process instead of a dictator of students.

Power is the base value for considering disciplinary techniques (method of student control) of the school, but the scope effect or outcome hoped for in the process is the promotion of high standards of rectitude. It should be emphasized that the teacher's role is one of upholding law—and due process of law—in the living and learning activities of children and to avoid the stigma of a government of men rather than laws as would be the case in the autocratic society. In a democracy, power, like any other value, is shared—shared by all members of the community with responsibility and with the expectation that all members of the community are informed concerning the laws and rules of behavior under which each is to perform. Further, it is expected that all members of the community participate in formulation of laws and of the disciplinary techniques which must be brought to bear on those who withhold values from others without merit or justification.

The general practice of the democratic school is to arouse and maintain expectations that all citizens will effectively participate in the sharing of values. A key word needs to come into the vocabulary of teachers and others who work with young people. That word is consultation. Children as well as adults must be consulted if they are to participate in the decision making of the community whether of the classroom or of the larger community, the nation, or the world. It apparently is never too soon to involve children in helping to make decisions which vitally affect them. Such involvement should, of course, be realistically geared to maturity level and to the acceptance of the responsibility by the children. The process of power sharing, as directed by the teacher, also includes, if consultation is to be effective, enlightenment as to what the common goals are which the group seeks, and, further, to reward every person who participates in decision making with respect. While the lust for power may be the mark of a mentally ill person, participation in intelligent decision making which affects one's own destiny is a healthy concern of the individual and should be encouraged.

The teacher who lusts for power over children is compensating against low estimates of himself—as contemptible, weak, unloved, or immoral. Such a teacher should not be entrusted with the supervision of the democratic process of power sharing in the classroom.

DEMOCRATIC FREEDOM IS LIMITED

Some have defined democracy simply as freedom or liberty. This, of course, does not take into consideration the true meaning of these terms. Freedom in a democracy is limited by constitutional provisions adopted by common consent in order to guarantee that maximum freedom for individuals will be maintained without encroachment on the privileges of other individuals. Thus, a democracy is an ordered and limited freedom which, while it guarantees maximum freedom for the individual, nevertheless presents a rather well structured process of law making and law enforcement by the community. Any classroom organized in September does so within the context of limitations imposed upon it by the world, national, state, and local community constitutions or policies. The community policies, of course, include those of the Board of Education. The special rules and regulations adopted by the administrators of the school also come to bear upon what may happen in a classroom. The area of freedom for a teacher and his students is still considerable and significant, but it must be defined carefully and out in the open so that all participants understand what is expected and what may not be permitted without application of sanctions. When the teacher and students make additional rules and regulations for classroom conduct, it should be for the purpose of further defining the freedoms of the individual. It should be the effect of such rules not to limit but rather to release the individual to search for ways to enhance his own values while doing minimum damage to the freedom of choice and value assets of others. Unbridled freedom of action resulting in gross withholding of values from others leads to the crippling effect of guilt. Ordered freedom promotes value sharing, creativity, and disciplinary measures which do not destroy a personality. It is well to have the class group consider by careful deliberation the setting up of duly constituted codes of behavior which, if broken, also call for the application of appropriate disciplinary procedures in order that the system will continue to operate for the maximum freedom of the individuals involved.

The teacher's role is not one of permitting the children to do as they please, obviously, but rather to help children set up rules and regulations of their own which are realistic, and then to set up realistic procedures for dealing with those who do not give reasonable conformity to these regulations. Overindulgence of the wrong-doer may lead to irresponsibility in the personality of the law breaker or the law enforcer. Since such overindulgence is corrupting, it is, therefore, deprivational. Power sharing as such must remain relatively dispassionate with the understanding that values such as affection and respect may be used in other contexts to rescue the individual as a personality, but power will be compromised unduly if soft attitudes on the part of the teacher or other children are tolerated. Instead, the *will to make law rule*—rather than the whims of men—is so vitally necessary to democracy, it is wise to build into the context of the classroom a relatively *impartial attitude* toward discipline.

Standards of discipline as set by parents and teachers often are eroded by good intentions resulting in overindulgence in other values such as affection. The child should not be permitted to get away with serious deviations from the norms of behavior in the name of love. A child's security is based not alone on love but on the limits set for his behavior. Every human individual has some aggressive and destructive drives. These are normal. These drives, however, need to be met constantly by social limits which help the individual to know when he is deviating from a social norm that he himself may have had a part in establishing. The child should be led to see that by depriving himself of rectitude, he is in effect also withholding respect from himself. Running up against these limits sometimes is painful and sometimes traumatic, but, nevertheless, every individual needs the security of knowing that if he goes too far with his destructive impulses, the society and his family and friends can help him *help himself* back to normal. Actually, antisocial behavior should be considered a "cry for help" in overcoming a previous condition of value deprivation which the child has suffered.

Even when children fail to get sufficient curbing of their destructive impulses in the home, the school has an obligation to set limits and, therefore, to try to set up a structure of security for the child. It is normal for the child to test the limits that have been set for him and to test the standards of adults. This is a part of his growing up process. As a very young child he feels very dependent upon adults. In order to grow up he must gradually establish his independence of adult control. This is a very gradual development, but specific events along the way sometimes precipitate violence in the relationship between children and adults. As children experiment with their new-found independence, it is important that adults not surrender their standards or the necessary limits to keep children from doing harm to themselves and to others. Children, as a matter of fact, need very much to feel these limits though they may not admit it even to themselves. In a way, adults let children down when they make concessions where social standards are concerned in trying to meet this new development of independence.

Although expectations for conduct should be firm, strategies and procedures for helping the child to use his increasing independence in constructive ways should be constantly developed by teachers and parents. While the standards need not come down, the techniques for dealing with children should change with the maturity level attained. The older child should not be constantly reminded that he is a child when he himself feels he is growing up. Obviously, freedom to develop independence and self-reliance within limits is necessary. If a child makes a mistake or an improper response in trying to achieve independence he should not be, as one teacher put it, "fussed at." Instead, his behavior should be challenged on the basis of the standards set up by society and dealt with fairly, impartially, and without passion so that he understands what the crucial limits of his actions are.

Another point that needs to be made time and again is that adults are models to children. Children need to identify with adults who are consistent, who have high standards of rectitude, who along with their feelings of affection, keep standards of conduct above reproach. If children cannot identify with such adult figures in the home or in the school they will likely identify with some other person in the community, and if that person's standards of rectitude are low the child's status of rectitude will likely be eroded.

It should be borne in mind that rules and regulations which obtain in the classroom or throughout the school are part of the larger context of social process prescribed by the educational system and by the society. That is why it is often so futile to prescribe isolated "tricks" for keeping order. The rules and regulations, the power sharing of the participants, and the disciplinary procedures applied to those who break the rules are all part of the larger social context of the classroom which includes, of course, the distribution of all values, not just the value, power. The application of disciplinary actions deprives the person of one or more of the values. In fact, the democratic management of value indulgences and deprivations are compatible with democratic goals. The interrelations of people often determine specific disciplinary events. It is important, therefore, when establishing patterns of control in the classroom, to think in terms of modifying the context of social action or interrelations rather than to prescribe specific or pat techniques. The process of developing law and order in the classroom, then, is in tune with the total process of democratizing the rising generation as it progresses through the school. This process in the school should contribute to the process which is going on in the larger society of developing mature personalities who can help make good laws and help enforce them, and at the same time help those who are not so mature to grow up to accept consequences of acts which deprive others of values.

THE RELATION OF POWER SHARING TO RESPECT FOR HUMAN DIGNITY

While the act of sharing power itself is a deference to the individual as a worthy participant in the social process, it is also true that failure to share power shows disrespect. Students who break rules should come to realize through consultation and guidance that they are depriving other pupils, the teacher, and themselves of respect. The student must see that discipline as applied to him is the automatic operation of a fair system of social retaliation for his own decision to deprive himself and others of one or more of the values. A child who can project consequences of his own action this way and still subject himself to such deprivations should be referred to a counselor or social worker. Reasonably healthy children respond positively to this kind of system. It furnishes a security within which the child works and within which he is able to launch himself into higher levels of endeavor. Such a child sees his own respect status related to that of others. He has a stake in the elevation of the respect status of all his associates. As the child grows in social insight, he realizes the great potential for creativity in a society which treats all people with respect.

FALLACIES IN APPLYING DISCIPLINARY PROCEDURES

One of the most common fallacies accepted by teachers is that they must first obtain order–order separate from teaching–through control of physical movement and noise. However, any such appearance of order must be accompanied by a psychological offensive if discipline and classroom order is to be educative for the child. Fear of the consequences of violating a process of law set up by the group should be substituted for fear of the teacher. As a matter of fact, appeal to fear as such should be avoided as a primary strategy because it has a serious crippling effect on the creativity of the child. Put another way, the child should be enlightened as to the value deprivations he will face if he breaks the law. He needs to understand that these deprivations will not be applied punitively or partially, but rather that they will be applied dispassionately in terms of prior decisions by the group. Nonetheless, he needs to evaluate rationally what consequences to him will surely follow his willful violation of rules–rules made by the group for the good of all.

Another fallacy often given credence by teachers is that of repeating a form of coercion because it succeeds. Here, again, is the use of fear in classroom management. It is possible to terrorize children and make them conform in certain ways which meet the approval of the teacher. There are certain well known teachers in every community who are praised by some parents and principals for their firm and even harsh control of children in the classroom. It is necessary to look at the context within which such a form of coercion is applied. Autocratic coercion stressing the personal relationships of teacher and pupil rather than the adherence to law and order may succeed in getting conformity, but, nevertheless, it is an unhealthy form of coercion and should be condemned.

An erroneous conclusion often given lip service by teachers is that power distribution in the classroom fails and therefore, because it fails in initial attempts, must be discontinued. Sharing power is something that all participants have to learn. It sometimes requires an extended educational process to yield really positive results. Democracy is not cheap nor easy. One cannot lead children to distribute power effectively until one is willing to begin this teaching with the prospect of possible failures along the route. As in the teaching of anything, some mistakes are to be expected, and mastery does not come necessarily on the first trial.

Another fallacious idea often expressed by teachers is that reactions of agitation and hurt feelings help in keeping children "in line." Again, it is important to emphasize that the teacher must maintain a professional and relatively dispassionate attitude toward law making and law breaking in the classroom in order to make the process work as it does in the larger society in which the children grow up. He should maintain relative calm in order to look behind the behavior symptoms to seek out the causes of the individual's antisocial behavior. Many discipline cases point up the kinds of emotional problems that children are having. Teachers can help with many; others give the teacher clues for referral of the student to counselors or social workers.

Still another fallacy is that some children *are born* with a tendency to be discipline problems. Psychological and biological evidence suggests, on the contrary, that discipline cases are a result of the human interactions surrounding the child, a symptom of his social environment which resulted in value deprivations. Therefore, children are not to be considered bad or good on genetic grounds. Some discipline problems are temporary, signifying little in the long term of a child's life. Many develop slowly from very complex emotional problems that occurred in the personality development of a child from his earliest years. Teachers sometimes can do little about modifying personality patterns that have already been well formed in an extremely deprivational environment and should not feel guilty about their inability to cope with some of these. Yet, personality always operates at any age within a social climate, and, if a climate is conducive to value sharing, teachers need not give up hope for most children.

CLASSROOM MANAGEMENT

There are no panaceas to which a teacher may turn in creating and preserving responsible classroom order. An important basis of good classroom management and control is the development of an ordered multi-valued classroom and teaching rationale. Within such a context the child may be expected gradually to develop responsibility (rectitude), courtesy (respect and skill), sympathy (affection), self-reliance (respect), and other enhanced value statuses.

The naive often think of "getting control" of the classroom as a first requisite of a good teacher. Respect for the teacher and acceptance of the power delegated to him is a necessary requisite to carrying on an efficient process of teaching. Carefully nurtured democratic process in the classroom community itself provides an inherent pattern of discipline. The class, with the teacher acting as the enlightened authority on essentials of the process, establishes its standards of conduct (rectitude) within constitutional limits and applies its own sanctions (power).

Students try out and experiment with the democratic process of justice as an integral part of the curriculum, not as an extracurricular activity. As they mature in the value analysis of such situations as enlightened and responsible citizens in the community of the classroom, they become more identified with the goals of their society. When they are engaged in constructive and challenging activities of value-oriented due process of law, the opportunities and compulsions for mischievious behavior decline. Problem-solving activities with their emphasis on clarification or justification of goals, elicit an intrinsic urge toward cooperation. The social process in and out of school should be a means of developing behavior patterns which will promote the realization of optimum potential in each individual. The development of self-discipline, governed by personal standards consonant with those of the society, is the distinguishing characteristic of mature self-actualization. The manner in which a teacher aids the development of inner controls will differ with each student. He should be alert to any child who seems not to find a harmonious social role in his group, who may dominate too much, is uninterested, is working at a pace out of gear with others, or lacks the intellectual ability to perform tasks he has chosen or been assigned by the group. On the positive side, the teacher, as a matter of course, seeks constantly to discover and promote the use of hidden strengths and abilities.[1]

Young people constantly imitate adults. They have mental pictures of good behavior and moral conduct from the adults they have known. They use these pictures to formulate their value goals.[2]

Teachers should provide an atmosphere in which the student can speak without fear or shame. The group should be led to see the contribution he is making and to appreciate his skills or knowledge. Each individual should be able to choose from a wide selection of participating roles.

Young people are expected to have some impulsive behavior in accordance with their individual personalities. The way in which a value goal is approached may differ in the amount of frustration which has been built up. For example, one who feels a need to move around physically may do so for reasons other than or in addition to physical well-being. Tasks which can use this physical and psychological drive should be provided as suit the needs and interests of the individual. This cannot be done successfully by a teacher until he has an adequate value profile on the student. Value-oriented guidance of learning quests gradually helps the student see not only the present worth but the future importance of the learning. It is a characteristic of good teaching that the pupil constantly is helped to become the kind of person he wants to be by tying his value goals up with his concept of the kind of person he wants to become and providing for essential steps along the way to this goal.[3]

Much antisocial behavior in school arises from the blocking of the individual's value demands, and this behavior is his way of dealing with the resulting frustrations. These blockings could be reduced if the teacher learns to interpret the student's behaivor in terms of his value profile and helps him achieve some of his goals in activities that make cooperation a rewarding experience.

---

[1] Inis M. Timson and Elizabeth H. Brady, "What Do Students Preparing to Teach Think about Discipline?" *California Journal of Elementary Education* (August, 1958), p. 16.

[2] James Hymes, *A Child Development Point of View*, pp. 12-18.

[3] R.H. Ojemann, "Based on Understanding," *Journal of the National Education Association*, September, 1958, p. 370.

GUIDING DEVELOPMENT OF SELF-DISCIPLINE

Discipline in a democratic society ultimately depends on a feeling of responsibility by the individual for the welfare of others, the ability to value-analyze oneself, and the habit of controlled deliberation in the search for truth. A student develops the ability to do these things as he learns to work cooperatively with others and to follow mutually-agreed-upon "rules of the game." Development of self-discipline cannot occur unless responsibility is gradually shifted to the students.

It is to be hoped that young people in value-oriented schools will learn techniques of self-discipline in all activities of living. Self-discipline is the highest form of rectitude.

The classroom teacher should be skillful enough to inspire most of his students to want to learn. Successful at this, he will have little trouble with group disorder. Since he has the cooperation of his class as a whole, he will be able to help the class deal with the individual offender with more detachment and professional concern.

The teacher who consistently and firmly guides a democratic classroom process often is regarded as a friend by the students. The group as a whole is encouraged to undertake and feel secure in adventures in learning because of the knowledge that respect cannot be lost even in the face of failure. The teacher is a partner in a mutual concern.[4] He should be determined to serve each and all according to their unique concerns within the arena of the democratic school.

CONCLUSIONS

It is clear that the young must be taught from an early age that values in a democracy are to be shared on the basis of merit, and that he as well as everyone else is expected to show some effort toward the distribution of these values. It is necessary that the adults around the young exemplify the kinds of mores and folkways desired, and that he get the identifications desired through good examples–especially his father, mother, and teacher. It is desirable that teachers point optimistically to the consequences following the performance of the acts of sharing values in a democracy. Expectations should indicate interest and respect for the individual and his performance, and every child has a right to expect that love from those around him will be continuous and unshakeable.

When desirable perspectives are made clear to the child in the school or in the home, half the battle is won. The remaining part of the task is to help the learner invent his own behavior–to live with reasonable independence but yet with normal dependence suggested by these perspectives, and to feel successful every day, if possible, in the performance of the total task.

When teachers are dealing directly with problems of discipline in the classroom the base value involved is power. In the application of power to discipline there are very special requirements. In a democracy, power must be

[4] Norma Cutts and Nicholas Moseley, "Four Schools of Discipline–A Syntheses," *School and Society*, February 28, 1959, p. 87.

shared and the educational process must help the child to gradually assume his responsibilities for power sharing. It is important to understand that the power that is shared is not power derived from the teacher. The teacher does not give to the student an increment of his own power, but power inherently is shared by the learner in the group because he is a citizen of our democracy. As teachers, we often say that we "allow" the student to choose. We must somehow get the personal factor out of power sharing if we are to help the young attain the security they need in the context of democratic control. The youth must never be led to feel, as he grows up, that power is something adults condescendingly give him if he is a "good boy." On the other hand, we must constantly cultivate the idea that power will be denied because of specific acts of the offender himself–that he deprives himself of power by depriving either himself or others of values. The major purpose of the disciplining process is the ever-increasing enhancement of the status of rectitude of all individuals who participate in the society which aspires to be free. Ultimately freedom depends upon the moral obligation of citizens to live not by the law alone, but also by the spirit of the law–and that which cannot be written entirely into the law: active concern in all human relations for the enhancement of human dignity.

DISCIPLINE CASES

The Case of Tom*

Tom T. is the talk of the school because of his outbursts and his unrealistic behavior. He will not make a constructive statement in class. His ridiculous suggestions provoke laughter, which shows deprivation of respect to his teacher and his peers. The children refuse to ask his opinion on matters which concern making a democratic decision.

Even though Tom is above average in intelligence, he does not try to do good work. This causes the class to withhold respect from him. He is not the fighting kind, but his egotism soars. He has only one brother, but most of the attention is centered on Tom who has the higher I.Q. This seems to flatter Tom's ego since he feels superior to his older brother. His peers detest this attitude.

Can Tom be taught to be a better citizen and a great leader in a democratic society? How can he gain the respect of his peers? What causes his egotism to be so rampant as to deprive others of their dignity?

The health folder on Tom was searched for clues to his unrealistic behavior. His achievement and I.Q. tests proved that he had superior intelligence. Nothing is wrong with Tom's ability to learn. Physically, Tom is in excellent health.

The permanent record shows that Tom would make all *A's* and then drop to *C's*. He had a perfect attendance record for two years.

Conferences with the principal proved that Tom had not been in serious trouble. He is likeable and accepted at times by his peers, yet, obnoxious and rejected at other times.

*This case was reported by Lois G.M. Willingham.

Mrs. T. visited the class on P.T.A. days and on special occasions. She threw light on some of the factors which caused some of Tom's unrealistic behavior.

Knowing right from wrong and attending church regularly, Tom should have a high status of rectitude but his behavior is not consistent with his knowledge. He has no trouble in giving credit where credit is due. No special demands are placed on him at home. Tensions do not seem to appear even when he is corrected about his unrealistic behavior.

Even though Tom does as little constructive work as possible in class, he is well-informed in most subject areas because he enjoys reading, watching T.V., going to movies, and visiting educational programs in the school auditorium.

Tom comes from an average income family. He has no deprivations of goods and services. His grandparents live next door, and see that their grandsons are well-cared for. Much affection is given to the boys, but the brother is quite different. His parents have had two years of college work. The mother does not work outside the home.

Tom's mother has a tendency to be somewhat haughty, but his father does not give that impression. His mother wants to have a higher prestige in social affairs and pushes her way into circles without being invited.

Tom participates in sports, especially baseball and football; however, he is sometimes taken from the games, for he does unfair things to his peers and then laughs as if it were perfectly all right.

Tom's irresponsible behavior leads one to think that he has been deprived of respect and consequently well-being. What can be done to restore his respect for himself and for others? He is courteous enough. Has his mother projected her feeling of superiority and haughtiness to Tom?

Visiting the classroom helped Tom's mother to realize his egotistical outbursts. She mildly and meekly corrected him. He laughed. How could Tom realize this was being disrespectful?

Tom was elected president of the Citizenship Club for six weeks. This made him gain some respect from his peers. He learned that he had to be a good citizen during that period to remain as president. He made the *A* honor roll, and seemed such a changed person. Everyone in school took note of the fact. Would Tom continue being a good citizen?

Many strategies for Tom's behavior were tried. Some worked temporarily. *When he overstepped the limitations of a good citizen, his peers were his judges, and he was deprived of play period—a rule in the Citizenship Club—because he withheld respect from his peers, his teacher, and himself.*

At the end of the fourth grade Tom seemed to have achieved a certain degree of maturity. His personality improved somewhat. His peers began to recognize him as a better citizen. He always seemed happy, even when he was so mischievous and egotistical.

Tom made the National Junior Honor Society in the eighth grade but had to be withdrawn in his freshman year. His grades dropped below prerequisite honor standards and he began to revert to his behavior of the past.

Tom T. is now a sophomore in high school and still seems to get "kicks" from causing humiliation to others. He has grown into a fine-looking young man.

Seldom does he date because girls resent his attitude and behavior. This does not seem to affect him. He continues to be boisterous and mischievous. His behavior ranges from punching his peers with his horn in the band to locking his buddy in the girls' restroom.

Tom has grown into a fair citizen, but could be a great leader if his potentialities were directed properly through high school and college, and if he learns to share the social values with his peers.

The question remains–What were Tom's most serious value deprivations? What strategies might have been employed to enhance his status in these values?

The Case of "David"*

David had great possibilities in life. He was polite to everyone. It was "yes, ma'am," "no, ma'am," "thank you," and "please," but David had a habit of losing his temper, fighting on the playground, and breaking other rules of discipline at school.

After his mother visited the classroom one day, David looked up and said, "Mrs. W., my mother and daddy hate me!" and began to cry. The teacher walked over to his desk, placed a reassuring hand on his shoulder, and told him that no real parents could possibly hate their child. He said, "You don't know the half of it!" His attention was diverted from this discussion by another child's entrance into the room. David was a big boy and did not want anyone to see him cry.

Could David be taught to be a better citizen? Could he curb his temper and learn to direct his decision making in a democratic way? These were questions considered for solving David's problem.

After David's outburst from his mother's visit, the teacher visited the principal's office. The principal enlightened the teacher with pertinent, confidential information about David's home life and his past discipline records in school.

The teacher's first reaction then was to study available records on David. His health folder, which contained achievement tests, I.Q. tests, reading-readiness tests, and his health record revealed many other things about David's past. David had average intelligence. This did not seem to be the source of his trouble. His permanent record card showed average grades, good attendance, but only fair citizenship rating. All seemed to be normal except the citizenship.

Why did David rate only fair in citizenship? One of his neighbors was a teacher in the same school. She was a chief source of information.

When his mother visited school, she was prone to degrade David. He appeared to be blamed for all misdemeanors at home, on the way home, and in the school. When the teacher defended David, by saying that he did not seem that radical at school, his mother assured the teacher that a "good beating" was the only way to "straighten him out." That was a critical clue to the teacher.

David has been deprived of all power status. His parents were very dominating and made all decisions. The mother insisted on perfection at all times.

*This case reported by Lois G.M. Willingham.

Being an unwanted child from birth, David had been deprived of affection, respect, well-being, power, enlightenment, and rectitude. Human worth and dignity had been denied David.

David had a sister two years younger than he. All wrongs done by the sister apparently were blamed on David, who was subjected to severe beatings with a "bull whip." This accounted, apparently, for his being extremely meek around adults. He had a generalized fear growing out of the severe punishment meted out by his parents.

David's mother was very active in community affairs. She was a Girl Scout Counselor, active in Parent-Teachers Association, and visited school often. She was a college graduate and had taught school. His father was an ex-officer in the Air Force. His mother maintained strict discipline according to her traditional method of teaching earlier in life.

The home life of David apparently was frequently traumatic due to the severe beatings and unjustifiable accusations of his sister. This resulted not only in the deprivation of well-being, but of most all other human values.

A highway patrolman moved next door, and after observing David's father "bull whip" him in the front yard, the patrolman threatened to notify the juvenile authorities. Afterwards, punishment was meted out indoors.

His teacher, other teachers in the school, the principal, neighbors, and townfolk became very interested in David. What was to be the outcome for David? What could be done to bring David and his parents closer together?

Under the leadership of the teacher, rules and regulations were formulated by the class for each peer to adhere to, with an understanding as to the punishment for breaking the class "bylaws." Each child participated. Officers were elected in the democratic way, and served a six-weeks tenure. This enabled all children to hold an office. David was chosen monitor and then fire captain. This proved to David that the class had respect for him. His peers were contributing to his well-being.

David began to move in a more constructive direction by trying to curb his violent temper. He turned most of his explosive energies into constructive directions. When he did forget and fought on the playground, he was punished according to the decisions made by the class. He had become over-polite for fear of punishment at first but grew to realize that respect of his peers and a high rectitude status were also good reasons for practicing courtesy and fair play.

The parents began to restrain themselves from beatings which contributed to the well-being of David, however, the mental anguish from accusations still continued but with diminishing severity. David has grown into a maturity which enables him to avoid the consequences of severe frustrations which he could not do in childhood.

David was happy when he was appointed monitor of the class. This accorded him respect, but it also recognized his capability of power sharing by being the leader of his class for a week.

David developed a more pleasing personality. His outbursts of temper became less and less frequent. He had a more secure feeling in becoming a citizen in the classroom, at school, and in the community. His self-expressions were more original, evidence that he was being released from much of his perceptual rigidity.

David learned about the overriding objective of his society, the realization of human worth and dignity. He sometimes forgets to curb his anger following value deprivations. He has never forgotten who first tried to understand his problems and often visits that teacher after school.

David has joined the R.O.T.C., a factor in bringing him and his father closer together.

SUMMARY

Power and rectitude loom large in the management of the problems of classroom discipline. Origins of these problems among young people which give rise to sanctions often are, however, traceable to other value deprivations, many of which occur in family relationships. Here as in most problems of man, the multi-valued approach will, in most cases, bear fruit.

Consideration of discipline problems illumines the principle that freedom in a democracy, whether at the level of the nation or at the level of the individual, is limited by constitutional or mutually-agreed-upon provisions. Democracy is a process of ordered freedom which can guarantee maximum freedom for the individual consistent with realities of social intercourse, such as a recognition of the rights of others.

Discipline in the classroom should be no different in general quality or in process from that to which the society at large aspires. The degree of application of justice should, of course, be consistent with the maturity of young people and the educational goals fostered by the school.

It is not the system of law or justice that should be compromised when individual circumstances are considered but, rather, the accordance of other values which may rescue the child from a pattern of progressive delinquency.

CHAPTER 6

•

Enhancement of the Self-Image by Teachers and Students

The changes in the classroom that have become the focus of this volume are primarily changes in the *people* of the classroom. Obviously, the person with the greatest influence on the other persons in the classroom is the teacher. This chapter describes how teachers can engage in self-study with generous rewards to themselves, to the children and their parents, and to the society.

Teachers should embark upon a journey toward self-knowledge that has no end, but must go on throughout life if maturity is to be achieved and maintained. Kubie makes a pertinent comment upon this point when he says: "Without self-knowledge in depth . . . we can have no adults but only aging children who are armed with words and paint and clay and atomic weapons, none of which they understand."[1]

The technique which has been found useful with adults who undertake to analyze and appraise their own personalities begins with the analysis of their statuses in each value category.[2] For each value category an analysis sheet must be planned which makes use of indices or criteria of the values. The person who is making this estimated appraisal of his value status levels is encouraged to consider his personality structure in terms of each of these indices. If his application of the indices is objective and uninhibited by the fear of facing up to his own characteristics, capabilities and lack of capabilities he will find that through this technique he will gain insights into his own personality which are extremely valuable in his continuing search for self-knowledge and maturity.

The teacher may be unaware of the consequences of value deprivations and therefore may suffer needless crippling tensions in his associations with fellow teachers, supervisors, and principals of his school. It is therefore of great importance for the teacher to be aware of the nature and consequences of such deprivations, whether real or imagined. Not only is such awareness necessary to his self-protection, but he also may be able to help any of his colleagues who may suffer such deprivations in their many human interrelationships incidental to carrying on the work of teaching. It is of great importance, also, to recognize

---

[1] Lawrence Kubie, *Neurotic Distortion of the Creative Process*, (University of Kansas Press, 1958), p. 133.

[2] V. Clyde Arnspiger, *Personality in Social Process*, (Dubuque: Brown, 1969), Chapter 5.

the possible damaging effects upon his pupils by the teacher, who responding unrealistically to value deprivations he has suffered, may in return deprive his pupils of one or more of their value assets. Then we see how contagious such personality damage really is and how seriously it may retard the entire enterprise of democratic education. It seems safe to say that one of the greatest obstacles to creative and productive behavior of pupils results from the transference to them by the teacher of his feelings of inadequacy or guilt in his relationships with them during the school day. The following reference may serve to make this point clear.

THE CASE OF MISS ALLISON

Miss Allison was a young teacher who had taught only two years in the elementary school. She was a seventh grade teacher and was very conscientious and dedicated to her job. She was very responsive to suggestions offered her by supervisors and principals and eagerly sought their help when confronted with problems which in her inexperience she had not faced before.

One morning in the course of studying the various transportation systems in the United States, she asked members of the class to name cities they or their parents had visited in the past. For some reason this provoked a great outburst by the children who vied with each other in trying to recall the names of such towns and cities. For a few minutes the good natured give-and-take of competitive discussions into which she had precipitated the class with her suggestion resulted in what to anyone unaware of her objective would appear to be uncontrolled behavior of her pupils. Her principal, who happened to be passing, entered the room to see what the noise was all about. It never occurred to Miss Allison that this was a case calling for discipline. Her pupils were doing precisely what she had asked them to do, and even though they were somewhat excited in calling out the names of the towns and cities, it was done in all good nature albeit with great enthusiasm.

To her principal, however, this was an obvious case of failure to control the situation by Miss Allison and he undertook to take over control himself, telling the children that he was surprised to learn that they apparently had little respect for Miss Allison and obviously had no regard for the other lawabiding citizens of the school.

Needless to say, Miss Allison was greatly disturbed by the event. Here was a case where her principal in the maintenance of strict discipline in the management of the classroom, had decided on the spur of the moment that he should help her "restore order." This was obviously a serious case of respect deprivation. It was a severe blow to her pride. She was at once deprived not only of respect but also of other very important value assets including power, skill (as a teacher), rectitude and affection. Her consequent deprivation of well-being was evidenced by the almost unbearable state of tension which she suffered.

At the end of the class period she went to the principal and tried to explain to him what her objective had been. To the uninformed principal, all Miss Allison seemed to be doing was trying to excuse herself for a lapse of discipline in her classroom. After she insisted on telling him what she had been trying to do, he said that while her objectives and intentions may have been good, she had allowed the class to "run away" with her, for as he said, they were obviously not under any kind of control. This, he said, he felt was a very unhealthy situation in any classroom.

Miss Allison finally gave up trying to convince her principal that she had been trying to promote democratic value sharing in the school. In reporting this incident, she pointed out that she felt she had been deprived of respect without merit because of the fact that her principal did not know what she had been trying to accomplish in this class. She reported that she had felt very anxious and tense the remaining part of the day and some two days later had not yet recovered from this very serious value deprivation. She reported that she had been impatient with the children and had several times punished them for behavior which she would have ignored in the past. In one instance, one of the boys in attempting to answer a very difficult question had failed completely. She had referred to his fumbling efforts to recite as "stupid." She reported that the boy had looked at her with blazing eyes, turned and looked out the window, and later had made a remark under his breath to a classmate that obviously indicated his rage at the respect deprivation he had suffered at her hands. She reported that she had asked this boy to remain after school and had tried to apologize to him. She said, however, that although he had in a mumbling sort of way accepted her apology, he had dropped his head and walked out without any clear-cut acceptance of her efforts to restore the value deprivation he had suffered at her hands. She reported further that she felt she had lost the friendship of this boy, for he had not even looked at her when he next came into the room and had studiously avoided any communication with her the following days.

In the discussion that followed, Miss Allison's colleagues had undertaken to analyze and appraise the events she had reported, in terms of the value deprivations suffered by the participants in the event. They made suggestions which occurred to them might be effective in restoring the value statuses that had been threatened. Some of these suggestions are reported below.

One teacher made the point that the principal's actions simply had reflected his previous education and experience and that Miss Allison should realize he felt he was being deprived of power and respect by her and her pupils in this incident. It was pointed out that his response was completely unrealistic and that it should be made clear to him that his power and respect statuses were not threatened. The group agreed that while her efforts to achieve the goals she set for the class had been very successful from her point of view, in the mind of the principal, she had violated all standards of "good class management." Another suggestion was that the teacher could go to the principal and explain to him that she had not intended to create this situation so as to embarrass him or to challenge his authority (power status), and certainly she had not intended to deprive him of respect. However, she was advised to insist that she had been trying to achieve certain objectives which she felt were indeed valid in terms of democratic education.

Another suggestion was that she call in for individual conferences any of her pupils who had suffered by her displaced hostility and transference of guilt during the days while she was in the grip of tension following her deprivations, and explain to these pupils that she had been very unrealistic in striking back at them in an effort to relieve herself of the tension she had been suffering.

Following this conference, Miss Allison did precisely as her colleagues had suggested and reported later that she had been amazed at the effectiveness with which her actions had relieved tensions they had all been suffering. In her conference with her principal, she said she had not been able to get more than halfway through her explanation before he insisted that he had been at fault and had acted precipitiously without really understanding what her objectives had been. His action, he had said, was inexcusable. He did thank her for coming to his office with this explanation and said that he had been thinking for several days of how to overcome the bad effects of his behavior which was not at all characteristic of the way he hoped to act as a principal.

Miss Allison said, also, that her conferences with the pupils involved had been very successful. The next day, when she had proposed that they name animals they had seen at the zoo, one of the boys had suggested, "Now, let's be a little more quiet about this," where upon the entire class had laughed uproariously. This, she said, was a real indication that the former status of congeniality in her classroom had been restored and with it her self-confidence and the feeling of friendliness and respect she had shared with her pupils had returned.

SYSTEMATIC ANALYSIS OF MISS ALLISON'S PROBLEM

From the events reported above, it is obvious that the most important techniques involved in the clarification of the problems to be solved and the creation of alternative ways of solving these problems have been employed during seminars in which the teachers analyzed these events as serious problems that warranted their careful systematic attention. At this point it will be well to review the intellectual tasks they performed in the systematic solution of the problems that confronted them. These tasks, also referred to as component operations of problem solving, can be employed in all areas of human living. Let us undertake briefly to examine these various ways of using the mind in the solution of the problems referred to above. Other similar examples could be cited as typical of the many problems which the teacher faces in the everyday management of interpersonal relationships occurring in the classroom. Let us see how the seminars held by the group of teachers mentioned above were organized and conducted.

Clarification of Goal

To begin with, certain necessary questions had to be answered regarding the nature of the problem. The first operation to be performed, as in all systematic or scientific problems, is that of goal clarification. This required that the goal be stated and justified. The goal, as stated by these teachers, was to restore the former amicable relationships between Miss Allison and the principal of the school. The justification of this goal lay in the fact that only through the restoration of amicable relationships could either of the participants work with the other in the wide sharing of values between them. Furthermore, continued failure to share values would seriously reduce their well-being status and thus greatly reduce their creative and productive capacities in their professional work. This goal, as can easily be seen, is certainly compatible with democracy's overriding objective.

Analysis of Trend

Trend thinking involves the analysis of past events pertinent to the problem. Answers to the questions asked by the group of Miss Allison lead to the conclusion that prior to the critical incident related above, the principal had been kind and considerate in his relations with her. As indices to support this conclusion, Miss Allison stated that the principal had given a great deal of his time to discussing her problems, had taken over her class so she could leave school earlier than usual to attend a theatrical performance in a neighboring city, and had written her a note of appreciation for her good work as a young teacher at the end of the first semester of school. He also had spoken in a complimentary manner about her work to one of the supervisors shortly before the critical event being analyzed. Miss Allison also said that prior to the unfortunate event, she had been quite conscious of sharing respect with the principal. She said she felt that their relationship had been very congenial and that her lowered status of well-being had resulted as much from her deprivation of respect and affection as from her threatened statuses of skill, enlightenment, and rectitude.

In order to achieve the goal set for themselves, it became obvious to the group that they must analyze the event in terms of the actual value deprivation suffered by each of the participants, since the problem demanded the restoration of the value assets that had been damaged in the critical incident. They began this analysis by considering first the deprivations suffered by Mr. Ainsworth, the principal.

In this way, they thought Miss Allison may be led to assume a more objective attitude toward the problem. That their judgment was good was evidenced by Miss Allison, who confessed that she had not realized the event had been threatening to Mr. Ainsworth in any way. However, it soon became quite evident that Mr. Ainsworth had thought his power status had been threatened. The index to this conclusion was his request to Miss Allison that in the future she discuss any "unusual" methods with him before "trying them out" in her classroom. The group also assumed that his reference to what supervisors may think, if they had witnessed the incident, indicated a threat to his respect status. Furthermore, his specific reference to the responsibility the school principal must assume for maintaining "order and discipline" was an index pointing to the threat, he felt, to his rectitude status.

Miss Allison stated that she had been greatly surprised to learn that Mr. Ainsworth had, because of these deprivations, suffered serious damage to his well-being status, just as she had. She stated that this insight into the reasons for

Mr. Ainsworth's actions had lead her to be more sympathetic with him and, consequently, her tensions had been greatly reduced. It is significant also to note that Miss Allison remarked that she thought her tension had been reduced partly because she had realized her own analytical skill had increased thus enabling her to achieve a more objective attitude (intellectual control of the situation).

Miss Allison remarked that she should not have expected Mr. Ainsworth to respond positively to this incident since he had not understood her objectives which necessitated the apparently permissive technique she had employed.

It was interesting to the group that Miss Allison took the lead with such a sure hand in analyzing her response to the deprivations she had felt she suffered. She quickly identified the threats to her power, respect, skill, and rectitude statuses growing out of the incident, and consequently to her well-being status. One of the group remarked that Miss Allison, at this point, seemed to be making remarkable progress toward facing up realistically to the problem and consequently was feeling much less anxiety and tension over the incident.

Analysis of Existing Conditions

In the consideration of existing conditions relative to the goal, Miss Allison volunteered the opinion that Mr. Ainsworth was still greatly disturbed by the event. She said he had obviously avoided her when she came to school the following morning and appeared nervous and anxious in a casual conversation with some other teachers in her presence. Other similar indices she offered led the group to conclude that Mr. Ainsworth's actions indicated serious tensions on his part, which they felt could be traced directly to the value deprivations mentioned previously.

Analysis of Future Probabilities

The group quickly decided from the analysis of past events and existing conditions that without intervention, further deterioration of interpersonal relations between Miss Allison and Mr. Ainsworth would likely persist and would result in further serious personality damage to each of the participants. This led them to decide to undertake the next important intellectual task in the solution of the problem involved in the achievement of their goal.

Creation of Alternatives

One of the most experienced members of the group suggested that in the course of their deliberations, Miss Allison had through her participation in the performance of the component operations of problem solving, and in the use of other tools of thinking, gained valuable insights into the nature of the problem involved. This opportunity, she pointed out, had been denied Mr. Ainsworth, and, therefore, Miss Allison's own high standards of rectitude demanded that she assume responsibility for taking the initial steps in creating and employing alternative ways of solving this problem. Further discussion led the group to conclude that the instrumental goal to be sought by Miss Allison was to restore the value deprivations suffered by Mr. Ainsworth. The question of why Miss Allison should assume primary responsibility for initiating remedial measures with Mr. Ainsworth was debated at some length. This debate ended when Miss Allison said she realized Mr. Ainsworth had suffered serious tension from value deprivations in the incident, and just as she would have employed all her skill to help him if he had suffered a physical damage so too, should she employ all the insight and skill she had acquired in trying to remedy the personality damage which she had come to realize he had suffered. She also said she realized that whether the value deprivation was actual or only threatened made little difference in the consequent depth of tension Mr. Ainsworth had suffered.

The following creative suggestions were offered in the effort to assist Miss Allison in her undertaking to restore Mr. Ainsworth's value status not only of respect, but also of power, affection and rectitude. The group assumed that as a result of the restoration of status in these values, his well-being status would be reestablished and he would be led to a more realistic appreciation of Miss Allison's position.

It was recommended that Miss Allison make an appointment with Mr. Ainsworth and open the conference by stating that she wished him to understand that she had not intended to withhold respect from him by acting in the undemocratic manner she had employed and that she wished to apologize for not having discussed with him the objectives she sought in the class which he had visisted, for she knew that if he had understood why her children were so enthusiastically noisy in their participation in the project, that he would have given her his support which she valued very highly.

It was further suggested that she tell Mr. Ainsworth he had acted within his rights and responsibility in interrupting a "noisy" class in the absence of any reasonable explanation of what appeared to be an overt breach of "good" behavior.

She was advised to tell Mr. Ainsworth she had appreciated the guidance he had offered her as an inexperienced teacher, that she had treasured the congenial relations which had existed between them prior to the incident, and that she hoped this mutually friendly and respectful relationship could be restored.

The group advised her then to proceed to explain to Mr. Ainsworth that she had been very disturbed by his conclusion that she had violated her responsibility as a teacher (rectitude), by her feeling that she had lost his respect, and by realizing that she had been so lacking in enlightenment and skill as to have failed to explain to him the objectives for the class period which had resulted in precipitating the problem. Miss Allison agreed to proceed as the group had recommended and immediately made an appointment with Mr. Ainsworth for the following day.

The group reminded her that one additional operation yet had to be performed in completing the intellectual tasks of problem solving. This task involved the appraisal of the alternatives they had created. Miss Allison said that she would probably have a sufficient number of indices to make a valid appraisal of the effectiveness of the suggested alternatives in the course of her meeting with Mr. Ainsworth.

Appraisal of Alternatives

As Miss Allison reported to her colleagues the following day, she had proceeded only partly through the suggestions made by the group when she was interrupted by Mr. Ainsworth who said that if anyone should apologize for undemocratic behavior, it was he. He said the incident had been a fearful blow to his feeling of self-respect and that he had acted irresponsibly in interrupting Miss Allison's class without knowing what her goals were. He agreed that he had felt (quite unrealistically, he realized now) that his authority (power) had been threatened.

Mr. Ainsworth then asked Miss Allison how she had come to make such a full and comprehensive estimate of his "feelings" after the incident and she told him she had asked for a conference with three of her fellow teachers at which time they had decided to attack the matter systematically be employing the component operations of problem solving. She then proceeded to describe this approach to the point of the final aspect of alternative thinking which required a valid appraisal of the alternatives suggested.

At this point, Mr. Ainsworth asked Miss Allison if she would allow him to participate in the project by presenting his appraisal of the alternative suggestions before her colleagues as a group. She readily consented and the group later agreed that Mr. Ainsworth had done a fine job of proving at first hand that their systematic attempt to restore amicable relations between himself and Miss Allison had indeed been successful. Mr. Ainsworth congratulated the group upon the mature manner in which they had so effectively employed the tools of thinking in solving this problem and asked their support in helping him solve many of the problems, which he as their colleague, would have to face in the future administration of their school. Miss Allison then told Mr. Ainsworth of how her colleagues had assisted her, also, in solving the problem she had faced in undertaking to restore the value deprivations her pupils had suffered because of her unrealistic behavior following the critical incident.

Still another important outcome of the practice of these techniques of self-study will be the increasing mastery and growing self-confidence of the teacher in dealing with the personalities of others including both pupils and parents.

Another technique which has been found useful in self-study is the "analysis of specific frustrations." Here the teacher employs a framework of analysis which provides practice in the manipulation of significant categories of the problem.[3] The categories of analysis presented in this procedure are typical of many other categorical arrangements which may be used by the teacher in planning for his interviews with the pupils, and with parents where such techniques are indicated.

---

[3] Arnspiger, *op. cit.*

Is self-study difficult? Are there elaborate rules to follow? At this point in the experience of the reader the answer should be in the negative for both these questions. One simply applies the tools already learned to oneself.

Begin with utter simplicity. Sum up your general reactions to your opportunity to view life through the value framework. No doubt you will find you have already done some informal self-study and evaluation like this anonymous teacher after only a short orientation to the science of values:

> I can truly say from experience now, that since I have analyzed the children in my room according to the framework I have a better understanding of them. When some problem arises, I find myself seeking the cause of it through some value deprivation. I have also taken an inward look at myself and tried to appraise my own value statuses. I am more aware of my obligation to society as a whole. Since teachers have such a great responsibility of leadership in a community, I feel that I am going to be more capable of providing opportunities for individuals to have access to the same values I have. In our different professional organizations, clubs, PTA and even in our churches, I think I can help these individuals who feel insecure in many ways to see their value statuses and value goals. There are many adults who are deprived of some of the social values. I am glad I have had the privilege of this 'bird's eye view' of the Value Framework. I think it is wonderful. I know it is going to help me a great deal in the future.

Another under similar circumstances made the following statement:

> After becoming aware of the framework of values, I have begun trying to practice value sharing with my own family and friends and my students. I have enjoyed trying to decide just what were the deprivations of the people with whom I am in contact and trying to accord them that particular value.
>
> After having written about the value assets and liabilities of each of my students, I find that I understand each of them better. It caused me to think very hard about what I could do to help each one and now I have four and a half months left in this school year to try to restore their values.

A more intensive experience with the science of values caused this very perceptive teacher to write the following:

> There are several important results which I attribute to having been introduced to the values framework. It has given me a definite set of tools by which to evaluate my life and my past relationships with my family. Without too much deliberate effort on my part, the whole experience has helped me achieve a greater understanding of myself. Although I had applied previously as much of my college psychology to understanding myself and my family as was possible, there were certain limitations in the various theories. The science of values seems to be the most complete rationale for introspection and self-evaluation which I have found.
>
> Here I could give a detailed account of how my mother and I used this rationale to analyze our family and its relationships and the written set of existing facts and attitudes we made, with plans for wider sharing of values by all family members now at home. The details are, however, still too sensitive to write about. Suffice it to say that whereas my mother and I had 'come to a parting of the ways,' now we are sharing affection and respect again.
>
> I feel that the values concept is essentially a very moral one, and as such, can be closely integrated with the Christian life. The value-oriented rationale is a very profound expression of the Golden Rule, and is extremely easy to apply to Christian living. Again, in relationships with others, it gives a definite form to evaluate by, and by which to attempt to live. The second effect on me, therefore, has been to work

this new method into my Christian living—that of according as many of the values as possible to others.

The third effect of the values framework has been to help me analyze and understand the true basic foundations of America. It is appaling, but nevertheless true, that this is the first time I've ever been introduced to the *true* meaning of democracy and realized so fully just what it means to me to live in a free country. This has prompted me to read a great deal about Communism so that I might more fully understand this great enemy to democracy and freedom that now exists. Perhaps in this area my vision has been expanded to include a greater number of realizations, new interests and avenues to learning than in any other. For the values have helped me to understand and truly believe in democracy!

None of these first three outcomes is unimportant. But perhaps the greatest impact the rationale has had on me is in my much revised educational beliefs. And although I had not planned to return to the teaching profession in the near future, I am now such an enthusiastic convert to these new ideas that I would like to put them into action. A very disappointing year of teaching under a stifling, depressing authoritarian situation left me with no desire to return to the field. My experience with the value framework has renewed my interest in, and my zeal for teaching. The value-oriented rationale has encouraged and inspired me so much that I should like to return to the profession as a teacher, supervisor, or perhaps sometime in the future, as a college instructor.

The value-oriented rationale is so important to the realization of democracy, I propose that it be required for all educators and administrators. It is vital to the contribution which education of this type should make to the future of our nation and to the world. There are others besides myself who need to know *where* they are going and *why*!

On Becoming a Democratic Personality

One of the early perceptions to be gained in the process of self-study through the value-oriented rationale is the comparison of one's present self-image with the ideal democratic person. Such a person places primacy on the realization of human dignity for all persons, including himself, according to merit. Dignity as the ideal is not to be achieved at the cost of balance in the value profile—either of undue deprivation or overindulgence. A high status of human dignity depends upon a relatively high status in each value category—a balanced value profile.

The rationale for achieving human worth and dignity through time is the *wide* rather than the *narrow* sharing of values. We do not have "special' neighbors with whom we may share values. All men are our neighbors. We are obligated to not merely love our neighbors, but, rather, we are obligated to share all values with them according to merit. By sharing values in our everyday human relationships, we internalize meanings which build up our self-image toward this obligation.

Sometimes the mature person must withhold values according to merit, for to accord values can, if undeserved, become over-indulgence. "According to merit" here refers to the degree to which persons accord values to others. The criminal deprives others of values without merit and is punished by being deprived of values. To overindulge violates the standards of rectitude. It is important, therefore, that the democratic person become more and more conscious of the value outcomes of each of his actions both for others and for himself. It does not follow that to accord values to others will mean a deprivation of one's own values. On the contrary, one cannot likely enhance value statuses of others without enhancing his own.

The following statements illustrate how thinking about democratic methods of teaching or behaving help to lead the way to self-improvement:

> I have always been a firm believer in democratic procedures in the classroom, but I must confess that I fall far short of the ideal democratic teacher. It is so easy to follow the path of a fixed routine. The teacher has such wonderful opportunities to accord values. I had never considered the democratic procedures in the light of the value framework.
>
> My pupils have always participated in the making of important decisions in the classroom, but I now pay particular attention to the procedure to see that all of the members have an opportunity to share values. The sharing of respect is one of the most enriching and rewarding of all, therefore, I try to develop practices in which respect is accorded every member of the class on the basis of merit. Every child should be accorded respect for work well done.
>
> Teaching pupils 'good behavior' is not enough. They should be taught that the moral person in a democracy is one who demands that other citizens have access to the values which he demands for himself. I realize that my own values will be enhanced when I accept responsibility for seeing that my pupils have access to the values.

— — — — —

> A working knowledge of the value framework has helped me, personally, to understand why I sometimes distrust, dislike, or disrespect others as well as myself. Now I not only understand why I have feelings of this nature, but I also know ways I can help to remedy them. I have a much closer understanding of 'self' as well as others.

— — — — —

> My reaction to the value framework was at first one of confusion and misunderstanding. I suppose this reaction was felt because I had to un-learn or turn away from the beliefs I formerly had about values. For the past four or five years we have been told at teachers' conferences to teach values to our students. 'Intangible Values,' they called them, but until I received a chart listing the eight values and defining values as needs and wants, I did not know what they were talking about.
>
> Then as we discussed values in teaching, I learned that we do not just ' teach" values, but actually accord them or withhold them. This knowledge has opened new possibilities for me. Actually, I believe I'm a better teacher because I've thought about the value deprivation of each pupil in my classes. When we try to understand why they act and think as they do, then and only then are we qualified to help them learn.

Teachers Analyze Unrealistic Behavior

The value analyses by the teachers in the statements above are highly significant in that really important insights into the self are achieved even without the benefit of systematic analyses which are made deliberately for that purpose. The experiences were contextual. The insights were achieved by placing the self in the social context.

How does one approach the systematic, deliberate study of self behavior? Again, the process is not mystical, mysterious, or beyond the power of ordinary persons. The truly mentally ill need the professional help of the psychologist or psychiatrist. For most people, the way to "know thyself" is to value analyze one's unrealistic behavior. These behaviors are not difficult to identify when it is understood that unrealistic behavior is that activity which is not likely to help one achieve his value goals on any lasting basis. Inappropriate, and therefore unrealistic, behavior blocks rather than opens the way to the achievement of goals. It is emotional, compulsive activity which is, as Kubie[4] says, "segregated from appropriate thought or action." In short, unrealistic behavior is the result of a "disturbance in the relation of the symbolic process to whatever it represents."

Unrealistic behavior intrinsically takes the form of defense mechanisms—defense of an ego that has suffered serious value deprivation. Briefly, they include among others: (1) compensation, (2) conformity, (3) daydreaming, (4) perceptual rigidity, (5) projection, (6) repression, (7) depression, (8) drugs and alcohol, (9) sublimation, (10) regression, (11) rationalization, (12) displaced hostility, (13) reaction formation, (14) shyness, and (15) hyperactivity. The following analyses of their own unrealistic behavior by teachers are offered as evidence that the science of values, when conscientiously applied to self-study, can lead to release from unnecessary rigidity, fear and tension, and to creative behavior.

SELF-STUDY NUMBER ONE

When I was a little girl, my eyes were very badly crossed. I knew how I looked and wondered how anyone could love me. Though I did not doubt the love of my parents and my brother, I certainly did doubt that of other relatives and acquaintances. This was a threat to me in that I feared loss of affection and respect, and certainly my well-being was affected. I also think my power status may have been threatened. An unrealistic behavior I indulged in at this time was daydreaming. I dreamed of becoming very successful, thus proving my worth and gaining respect and perhaps affection.

Surgery during the year I was thirteen brought about a measure of correction and a great deal of relief from tension for me. I still, however, continued to worry about this matter and dreamed of success in some field which would bring about respect for me. I went to college, graduated, became a secretary, and still this problem persisted to some degree. I had by this time, however, proved that I was capable, and my self-respect increased. I also by this time had some boy friends. This, too, increased my respect status.

When I was twenty-two, I again tried surgery for a little better correction. The specialist discouraged me at first about having this surgery. I was very disappointed, because I had dreamed of having eyes that were perfectly straight. The doctor consulted with other specialists and decided that surgery might be tried again if it were done on my 'good' eye. I had long

[4]Lawrence S. Kubie, *Neurotic Distortion of the Creative Process.* Lawrence, Kansas: University of Kansas Press, 1958, p. 19.

since suppressed the vision of the other eye (or perhaps may never have seen with it). The correction which resulted was not perfect, but it seemed satisfactory to me, and the specialist advised me never again to have such an operation, since the muscles had been shortened until a degree of receding of the eye into the eye-socket would result from further attempts. I had long before this time discovered that a person's looks were certainly not the only cirterion by which he was to be measured, and had gained enough self-respect and confidence that I was no longer so thoroughly miserable about my looks. Having done what I could to correct a physical situation which I felt robbed me of respect, I continued to gain self-respect and the respect of others.

I feel that out of the escape I sought in daydreaming may have come some good. I did gain what at least to me is a measure of success as a productive, creative human being. I decided I would like to be a school teacher. I had leaned on my family for assurance of affection, and respect, and I now wanted to get far enough away from them to prove to myself that I could be successful and well-respected by those other than my family—and this on my own. I took a school teaching job in New Mexico and was able to do a good job there, acquire friends, a place for myself in the community, was asked to take a part in the faculty play presented to make money for scholarships, to take part in a show done by a local service club, and felt generally that I had proved to myself that I was secure enough to gain respect on my own, away from my family. I enjoyed these years of teaching in New Mexico and came back home to East Texas only when I became engaged to marry an East Texan whom I had met here during the summer at home.

Some of the things concerning my father-in-law which I shall relate are hearsay from members of the family, and I hope I have not been unduly biased against him by them; nevertheless, I heard them, and have put them together with things I have witnessed for myself to form my ideas of his personality.

My father-in-law is not able to read and write, a fact which he has managed to let very few people know. He was said to have had epileptic seizures when he was quite young. Thus, his parents did not make him go to school and learn to read and write. I wonder if this was really what he suffered from and if it was the real reason he did not attend school, for at the age of fourteen he began to make a living for his father, who was terribly crippled, and the entire family. His father and mother lived with him and his family until their deaths. All of this has been intended to give background information before I describe some of Papa's actions. From family hearsay I have heard he was in his youth a 'wild one' who drank, 'chased women' etc., (this being after his marriage). He has beaten his children, beaten his wife in the head with his fists while he had her hemmed up in a closet, and has threatened to kill himself in the presence of his wife and children. I can attest to the fact myself that he is overbearing and has an uncontrollable temper (which has on occasion been directed to me). He demands that he be waited upon by Mamma S. 'hand and foot.' He sits while she gets him a glass of water. She combs his hair. If he wakes in the night with a headache, she gets up and gets medicine for him (he literally eats medicine).

My specific problem is that I have consuming fear my husband might get to be like his father. I literally daydream about this. I try to imagine what I would do if he ever become so demanding upon me. I know this is certainly unrealistic. I have talked with my husband about it (talked? no, berated him about it), and he tells me how unrealistic this is. He asks me what action of his has suggested to me that he might ever treat me as his father has treated his mother. He states having witnessed such behavior would make anyone more and more determined not to practice such cruelty. I do know my behavior is unrealistic. I have known that my father-in-law is truly a sick man. There was a time when he should have had psychiatric treatment, perhaps he still should have.

Recently, with the aid of the value framework, I have been able to accept Papa somewhat better. I have been trying to think of ways to make him feel respected. I could go on and on about deprivations he has suffered and is, I think, still suffering which I feel have contributed to making him the way he is. I feel that the people involved right now, in depriving him of not only respect, but also affection, are unaware that they are doing so. I believe that in the act of restoring his respect and giving him affection I can further correct my own unrealistic fears and behavior. Everyone in the family says Papa's behavior is much improved.

Summary of Unrealistic Behavior

1. I used to dream (daydreaming) as a little girl of becoming famous and successful in order to gain respect and affection I felt were not mine because of my terribly crossed eyes.

2. I daydream now of my husband's becoming cruel and demanding toward me as his father has been toward his mother.

3. Daydreaming was an unrealistic behavior indulged in as an escape from my physical handicap. As I think more about it, I believe also this became a step worse, and a real shyness resulted.

4. Recent daydreaming has been a result of my imagined threat of deprivation of respect and affection of my husband.

SELF-STUDY NUMBER TWO

Two years ago in August I began to notice a sore, touchy spot on the back of my head. At first it bothered me only when I combed or washed my hair and touched my head. In a few weeks I began having sharp shooting pains first in the back of my head and then in the front. Especially at night did I notice these pains and finally to the extent that because of the pain and the emotional distress I was unable to sleep. I postponed going to the doctor for the stupid reason that I feared the loss of my power to carry on in family affairs. Finally in November when I took my mother to Dallas to a specialist in the field of radiology who has been treating her for the last three years, I revealed to him and to her this pain and fear I had been suffering. After examination of the spot he immediately sent me to a tumor specialist who removed the benign tumor which, he said, was a result of injured tissue of long ago with surrounding infection accompanying it.

I am aware that I behaved in many unrealistic ways. First, I had a great phobia that I was the victim of a malignancy because of a recent experience with a close member of my family and a friend. I suffered feelings of guilt at the thought of being sick. Also, I practiced repression in trying to convince myself that this pain did not exist or would disappear. I certainly was not mature enough to face the problem realistically. In addition I became more withdrawn and preoccupied in the hiding of my pain and fears. I believe this frustration was caused chiefly by the fear that I might suffer the deprivation of respect, power, and affection of my family if I were unable to fill a needed place in helping them rather than in needing to be helped.

I feel that much of my behavior in the past has been unrealistic. In the first place I have had a constant struggle with feelings of guilt at the fear of incurring disapproval of my actions and choices from other people. I limit myself to a few activities which I try to do perfectly, and when I fail to live up to my hopes, as I often do, I am miserable.

Also, I am extremely timid and shy. I have always felt that I should be very quiet and not attract attention to myself. This has resulted from my feelings of inadequacy.

In addition to the particular incident I have related and the examples of unrealistic behavior evidenced in it, I believe I can list other examples of unrealistic behavior which I have shown in the past.

Probably shyness is the type of unrealistic behavior which I have engaged in all, or most, of my life. I have always desired to keep out of the limelight as much as possible and to compensate for my inability to be at ease by working laboriously 'backstage,' so to speak. I am very easily embarrassed, especially at complimentary remarks. Since I feel inadequate in many fields, I have a feeling of guilt when praise is given.

I also often practice compensation. Feeling inadequate in many ways, especially in the ability to be friendly, I seek status in other values. I believe I pursue music for this reason. It seems that I strive for perfection, an impossible goal, in a few things which I feel I am able to do well. In trying to be perfect in one thing, I attempt to compensate for my inadequacy in so many other things.

I really have not been aware of my unrealistic behavior so much before these last few weeks. Certainly I am beginning to analyze these behaviors in the light of the value deprivations suffered.

There are many indices to support the conclusion that much of my unrealistic behavior should be classified under the defense mechanism of shyness. I find myself continually trying to avoid exposing to the eyes of the world that I am inadequate and generally ineffective. In this way, I do not feel so much threat of deprivation in the value status of respect. I become very tense when forced into a position that draws attention to myself, especially in speaking before a group. Being a teacher of English, I have come to realize that this also is a threat to my respect status. Definitely I feel this withdrawal mechanism provides me with only a temporary release of tension from this deprivation.

Another index of my practice of the defense mechanism of shyness is that many times I have been told by a friend after knowing her for some time that in our early association she felt me to be snobbish and that I appeared to reject friends. This is far from the truth, of course, and although I do not have a wide circle of close friends, the people who are close to me know this to be untrue. I realize now that I have many times refused to offer affection and respect to people because of the fear of suffering deprivations in these categories if they should reject my efforts.

There are also many indices to support the belief that I have always practiced the defense mechanism of compensation. For example, all my life I have tried to excel in scholarship to achieve high status in respect and enlightenment. In addition, it has been my desire to become a skilled musician to compensate for some deprivation of which I have not been aware. Looking back on my childhood, I find that I was encouraged to practice compensation as a result of the deprivation of affection. Being an only child and often lonely, I was given things of material value to compensate for the deprivation of affection. Certainly there was no lack of affection from my over-solicitous and loving parents. However, since my early playmates in the neighborhood were members of larger families, I realized at an early age that I must relieve much of my lonliness with toys from the store.

Being the member of a small group of friends and relatives who always held very high standards for themselves and me, I believe I have used repression for a long time also. Many of my decisions since a young age have been made in an effort to please these few people in my circle instead of myself. I have always leaned very heavily on the advice and decisions of several of these people rather than on myself. However, I realize now that this has made me have many feelings of dependency and insufficiency and has caused me to suffer the deprivation of power (freedom of choice). I have repressed much anxiety about my ability to achieve certain important goals. This anxiety, in turn, has caused me deprivation of well-being with occasional occurrence of symptoms of psychosomatic illness in the form of headaches and insomnia.

In my self-analysis of the last few weeks I believe I have made a shocking discovery. Could it be that I have been suffering from deprivation of affection, not because of lack of affection from my parents, but from other people? I realize that I have been seeking to enhance my respect status to compensate for affection deprivation, but I realize too that I must face my problem realistically. The following suggestions are constructive plans I have made to build up or to restore value statuses that appear to have been withheld from me.

Summary of Unrealistic Behavior

1. I have always tried to be perfect in everything and I know this is an unrealistic goal.

2. I have wrongly believed that most people were unfriendly. I must realize that to have a friend I must be a friend. I must concentrate on sharing values with others as well as having concern for my own needs and wants in order to avoid embarrassment and other selfish feelings.

3. I have tried to fill the void of loneliness in my life by compensating with material things. I have cultivated hobbies which do not bring me into contact with people or cultivate interest which involve people. I must correct this by seeking the company of others in many activities.

4. I have refrained from talking freely about my problems and my desires with those interested and close to me. I have withdrawn and suppressed my own desires and have not aspired to valid goals. This I must correct.

SELF-STUDY NUMBER THREE

Several months ago I suddenly came to the conclusion that my husband surely must not love me any more. As a result I became sullen and depressed. Naturally it took my husband only a short while to notice the change. After a serious talk, and the reassurance of his love for me, things returned to normal.

I realize now that the feeling must have been due to fear of not being the type of mother and wife I've always set out to be. To my notion, a day had too few hours according to the numerous household duties I had to perform. Actually my family wasn't demanding all of this. An inner need for recognition of perfection led me from one job to another, until at the end of the day I was extremely tense and nervous. This is when my family would really 'catch it.'

Finally realizing that my role in the family involves many trying moments, but that we all make mistakes, I no longer strive for complete perfection. After all, what husband would really want a perfect wife (if one could be found)? My goal now is to fulfill my obligation to my family to the best of my abilities. After all, what more can anyone possibly do?

Summary of Unrealistic Behavior

1. I felt my husband no longer loved and respected me; I became very sullen and cold toward him. At times I acted harshly toward my children even when they were not at fault. Displaced hostility–rather than facing up to my problem, I fussed at my husband and children. Depression–this mechanism I used mostly to avoid the feelings of guilt and unworthiness since I had not been a perfect wife and mother. Hyperactivity–the busier I kept myself the less time I had to think of my many problems. Repression–I repressed into my unconscious a remark my husband had made only weeks after our marriage.

2. The remark, 'You'll never make a good wife,' made in fun, led me to set the goal of unrealistic perfection.

SELF-STUDY NUMBER FOUR

My most serious or baffling frustration is not being able to get up and talk before a group. When called on spontaneously, I would become completely blocked. This puzzled me because some things do not bother me while others do. I remember when I was in high school I took a speech course in an attempt to overcome this. I was doing all right until I had a three minute talk on some personal experience, which the teacher said was quite good but then asked if I had really done this. Her withholding respect from me caused me to fall apart again.

In college I took a parliamentary procedure course again seeking help with the belief this type of knowledge would be useful and reassuring to me, but again when I was called upon I froze.

It was only after finishing college that I decided to teach and the prospect of standing before the students was terrifying, but I mustered courage and found working with young people so challenging, so rewarding, and so completely enjoyable, it opened up a whole new world for me. Encouraged, I proceeded to take some graduate work in a summer session and was in a course the second six weeks term under a Professor I had had the pervious term. One day when his nose began to bleed, he said, 'Miss R., will you take the class for me,' and he walked out of the door. I was petrified, everything became still and quiet and one kind neighbor whispered, 'He meant you.' I shook my head, got up, and went to the desk, and did the best I could, but I could never remember afterwards a word I said. Again, recently when I was serving as Vice President in P.T.A. I had to preside. I did try but nothing seemed real.

Speaking before a group has been a problem to me all my life and since taking this course I asked myself how I got this way in the first place. Theoretically, I had explained it by the fact that mother had changed me from being left-handed to right-handed.

So I began to think back into my childhood. First, I remembered Mother's frequent remark that Daddy had said I walked and talked before I had any 'sense.' I was 'into everything' and it was impossible to keep me clean.

Then I recalled my inability to pronounce words clearly and how my older sister's friends, especially the boys, teased me about the way I talked. This was pre-school and somehow after starting to school, this cleared up. Later mother said she had changed me from being left-handed to right-handed. I had supposed this caused my speech difficulty and that my present problem was possibly a carry-over from it.

Another incident was a skull fracture I suffered about the age of 3½. The only conscious memory I have of this experience is that I was not allowed to go to sleep until we drove to the nearest town for X-rays and that when I was placed on the X-ray table it was so hard and my head hurt so I begged for a pillow. The pillow evidently became a symbol of pain because when I had uremic poisoning before my son was born and required a section, after surgery I fought having my head on a pillow until I became conscious enough to know what they were doing.

My little brother died when I was nearly six years old, and I witnessed this. The three of us were sick, he worsened, and took pneumonia. He lay looking up to my mother saying, 'Watie, Mottie, Watie,' to which she answered, 'Just a few minutes more and you can have some water,' but he choked to death. I was very much afraid and would not go up to the casket, but finally my father took me. However, the image of the boy in the casket was unreal–I could not accept this as my little brother.

At a later date I had a bad case of croup. Members of the family related to me afterward that I said, 'I am going to die,' but I do not remember saying this. Apparently I associated my choking with the choking to death of my little brother.

I have often wondered why I do not remember more of my early childhood as other people do, but suppose that I have repressed it as too painful to recall. I do not recall any other incidents. I feel that many of my childhood memories were associated with watching my little brother die begging mother for water.

Summary of Unrealistic Behavior

1. The tremendous fear of death was so great, following the death of my brother, I repressed it and blocked it out of my mind.

2. I have felt guilty because I blamed my mother for not doing more for my brother (deprivation of rectitude).

3. I tried to compensate for my feeling of guilt by trying to do everything I could to make my mother proud of me. My goals were conditioned by the desire to please my family and when these conflicted with my own desires I was frustrated by not knowing whether to be myself or what others expected me to be.

4. I sought respect and affection by overindulging others with affection.

5. My feelings of guilt must have contributed to my lack of confidence (self-respect) and thus to my fear of appearing before groups.

SUMMARY

This chapter points up the ultimate function hoped for in the process of value sharing, namely, through self-study, the individual will come to terms (share values) with himself. Changes must come also in him who would effect change in others. The process of value sharing cannot be characterized as a mechanical, manipulative device for human interaction. It is intimately tied up with the dynamics of personality.

The science of values, then, must be applied by teachers not only to pupils in the classrooms but also to the study of themselves. These two aspects of the process of analysis are really different sides of the same whole. Teachers who are convinced that value analysis has made a difference in their own lives have, as is so dramatically illustrated by the anecdotal material in this chapter, made a difference in the lives of those with whom they work and live.

Self-study for the persons contributing statements in this chapter has led to clarifications of many confusions and ambiguities in their lives. Democracy, Christianity, the Golden Rule, etc., all took on new meaning and significance through value clarification. The value framework focused upon the constant effects of one's behavior on all those around the individual and produced sobering and thoughtful contemplation of what is really meant by the phrase, "Freedom with responsibility." These persons found with compelling urgency that they were, indeed, their brother's keeper.

CHAPTER 7

•

Self-Study and Appraisal of Memory

The techniques employed in the analysis and appraisal by the individual of specific memories of his past experiences emerged from instructional experiences in experimental courses in personality during a period of eleven years.[1] This model for self-study was created to present significant events in the emergence of personality in social process, and involved the following exercises:

1. The appraisal by students of their statuses in each of eight categories under which the human values can be classified. In this procedure human values are defined as human needs and wants, which again may be said to refer specifically to the events sought by men in varying degrees in all societies and subcultures.

2. The coding of the events recorded by students in their individual diaries over a short period of a day or two in terms of the value consequences of these events in their lives. The results of these efforts to code their behavior led students to recognize such phenomena as relatively specialized to the values consciously or unconsciously sought as goals as well as the value indulgences they enjoyed, the value overindulgences they experienced, and the value deprivations they felt they had suffered. Here it can be seen that students in the process of coding their aspirations and personal strategies are led to take their first steps into the systematic study and appraisal of their own behavior as well as that of others.

3. Another instrument of thinking introduced at this point involved the analysis of human behavior in the search for goals. Pursuit of all goals is attended by tension in varying degree. If the goal sought is achieved, this tension is relieved and the individual is freed to pursue other goals in his attempt to achieve status in one or more of the human values. If, however, his search for the goal is denied or frustrated, he enters a state of fear always accompanied by an increased state of tension which is a significant index of his reduced status (deprivation) of well-being. Thus, a useful working definition of fear emerges. Fear (and/or anxiety) is the response of the individual to actual or threatened

[1]At East Texas State University, in A Program of General Studies. V.C. Arnspiger, Director, conducted this research.

deprivation of one or more goals which can be classified under the value categories.

It has long been recognized that the tension of frustration distorts and inhibits the creative and productive activities of the individual. For this reason one of the major purposes of the educational program is to release the student from this debilitating tension so as to free him for the creative and productive use of his mind in the performance of the tasks demanded in a truly effective program of education. In order to develop a theory for dealing with this problem, let us take into account the following factors. When a goal actively sought is denied, the individual's status in one or more of the human values is reduced. This frustration leads to a state of fear that is always accompanied by the tension of frustration which is an index of well-being deprivation.

Release from this tension is always sought by the individual. He may act realistically in his efforts to remove this tension by facing up to his problem, in trying again to achieve his goal following an amendment of his strategy, by reinterpreting it, or by establishing a more realistic goal in terms of existing conditions. Such strategy may be said to lead to the realistic release of tension.

On the other hand, goal (value) deprivation may lead the individual to behavior which may be classified as neurotic (or unrealistic) in the sense that it provides only temporary release from accompanying tensions. Such behavior we may classify as mental mechanisms employed by the victim of value deprivation in his efforts to escape the consequences of his frustration. Such mechanisms may be classified as substitution behavior, self-deception or withdrawal. We may say that such behavior, if practiced extensively leads this individual into a state of mental or even physical ill-health (deprivation of well-being) which distorts and inhibits his creativity and productivity. In such a state the student may perform the acts necessary to rote learning, but he cannot do the creative thinking which he must do if he is to direct his activities toward the systematic solution of his own problems.

4. In the effort to deal with other dynamic factors of personality, students were introduced into another exercise of the course which involved the analysis and appraisal of what they have specified as one of their most damaging frustrations (value deprivations).

The framework of analysis and appraisal provided to guide the student in this project introduced him to the process of placing events of his experience in social context. In other words, he was led to see the consequences of the event which led to his value deprivation (frustration) in terms of its value consequences for other individuals involved with him in the event. This leads to a more objective analysis of the event and, of course, to a more realistic appraisal of many of its aspects which he had formerly felt were very deprivational for himself. In this situation, the student often came to realize that many of these aspects may have been more deprivational to those associated with him in the event than they were for himself, and he may have become somewhat relieved of his tension-filled feelings of guilt (rectitude deprivation), of respect and affection deprivations and so on through the other value categories.

5. The technique of placing events of one's experience in social context was employed also in the intellectual framework provided for students in their analysis and appraisal of the breakdown of interpersonal relationships. Here again, they were led to a more realistic understanding of the value consequences for others with whom they had been in conflict before they considered their own deprived feelings, and consequently were led to recognize that many of their fears and tensions had resulted from deprivations which were more imagined than real, thus relieving themselves of significant debilitating effects of their experiences which formerly had been misinterpreted as deprivational.

These experiences in actual practice in the classroom have reinforced the concept that one's deprivational memories support his own damaging self-image, which tends to distort and inhibit the development of his creative and productive capacities. This experience led to the formation of the following theoretical model or prototype to be used as a guide in the collection and processing of data to be collected in the analysis and appraisal of student memories.

THE EXPERIMENTAL MODEL EMPLOYED AND OTHER CONSIDERATIONS

I. A number of experimental models may be developed to explore the various ways in which the memory appraisal technique operates and why and when it attains effective results for various kinds of personalities, subcultures and types of problems. Needless to say, such models about the whole or significant parts of the processes tapped by the technique may also suggest further alternative modifications of the technique itself so that a continual back and forth movement between theory and technique results that further fits an emerging field of facts brought to light by either new clarification or perspectives and/or further refinement in procedural matters.

II. A model of considerable scope employed since the beginning of this enterprise is the following: (1) To the degree that any personality has problems, we can say that part of the conditions leading to the problems stems from a *faulty and damaging self-image* usually of a deprived nature that keeps the person from realistic problem-solving. (2) Failure to solve these problems may be reflected by symptoms of many sorts—migraine headaches, tics, ritualistic worrying about the safety of a child, etc. (3) In turn, these damaging self-images flow from and are supported by deprivational or overindulgent memories about one's past experiences. We choose to recall those events that we feel we will be better off recalling. Some persons with deprivational problems feel that they will be better off recalling deprivational events—to find "excuses" that maintain a life of partial symptomatology. Others may have deprivational problems that are so threatening to them, such as behavior which they may feel is immoral, that they try to repress all memory of them.

III. We can measure each of the three factors we have pointed to above. It is possible to get a person to give some indication (by checking traits relevant to himself) of his own self-image at any point in time of contacting him. It is also possible to get a list of symptoms, problems or worries. Lastly, it is possible to get a list of his memories that act to "support" relations between both of the other two. At present, we *infer* the first two or have case history data pertaining to them, while only the last–the supporting memories–are directly and systematically tapped.

IV. This section is intended to present the technique now employed in memory analysis by students. It consists of three phases which are outlined below:

A. Phase I of the Project.

1. The Recall of Events from the Past.
   a. Begin recording with the earliest event you can recall during your lifetime. Be brief in making this first written record.
   b. Beginning with this earliest event, record or write all of the content of consciousness that occurs in your mind until fifty events have been recorded. You should undertake to do this with a minimum of censorship over the content of the events recalled.
2. Conditions for Preparing the Recalled Memory Record.
   a. *Place*: Be sure to select a place to make this record in which your privacy will not be interrupted. If any external interference occurs, start again at the beginning, i.e., with the earliest event in your life which you can recall.
   b. *Length of period*: The initial memory recall period will be continued until fifty separate events have been recorded.
   c. *Mechanical recording*: A tape recorder or other mechanical recording device may be employed if desired. If, however, these memories are mechanically recorded, the record shall be transcribed so that it can be typed for later analysis and appraisal.
3. Value Coding of Recorded Events.
   a. *First Phase in coding of recorded events.*
      In preparation for value-coding, the memory record should be broken down into specific events which are then listed and numbered consecutively from beginning to the end of the list. These numbers provide reference points to the events for value coding and appraisal. At this point the approximate age of the student when each event occurred should be recorded along with the event.
   b. The first task to be performed in the project of analysing and appraising the events recorded will be to code these events in terms of their value consequence for yourself (the student conducting each personal memory project).

c. The form to be used in coding and appraising the events recorded in the recalled experiences is shown on page 144. Each of the recalled events should be coded in terms of its consequence for the individual whose memories have been recorded. That is, each event should be classified in terms of whether the individual considers the event to have been a value deprivation, a value indulgence, or a value over-indulgence. The entire list of recalled memories should be coded before proceeding to Phase II of the project.

B. Phase II of the Project.

1. Elaboration of Specific Events in the Memory Recall Record. Before proceeding further into the process of coding and appraising the events recorded, you should review each event and undertake to elaborate it so as to include additional significant aspects of that event which you can recall that provide a more detailed picture of the total event, for example, in addition to stating your age at which each event occurred, include significant participants in each event or any other circumstances which will serve more completely to place each event in social context. You should prepare these more elaborate statements of the events recorded in writing and value code them on another copy of the form provided.

2. Value Coding of Recorded Events After Being Elaborated in a Broader and more Realistic Social Context.

a. After you have elaborated the events as originally recorded by recalling the additional facets which enrich each total experience, you will see that a large portion of them will involve interpersonal relations with other participants in the recalled experiences. This is an important aspect involved in placing your memories in social context.

b. Your second task to be performed in the analysis and appraisal of the events recorded in the memories will be to classify each event that has been elaborated to include other participants in the events, in terms of its value consequences for these participants (other than yourself).

c. This will involve value coding these relationships in terms of other participants. The method of referring to these participants shall be to letter them "a," "b," "c," etc., in the order in which they are introduced in the memories recorded. You will place and encircle these letters a, b, c, etc., indicating the other participants involved in the event in the order in which they appear in the elaborated form of each event. Furthermore, the identification letters should be placed with the number of the event when posted on the analysis form used in coding.

d. The coding of this second phase shall be done on another copy of the coding form. You will of course discover that in all these relationships recorded in the recalled event the other participants will also have been deprived, indulged, or overindulged in specific value categories and are to be coded accordingly. For an example of coding in Phase II see page 145.

C. Phase III of the Project.
The third task you are asked to perform shall be to review and to code event-by-event the value consequences (deprivations, indulgences, and overindulgences) for yourself of having made the analyses and appraisals as recorded in the two previous phases of the project. This shall be done on still another copy of the coding form. The second step in Phase III shall be for you briefly to justify the coding of these value consequences for yourself in a separate document. This procedure is intended to lead you to a more realistic consideration of the "deprivational" events of your past so as to give yourself a more realistic appraisal of the consequences of the events you have recalled from your past experience.

Following are typical completed forms used in the tablulation of memory analysis data by a student through Phases I, II and III in his self-study of recalled events. A comparison can be made of the coding of remembered events in Phase I with the coding of these events in Phase III following their reinterpretation after being considered in a broader and more realistic social context in Phase II. This comparison will indicate the marked degree to which events of this student's past that he had formerly considered to be value deprivational, had through his reinterpretation in Phase II, lost their deprivational, and apparently tension-provoking effect. It can be noted further that this student in Phase III coded the effect of most of these remembered events as value indulgent for himself. It is expected that this process will have removed many of the factors of this student's past (in the form of deprivational memories) which supported a damaging self-image, and replaced them with factors in the form of value-indulgent effects of these memories which will, through the enhancement of value statuses, contribute also to a new and improved self-image for this student with increased creativity and productivity in his future activities.

V. In Phase II of the technique, a "corrective" process is assumed to occur.[2] The person is asked to review the same events from the standpoint of all other persons involved in them. Here, there is a shift from an "I" and "me" frame of reference—an ego reference—to one of "we' or self-reference. The "I" and "me" sense grows out of encounters with other egos in which a sense of "we" or "not-we" is involved—acceptance or rejection of others. In Phase II, the past event is more *fully* recalled by requiring that the standpoint and perspective of all the others be taken into account within

---

[2] The theory underlying this technique of self-study was advanced by Arthur J. Brodbeck.

VALUE CODING OF EVENTS RECORDED

(Analysis and Appraisal of Recalled Events)

Mark "X" in the square indicating which phase of the analysis you are engaged in on the form below:

PHASE 1. [X] in terms of consequences for you, the person making the study.

PHASE 2. [ ] in terms of consequences for others involved in the events recorded.

PHASE 3. [ ] in terms of consequences for you of having made the above analyses.

Values Involved	DEPRIVATION Event Number	INDULGENCE Event Number	OVERINDULGENCE Event Number
POWER	15, 24, 27, 28, 30, 31 37, 43 [8]*	8, 19 [2]	19 [1]
RESPECT	1, 2, 4, 8. 13, 15, 24, 26, 27, 28, 29, 30, 31, 37, 43, 47, 50 [17]	3, 6, 7, 8, 10, 12, 14 16, 17, 20, 32, 33 [12]	18, 19, 34 [3]
WEALTH	2, 26, 39, 41, 45 [5]	7, 8, 40, 44 [4]	[ ]
SKILL	2, 24, 47, 50 [4]	3, 8, 10, 12, 13, 14 17, 19, 20, 25, 36 [11]	[ ]
ENLIGHTENMENT	2, 24, 43, 50 [4]	3, 7, 8, 10, 11, 16 20, 25, 38 [9]	[ ]
WELL-BEING	1, 2, 4, 5, 8, 10, 13, 14 18, 21, 22, 24, 26, 27 15, 28, 29, 30, 31, 37 39, 41, 42, 43, 45, 46 47, 48, 49, 50 [30]	6, 7, 9, 11, 12, 17 20, 23, 25, 32, 33 34, 35, 36, 38, 40 44 [17]	[ ]
RECTITUDE	1, 5, 15, 22, 27, 30, 37 42, 43, 48, 49 [11]	14, 38 [2]	[ ]
AFFECTION	4, 5, 15, 18, 21, 27, 28 29, 31, 37, 43, 46, 47 50 [14]	1, 3, 6, 7, 8, 9, 12 16, 17, 20, 23, 32, 33 36, 38 [15]	23 [1]

***Small squares are for total number of events recorded in each category.**

VALUE CODING OF EVENTS RECORDED

(Analysis and Appraisal of Recalled Events)

Mark "X" in the square indicating which phase of the analysis you are engaged in on the form below:

PHASE 1. [ ] in terms of consequences for you, the person making the study.

PHASE 2. [X] in terms of consequences for others involved in the events recorded.

PHASE 3. [ ] in terms of consequences for you of having made the above analyses.

Values Involved	DEPRIVATION Event Number	INDULGENCE Event Number	OVERINDULGENCE Event Number
POWER	A4, B4, A14, B18, A21 A22, A26, B27, A31, B31 A40, A42, B44, A45, A46 A48, A49, A50 B21 19*	A1, A2, A3, A5, A7 A12, A13, B13, A16 B21, A25, A28, A29 A30, A32, A34 A38, A41 18	
RESPECT	A1, A2, A4, B4, A5, A7 B13, A14, A15, B48, A21 A22, A24, A26, B27, A28 A29, A30, A31, A32, A40 A43, A44, B44 A48, A49, A50 27	A2, A3, A6, A9, A10 A11, A12, A13, A16 A17, A19, A20, B21 A23, A24, A25, A27 A32, A33, A34, A35 A36, B36, A38 A41, A46 26	A7, A8, A18 3
WEALTH	A21, A22, A26, A31, A33 5	B1, A3, A12, A32, A36 A38, A47 7	
SKILL	A4, B4, A5, A8, B13 A21, A22, A24, A31, B31 A40, A42, A43, A48, A49 A50 16	A3, A6, A7, A9, A13 A16, B17, A19, A20 B21, A23, A25, A33 A36, A37, A38 B41, A44, A47 19	
ENLIGHTENMENT	A4, B4, A5, A8, B13, A21 A22, B27, A31, B31, A42 A43, B44, A47 A48, A49 16	A10, A19, A20, A24 A30, A36 6	
WELL-BEING	A1, A2, A4, B4, A5, A14 B14, A15, B18, A21, A22 B24, B26, B27, A28, A31 B32, A37, A40, A42, A43 A44, B44, A45, A47, A45 A46, A42, A49, A50 30	A3, A6, A7, A8, A9 A11, A12, A13, B13 A16, A17, B17, A18 A19, A20, B21, A23 A25, A27, A29, A30 A32, A33, A39, A34 A35, A36, B36, A38 A41, B41, A42 A44, A46 34	
RECTITUDE	A1, A4, B4, A14, A21 A22, A24, A28 A31, A50 10	A2, A3, B13, B21, A30 A34, A35, A38 A39, A42, A43 11	
AFFECTION	A2, A4, B4, A5, A7, A13 B13, A14, B14, A15, A21 A22, B27, A28, A29, A30 A31, B31, A37, A40, A42 A43, A44, B44, A48, A49 A50 27	A1, A3, A6, A7, A8 A9, A11, A12, A13 A16, A17, B17, A18 A19, A20, B21, A23 A24, A25, A27, A32 A33, A34, A35, A36 B36, A38, A39, B41 A41, A44, A45 A46, A47 34	

*Small squares are for total number of events recorded in each category.

VALUE CODING OF EVENTS RECORDED

(Analysis and Appraisal of Recalled Events)

Mark "X" in the square indicating which phase of the analysis you are engaged in on the form below:

PHASE 1. [ ] in terms of consequences for you, the person making the study.

PHASE 2. [ ] in terms of consequences for others involved in the events recorded.

PHASE 3. [X] in terms of consequences for you of having made the above analyses.

Values Involved	DEPRIVATION Event Number	INDULGENCE Event Number	OVERINDULGENCE Event Number
POWER	30, 31 * 2	1, 4, 8, 10, 11, 12, 14 17, 20, 24, 32, 34, 35 36, 38, 39, 41, 44, 45 46, 48, 49 22	
RESPECT	4 1	1, 2, 3, 6, 7, 8, 10, 11 12, 13, 14, 16, 17, 20 23, 24, 25, 30, 32, 33 34, 35, 36, 37, 38, 39 40, 41, 42, 43, 44, 45 46, 47, 48, 49, 50, 9 38	18, 19 2
WEALTH		8, 36, 40 3	
SKILL		3, 6, 7, 8, 9, 10, 11 12, 13, 14, 16, 17, 19 20, 23, 24, 25, 34, 36 37, 38, 39, 41, 44, 46 47, 50, 4 28	
ENLIGHTENMENT	4, 5 2	1, 2, 3, 7, 8, 9, 12, 13 14, 16, 17, 18, 19, 20 23, 24, 25, 28, 31, 32 34, 36, 37, 38, 39, 42 43, 44, 46, 47, 48, 50 4 33	
WELL-BEING	48, 49 2	1, 2, 3, 6, 7, 9, 10, 11 12, 14, 16, 17, 18, 19 20, 22, 23, 24, 25, 28 30, 32, 33, 34, 35, 36 37, 38, 39, 40, 41, 42 44, 45, 46, 47, 48, 50 4 39	
RECTITUDE	49 1	14, 17, 23, 25, 27, 37 38, 42, 45, 46 10	
AFFECTION		1, 2, 6, 7, 8, 9, 10, 11 12, 16, 17, 18, 19, 20 25, 27, 28, 32, 33, 34 35, 36, 37, 38, 39, 40 41, 42, 44, 45, 46, 47 48, 50 35	3, 23 2

***Small squares are for total number of events recorded in each category.**

the memory. The ego is thus put in social context to make it part of a self or group life. It may well be that other "expanding" recall occurs too—such as remembering the *long-term* indulgent effects of a momentary deprivational experience—which the technique more incidentally promotes and does not directly capture and measure. In any event, it is assumed that the ego is placed in social context and in relationship to a larger "we" concept than it had previously been. In this, the technique may act as an antidote to overconcentration on the ego, as in traditional psychoanalysis, and reduces attention to the self as well as allows the past to be used for injustice collecting in the name of "causal" scientific explanation.

VI. The result of Phase III is a recoding of these same events for their ego significance in a way that allows neither the deprivational nor over-indulgent features of them to remain as they were before the ego was expanded to include the other comprising the self. The person is no longer "better off" by recalling such experiences, since they no longer support a damaged or faulty image of the self as much as they had previously. Indeed, the result of Phase II is in all probability a revised image of the ego as a result of having to consider the past events more fully and in richer configurations than previously. The revised image in turn makes the future look more promising and releases potentiality for problem solving rather than a partial sense of powerlessness or need to further impose deprivations on others by being overpowering. Hence, the recoding in Phase III leads to less deprivational "interpretation" of past memories—and, after all, an indulgence or deprivation is ultimately a subjective event of interpretation that shifts as the considered context of the event shifts. It is possible, additionally, to test to see whether a new set of remembered events—even one demanding a totally new set of nonoverlapping events—will move toward more indulgent ones. Having reduced the "low" position of the isolated ego by the technique, the problems and symptoms are likely to wane and subside, either in part or as a whole.[3]

VII. The hypotheses suggested can be refined in many ways and further work should focus on so doing as well as seeing whether the general model has validity and/or needs further revision. For instance, one may discover the shift occurs primarily for certain values more than others—and with certain groupings may be easier to obtain for some values rather than others.

VIII. An especially important refinement would be the following. Do the memories scatter evenly over the *whole* preadult span or *center in one* age bracket? Do the figures who enter into the memories involve many different persons or only one or two people? We know the neurotic is characterized by poor recall for early childhood while the psychotic has fantastically vivid early memories—while the normal tends to have better "control" over the whole past arena of memories. How will the pattern of scatter of recall affect successful shift with the technique? We would

[3]This assumption was valid for a small sampling of twenty student cases.

A MODEL FOR EMPLOYING THE TECHNIQUES OF FREE RECALL

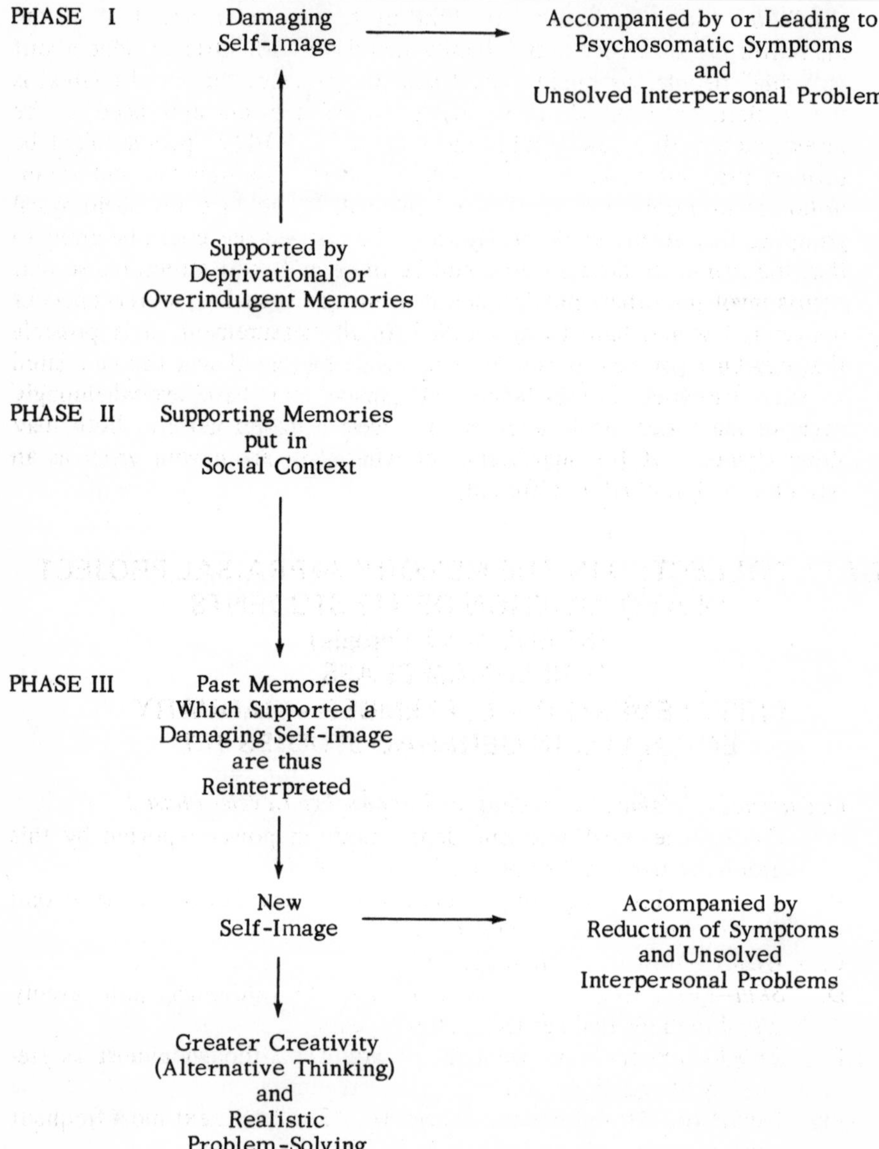

predict that less change of coding and symptoms would be possible with severe neurosis since it is likely to be characterized by memory primarily of adolescent events and is likely to be poor on recall of early childhood memories. We will probably get a pattern of clustering of memories in early childhood too infrequently to allow us to say much about it. If the memories are primarily about family members with little or none about "outside" people, we might expect less change, since the social context is too limited. But all of these are empirical matters and need to be investigated with a few guiding ideas in mind. "Other" people might be divided into intimates vs. strangers or peers, subordinates and superordinates or males and females and so forth to embrace any sociological grouping that seems workable. Indeed, the instructions could be given so that the memories dredged up could be more and more structured so that events involving others not frequently mentioned (such as storekeepers or policemen) would have to be recalled. In all measurement, it is possible that *baselines* for each person be established so that change can be related to such baselines. For instance, one person may have overwhelmingly negative memories, while another may have a mixed pattern. Both may show change—but the significance of what they are moving *from* as an outcome in Phase III is different.

DATA COLLECTED IN THE MEMORY APPRAISAL PROJECT IN A POPULATION OF 112 STUDENTS (65 Male – 47 Female) FRESHMAN CLASS FIRST SEMESTER – SEPTEMBER – JANUARY ENROLLED IN GENERAL STUDIES 161

I. *Occurrence of Value Deprivations at Various Age Levels—Phase I*
   A. *Power*—The most frequent deprivations in power reported by this group occurred at the age of 17.
   B. *Respect*—Most frequently experienced at ages 16 to 18; the second most frequent at ages 6 and 7.
   C. *Wealth*—Most frequent at age 18.
   D. *Skill*—Most frequent at ages 17 and 18, although quite evenly distributed over all age levels after 5 years.
   E. *Enlightenment*—Most frequent at age 18, although almost as frequently at ages 6, 10 and 14.
   F. *Well-Being*—Most frequent at ages 16, 17 and 18; next most frequent occurrences at age levels 5 and 6.
   G. *Rectitude*—Most frequent at ages 17 and 18, but also quite evenly distributed over all age levels from 4 to 15 inclusive.
   H. *Affection*—Most frequent at age level 17 and 18 years, but quite evenly distributed from age 4 through age 16.

II. *Frequency of Deprivations by Value Categories as Reported by All Students (112) in Project (including all ages from 1 to 18 and over).*

The frequencies of deprivation reported by all students were as follows:

Well-Being–2376 deprivations were reported in this category which, of course, was expected to be more frequently experienced than in any other single value category because serious deprivation in any of the other value categories results also in deprivation of *well-being*.

Respect	–	1190
Affection	–	1070
Rectitude	–	879
Power	–	485
Enlightenment	–	388
Wealth	–	309
Skill	–	306

If this population of 112 students is typically representative of college students at the freshman level, then it can be seen from the frequencies listed that the origin of most of the tensions which give rise to the mental ill-health of college students lies in deprivations in the value categories of *respect, affection* and *rectitude*. From the data given in the above figures, deprivations in the other categories– *power, enlightenment, wealth* and *skill* are markedly less frequent. However, it must not be assumed that deprivations in these categories are insignificant for students who report them. On the contrary, deprivations in these value categories have uniformly been coded by these students as leading to deprivations in *well-being*.

III. *The Reinterpretation of Remembered Events in PHASE III.*

The following trends in the reinterpretation by students of their deprivational memories occurred. The process of placing remembered events in social context as in Phase II of the project, had a significant effect in reducing the number of value deprivations which students felt they had suffered and which they still felt they suffered from remembered events as coded in Phase I.

For example, the reinterpretation of memories which were originally coded by the students as *power* deprivations was reduced in Phase III from 485 in number to 88. Similar data for the other value categories follow:

Respect deprivations	from	1190 to 309
Wealth	from	309 to 110
Skill	from	306 to 93
Enlightenment	from	388 to 112
Well-being	from	2676 to 596
Rectitude	from	879 to 274
Affection	from	1070 to 298

The reduction of deprivations as coded in Phase III when compared with Phase I ranged from the lowest of 64% in *wealth* to the highest of 82% in the case of *power*.

The percentage of reduction in the *well-being* category was 75%. The computer was employed (analysis of variance) to arrive at the statistical significance of the degree of difference in the value deprivations in Phase I and Phase III. These results were shown to be statistically significant within the 1% level.

The computer was used also to determine the statistical significance of the degree of difference in the number of coded deprivations in Phase I and Phase III for each of the *value categories.* The T-Scores ranged from 5.07 in the case of *rectitude* to 20.8 in the case of *well-being.*

IV. *Origins of Value Deprivations*

The value deprivations as coded by students in Phase I of the object had their origins in events from the past which involved both non-interpersonal and interpersonal relationships.

A. Non-Interpersonal Relationships.

Value deprivations growing out of contacts with the physical or biological environment, but which did not involve significant relations with other persons are classified as non-interpersonal relationships. This category provided the origins of more value deprivations (942) than any other. Such relationships for example may involve accidents which occurred when the individual was alone which resulted in the deprivation of physical and often mental *well-being.* Such an accident may have been reported by a student which resulted in his being entangled in a fence on a hunting trip for an extended period of time. In Phase I he may have coded this event as deprivational in *well-being,* and possibly also in *respect* because he felt inept or *unskilled* as a hunter. He also may have coded this event as *rectitude* deprivation because he failed to employ practices which he knew very well would have prevented this accident to himself. So it can be seen that many of these accidental events classified as non-interpersonal which resulted in *well-being* deprivations also may have other significant deprivational consequences. A further circumstance which added to the number of deprivations classified under this category was that while the research staff classified the initial aspect of an event, such as a broken leg, as a non-interpersonal relationship, the elaboration of this event in Phase II to bring out its larger social context may have revealed other deprivations that had their origins in interpersonal relationships.

B. Interpersonal Relationships.

The categories selected for the classification of deprivational events which had their origins in relationships with other persons include mothers, fathers, brothers, sisters, grandparents, opposite sex (of approximately same age) teachers, and significant others.

Data are available which indicate differences in age and sex with respect to the types of interpersonal relations which most frequently provide the origins of value deprivations.

It may be more useful at this point, however, to consider the relative frequencies of the various categories in terms of those which provide origins for value deprivations at combined age levels and for males and females also combined.

1. The interpersonal relationships which provided the origin for the greatest number of deprivations were classified as *significant others*. This category included friends, acquaintances, and others of the same sex and of approximately the same age levels as the cases studied. Others in this category included cousins, uncles, aunts, policemen, supervisors, foremen and fellow employees. The value deprivations in this category were 845 of a total of 3317 reported.
2. Mothers made up the category in which the greatest number of deprivations involving persons in the immediate family occurred. This category totaled 449.
3. Fathers provided the origins of 320 reported value deprivations.
4. Teachers followed fathers in providing the origins of the next greatest number of deprivations reported; a total of 293.
5. Opposite-sex relationships provided the origins for 211 reported value deprivations, but it is interesting to note that the deprivations reported by females in this category were three times those of males. The ages of greatest deprivation in this category in the case of both sexes were 17 and 18 years.
6. Contrary to much that has been written and said about the extent of interpersonal conflict traceable to sibling rivalry, the reported value deprivations which had their origins in relationships with brothers (101) and sisters (58) were much lower than in all other categories except in the case of grandparents (98).

V. *The Reinforcement of Indulgent Memories.*

It is assumed that in addition to a more realistic appraisal of value deprivations, two other factors are operating which also contribute to the reinterpretation of damaging self-concepts. First, are the indulgent memories of the past that have been more objectively and realistically considered by students in the process of placing them in social context than was the case in coding of these events in Phase I. This process appears to have been significant in the personal amendments by students of their own self-images and seems to have taken place when, in considering indulgent memories in social context (Phase II), such memories are more often coded as enhancements of *well-being* and of other value categories than in Phase I where it appears that the impact of remembered value deprivations is greater in producing deprivations in *well-being* than are recalled value indulgences in producing the enhancement of status in this value (well-being).

The second factor in this approach to self-study which appears to contribute to the amendment of their self-images is the degree to which, in Phase II, students through more realistic and objective appraisals of remembered events in social contexts tend to realize that in this process they have gained status in a number of value categories. For example, they appear to feel that they have enhanced their statuses in *enlightenment* (knowledge of the relative effects of value deprivations and indulgences), in *skill* (the ability to appraise and to code events in terms of their deprivational and indulgent characteristics), in *respect* (as reflected in the increasing confidence with which they discuss human behavior in terms of its value consequences, for example), often in *power* (through the realization that their goals and decisions can be more realistically validated through the application of a value-oriented rationale which is compatible with the perspectives of a society that aspires toward freedom), often in *rectitude* (the acceptance of responsibility for facing problems realistically and undertaking to solve them through the performance of the intellectual tasks which constitute the component operations of problem solving), and, of course, consequently in *well-being*, since significant value indulgence in any of the other categories tends to enhance status in this value.

The extent to which enhancements in value statuses of students have occurred is expected to be reflected not only by decreases in value deprivations shown in Phase III coding, but also by increases in the value indulgences coded from remembered events in Phase III when compared with Phase I. Increases in the number of codings of value indulgences occurred in all except one of the value categories, *wealth*, where indulgences declined from 404 in Phase I to 356 in Phase III.

The greatest increase in value indulgences coded in Phase III over Phase I occurred in the *enlightenment* category from 1350 in Phase I to 2759 in Phase III. The second greatest increase was in *well-being* indulgences, from 1452 in Phase I to 2494 in Phase III.

Codings in *skill* enhancement increased from 940 to 1805, in *respect* from 1044 to 1623, in *rectitude* from 324 to 706, in *affection* from 1279 to 1572, and in *power* from 502 to 551.

The data shown in the following chart record the results of self-study conducted by 47 graduate students (practicing teachers) ranging in ages from 25 to 63. With these students, apparently significant modifications in their self-images occurred also in all the value categories, again with the highest apparent degree of change in the categories of respect, affection, rectitude, and well-being.

It should be recalled that reinterpretations of recalled events which indicated enhancements of status rather than deprivations in any of the values resulted also in the enhancement of the status of well-being as indicated by student's appraisal of their feelings in this category following their completion of the self-study project.

Other projects in memory analysis and appraisal involving 520 freshmen students and 250 graduate students have produced data which closely coincide with the data of the projects reported above.

STATISTICAL SIGNIFICANCE OF THE SELF-STUDY AND APPRAISAL OF RECALLED EVENTS BY GRADUATE STUDENTS

This chart shows the difference between Phase 1 and Phase 3 of the memory analysis project involving 47 graduate students (practicing teachers).

Meaning of Symbols:
Ph 1 - Phase 1
Ph 3 - Phase 3
M - Mean
T - T Score
SD - Standard Deviation

Values Involved	DEPRIVATION		INDULGENCE		OVERINDULGENCE	
	Mean No. Of Events	Statistical Significance	Mean No. Of Events	Statistical Significance	Mean No. Of Events	Statistical Significance
		T- 8.28		T- 4.92		T- 2.00
POWER	M	SD	M	SD	M	SD
Ph 1	8.30	4.78	7.79	7.91	2.06	3.02
Ph 3	2.49	3.74	13.51	10.27	1.02	1.91
		T-11.75		T- 8.89		T- 2.27
RESPECT	M	SD	M	SD	M	SD
Ph 1	14.47	6.61	9.85	5.87	1.79	3.15
Ph 3	2.81	3.22	18.64	10.10	.62	1.87
		T- 6.93		T- 5.81		T- 3.61
WEALTH	M	SD	M	SD	M	SD
Ph 1	7.55	4.73	5.89	4.62	2.04	3.06
Ph 3	2.57	3.23	10.26	8.01	.38	.84
		T- 6.34		T- 5.33		T- 1.77
SKILL	M	SD	M	SD	M	SD
Ph 1	4.94	3.91	6.45	4.33	1.13	2.61
Ph 3	1.40	2.86	13.87	10.71	.40	1.20
		T- 5.73		T- 7.34		T- 2.22
ENLIGHTENMENT	M	SD	M	SD	M	SD
Ph 1	6.09	4.95	7.79	5.73	1.51	2.92
Ph 3	1.70	2.34	18.62	12.04	.49	1.46
		T-11.71		T- 8.98		T- 1.84
WELL-BEING	M	SD	M	SD	M	SD
Ph 1	27.49	9.20	13.53	8.55	3.06	5.75
Ph 3	7.55	6.95	27.40	12.56	1.17	4.15
		T- 6.98		T- 6.93		T- 2.40
RECTITUDE	M	SD	M	SD	M	SD
Ph 1	11.47	7.92	5.43	5.14	1.98	3.56
Ph 3	2.60	2.84	14.91	11.40	.72	1.83
		T-11.77		T- 7.55		T- 2.35
AFFECTION	M	SD	M	SD	M	SD
Ph 1	13.38	6.03	10.36	6.15	2.15	3.14
Ph 3	3.43	3.88	18.38	10.67	.94	2.20

SUMMARY

When we project into the future the possibility that this technique in its further elaboration and enrichment will provide a framework the individual can employ in a life-long study and appraisal of the events in his life, we can predict that most events which may seriously threaten him with deprivation in one or more values can be met successfully and creatively. The ability to place such events in comprehensive social context should enable a person to avoid the crippling effects of tension following many serious deprivations which may distort and inhibit his creativity and productivity as a fully participating individual in his society.

CHAPTER 8

•

Appraising Mood and Feeling in the Classroom

It is becoming increasingly clear that mood may function as a conditioner of what it is that one selects to remember and learn. In moods of gloom, one tends to select experiences from the past that substantiate the mood, whereas in more hopeful moods, opposite experiences will be remembered. Current interest patterns often follow the path of one's moods. It is quite likely, too, that moods may act to some degree as conditions of what one selects to think about and imagine with regard to the future. In a gloomy mood, it is difficult to view the social process in which the self is embedded as moving toward a bright and sanguine future outcome. In this way, mood may inhibit alternative thinking of how to move toward the future. In short, then, *the way one feels often conditions the way one thinks.* Since education is concerned with training and developing the human resources for thinking, it sooner or later must come to grips with the way in which mood and feeling enter into the thinking process.

Unfortunately, we have little by way of a standardized vocabulary by which to investigate and code the varieties of mood and feeling, and without such a language in terms of which these subjective factors may be effectively shared through communication, there is an unnecessary curtailment in the tools by which we can observe how mood and feeling condition both thought patterns and other practices in the classroom. The learning about the self that is part of psychotherapy puts a good deal of emphasis upon the examination of mood and feeling, rather than upon isolated "intellectual" processes. Yet, we have been impressed, when examining the protocols of the word exchanges between patients and therapists, to discover what a paucity of words either patient or therapist have at their command by which to analyze moods. Often, *one* word is used to refer to many *different* subjective states, such as the vague word "upset." Many times, too, the resort is to image and metaphor. When we use such expressions as "I feel like a motherless child" or "I feel like a feather in a breeze" or "I feel as if I were bottled-up," we are using the *images* the mood or feeling has brought into being, rather than concentrating directly on the mood itself. Often, however, there is no difficulty in making an inference from metaphor about mood. Yet, much is to be gained by developing less literary devices for the scientific study of the feeling events within persons.

The framework used throughout this book is designed to be comprehensive. Hence, we should be able to extend it to deal with the problems of the relationship of mood and feeling in learning, so that significant educational problems can be formulated and put to inquiry by practitioners and researchers in the educational disciplines.

Since mood and feeling are subjective events, they form part of the perspectives of persons. Hence, the way we have analyzed perspectives should be equally applicable to mood and feeling. We would expect moods to be relatively specialized to each of the three components of perspectives–i.e., demands (values), expectations and identifications. And, indeed, our expectation does turn out to be substantiated.

If we turn to moods which could be considered relatively specialized to identification, for instance, we discover "feelings of alienation" and "moods of loneliness." On the more positive side, there are "moods of belonging" and "feelings of commitment." Moods of "boredom" are often troubling to teachers not only when they seem to be present among the members of a class but equally so when the teacher struggles with them. There is more and more reason to believe that such moods are actually related to changes in the identification process. Adolescents, for instance, experience "boredom" with great frequency and intensity during a stage of socialization when they are moving from one identity (preadult) to another (an adult one). Yet, such moods vary from person to person a good deal, even when we standardize for their general backgrounds, and a significant problem of education may be to discover how education as part of the total socialization process can be considered so as to minimize such subjective states of alienation, boredom and loneliness, since they tend (as far as we now know) to impede the smooth progress of education and contribute high deprivational costs during it. With regard to the deprivational aspects, it may be that part of education should be concerned with getting youngsters to learn to tolerate feelings of boredom by seeing them as transitory states in a growing identification process. The management of boredom may be one of the essential features in developing the thinking process itself successfully.

When we turn to moods and feelings that have bearing upon expectations, we discover moods of hopelessness and despair and, on the other hand, moods of hope and faith. These refer to very *general* expectations. And, as a matter of fact, one of the salient characteristics of all moods appears to be that they are *suffuse* rather than related quite specifically to any one *particular* context. The more moods and feelings get expressed in images, and they do when they are described in terms of metaphors, the less we become aware of the way in which they tend to permeate *all* perceptions, memories and other intellectual processes. A mood of hopelessness is likely to produce gloomy images no matter what context is under focus on the part of the person experiencing the mood. Furthermore, unlike the images they give rise to, they tend to be more *enduring*, not quick to change, although there may be remarkable individual differences in the relative duration of moods undergone in the subjective experience of persons.

When we turn to the value dimensions of moods, we become aware of both the positive and negative demands that moods may exercise upon the personality and, then, in the most general and suffuse way, rather than in relationship to a specific context. Value demands of a person we now know shift somewhat as that person shifts from one situation to another and as his roles in those situations differ. Because of this, it is frequently difficult to get at a stable value profile for a person, since the measurement is necessarily relative to specific contexts. It may well be that the measurement and observation of characteristic mood patterns will, precisely because they tend to transcend specific contexts, allow us to get at relatively stable value profiles more reliably and validly.

It is informative to discover the moods which are exemplifications of each value, since it soon becomes apparent that we have developed a rich variety of terms to refer to moods relative to one value while a certain paucity of terms exists with regard to mood exemplifications relative to other values. Let us take the *wealth* value, for instance, as compared with the *well-being* value. The number of terms referring to the well-being value are extremely rich, both in positive and negative directions. It is customary for people to report that they "feel peppy," "feel content," "feel full of vim and vigor," "feel comfortable," "feel at ease," or, on the contrary, "feel fatigued," "feel faint," "feel anxious," "feel ill at ease," "feel lethargic" and so on. During the socialization process, much effort is apparently expended into paying close attention to mood states of well-being. The terms covering moods that exemplify the wealth value do not, despite what is supposed to be a strong wealth-centered strain in our culture, come in for the same elaborateness of subjective coverage. Nonetheless, we do find that people report "prosperous feelings," "luxurious moods," "moods of resourcefulness" and, on the negative side, "feelings of impoverishment," "penurious moods" and so on. Part of the reason for whatever discrepancy may exist between the importance of the wealth value in a culture and the subjective attention given to it may reside in the degree to which the science which has been specialized to the value has focused attention upon subjective processes. It is no secret that economics has tended to make many assumptions about "human nature" without resorting to empirical check upon the subjectivities that are supposed to operate within economic transactions, although there is a drift now in this more empirical direction as economic theorists examine economic systems in greater detail. It would be strange, indeed, if the life of mood and feeling had no bearing upon the practices that relate to the management of goods and services.

Both *rectitude* and *affection* receive a good deal of attention when the subjective life of moods and feelings are examined in our culture. Few people do not make some reference to the rectitude value when they speak of "feelings of guilt," "feelings of remorse," "irresponsible moods," "wicked moods," "carefree moods," and, on the more positive side, "moods of righteousness," "holy feelings" and "earnest moods." Interestingly, moods relating to rectitude may often take the form of expectations. Thus, a person who feels guilty may often experience "a nameless dread" for the future. The mood is one of anticipating something terrible to come which does not receive any concrete form but it is left "free-floating." Many times, such overpowering moods of expectation may supplant the mood-demand in consciousness, so that the person is more aware of the mood of expectation than the mood of demand with which it is associated.

Guilt is not experienced so much as the dread of something bad that may be coming.

The mood counterparts for *affection* also have many key terms in conventional speech by means of which they may be easily communicated. On the positive side, there are "feelings of warmth," "moods of empathy," "congenial moods," "feelings of openness," "intimate moods," "moods of tenderness"; on the negative side, there are "feelings of being unloved"; "moods of indifference," "feelings of coldness," and so on. It is frequently the case that many more terms are developed to deal with the negative aspects of a value as it is exemplified in moods and feelings than with the positive aspects or vice versa. Thus, the rectitude value tends to be noticed as a mood or feeling primarily in *negative* terms. Much more is written about guilt as a feeling than there is about righteousness as a mood. On the other hand, affection comes in for a good deal of *positive* attention. To some degree, it is much more ambiguous to designate what the negative side of affection may be as a mood than there is in designating the positive side. One can describe "loving" moods much more easily with the conventional array of terms than one can the "nonloving" moods. This may often make it possible to bring in other values so as to confuse an analysis of the subjective life of feeling. "Hatred," for instance, may be taken as a sign that the affection value is operating negatively. Yet, insofar as the term "hatred" refers to a mood in which the predominant feature is one of wanting to get rid of an object, it is more probably a designation of the *power* value. There is, thus, a tacit assumption being introduced into a mood-value analysis that, if a loving mood is not present, the power mood will be and vice versa. The assumption is highly questionable and, in any event, subject to empirical test rather than to be taken as an axiom for mood analysis. When we start to survey the way in which moods are currently examined, we frequently find such tacit assumptions about the relationship among values running through the analysis of the subjective life which are frequently no more than wishful perceptions, often culturally reinforced.

Both *power* and *respect* do receive attention in their own right, and come in for fairly elaborate scrutiny. Reference to power is positively present when people report "willful moods," "feelings of domination," "hostile moods," and the negative emphasis occurs when self-reports indicate "feelings of weakness," "feelings of submission," and "moods of powerlessness." The negative reference to respect is primarily and conventionally organized around "feelings of shame" but may also be present in self-reports that emphasize "feelings of insignificance," "feelings of embarrassment," and "worthless feelings." The positive side may be indicated by phrases such as the following: "heroic feelings," "feelings of pride," "feelings of importance," and so on. Generally, the concern with feelings of "self-esteem," and with the rise and fall of such feelings, is a general measure of the subjective life in it's *total* success and failure to the person who is under scrutiny. When one is meeting or maintaining all demands upon the self, feelings of self-esteem will be high, and they will drop when there is a failure to meet or maintain them. Despite wide variance between persons in the specific pattern and intensity of these demands, we can nonetheless chart rises and falls of self-esteem, since the latter term refers to a total outcome of feeling. Because there is no one pattern of demands which creates high self-esteem in all, we are, therefore, able to look upon self-esteem as a general measure of *respect* of the self for the self. It might also be wise to draw attention to the fact that we have been speaking of relatively unmixed feelings and moods that exemplify the working of each value in relative isolation from the rest. However, some moods may be resultants of two or more values coalescing to give a stable mood pattern. "Cowardly feelings," for instance, appear to be an exemplification of respect, but there is also some reference to responsibility and, hence, the rectitude value. When we speak of a value profile that characterizes a personality, we seek to find which of the eight values tends to *govern* the rest. It frequently will happen that the product of such an analysis shows that two or more values more or less govern all the rest together and, hence, take on high priority in the life of an individual. We would, therefore, expect to find many mood combinations of those values which act powerfully together to govern the rest of the potential moods people are capable of experiencing.

Like wealth, but not to the same degree, we have a rather less clear-cut vocabulary to designate the moods that relate to enlightenment. One interesting possibility that emerges from a mood and feeling analysis in terms of values is that *consciousness may be looked upon as a mood itself*, and a primary positive designation of the working of the enlightenment value. It will be remembered that a characteristic of mood is that it is both enduring and suffuse. In a state of high consciousness, it is not any *one* image that is entertained clearly, but *all* perceptions have taken on an added clarity and definitiveness. The negative side of enlightenment in the feeling life of the individual would be indicated by such phrases as "feeling of confusion." A high state of enlightenment would be present if people report "feelings of illumination," when all of the elements around one appear to be known in their fundamental relationships to one another and no matter where one looks one has a feeling of seeing things extraordinarily deeply and clearly. A lesser intensity of the positive aspect of enlightenment in the mood dimensions of the subjective life would be present when people reported "feelings of alertness." One is often impressed both as teacher and as student with how a high state of consciousness may appear suddenly and last for considerable lengths of time and then evaporate into feelings of growing confusion. An image that one had entertained clearly in a positive state may be difficult to recapture in a subsequent state of lowered consciousness. To be in a mood to be conscious or confused does not mean that the process is under voluntary control any more than to be in a mood to feel guilty or to feel guilt-free and righteous. Because we have made of education so much a product of the non-feeling life of individuals, we are slow to see how it itself is conditioned by moods of consciousness, as well as slow to see how much of the mood of consciousness may be interacting and be conditioned by other moods relating to other values. Like the wealth value, the investigation of the mood components of the enlightenment value have been relatively neglected and need our continued scrutiny. There are moments which most skillful teachers experience when students seem to see clearly every complex idea being presented to them as though there had been induced a group sharing of high level moods of consciousness. The tracing of the rise and fall of such moods of consciousness over time in the teacher-student relationship would be interesting to explore so as to discover what conditions may explain the shift in the mood movement toward or away from enlightenment.

The *skill* value is easier to find designated in the conventional vocabulary of mood and feeling. For instance, on the negative side, there are "clumsy feelings," "moods of awkwardness," while on the positive side, there are "moods of cleverness" and "feelings of adeptness." One might ordinarily think that the positive moods of skill and enlightenment would occur together, but with some reflection, we indeed discover that this is not always the case. For instance, there may be an intense mood of consciousness but a mood of clumsiness and awkwardness accompanying it, so that it is difficult to make articulate what flights of consciousness may convey to one. Perhaps much of what we call "intuition" is sometimes to be characterized in such a way.

When we survey attempts to deal with the feeling side of the subjective life of persons, we instantly become aware of how much emphasis has been put upon "the emotions" as compared with the more enduring, stable and regular paths of feeling. It seems quite possible that we can look upon emotions as *a state of crisis* in the feeling life of the personality. Thus, there need be no sharp division between mood and emotion. Emotion is merely an intense state of mood pressing for expression. Guilt, for instance, is often classified as an emotion, as is shame. Yet, we have made clear that these two feeling states are relative extremes of moods specialized to the rectitude and respect values. Surprise is often classified as an emotion; yet, it is clearly related to the enlightenment value in terms of expectation. In principle, then, we meet no untoward difficulty when we extend the analysis to deal with what is conventionally labelled as emotions.

Although we now have many longitudinal and developmental studies on a great variety of the practices involved in thinking and doing, we have very few on feeling. Perhaps the absence of the study of how mood patterns arise in the life history, and in what sequence, curtails a value analysis of socialization processes, since the mood data provide one of the raw materials needed to work out a value analysis of socialization in any detailed way. There is no ultimate substitute for observing systematically all the sequences in which students interact with teachers so as to discriminate and communicate subjective states of feeling. Yet, there may indeed be certain trends in the learning and communicating of moods and feelings that can be roughly ascertained and isolated. It seems likely, for instance, that the child's attention would be brought first to feelings centering around well-being than it would be to feelings centered around rectitude or enlightenment.

Given such a perspective, can we construct a provisional map of *the relative sequence* in which attention is brought to feeling and mood in each one of the value categories? It seems quite possible to do so. We need not assume that the attention is always initiated from the teacher, although it may be more important when that condition prevails, nor do we need to assume the attention is always expressed in words. A teacher may make interpretations of what the mood of the infant or child is and take steps to give it expression by supplying an environment appropriate to it. For instance, the teacher may interpret the mood of an infant as indicating one of playfulness or friskiness or, more generally, one relevant to the skill value, and give the child a situation and materials upon which skill may be expressed. Using this type of phasing analysis in the growth of mood and feeling in terms of the value categories, it is possible to set up four provisional phases of teaching.

In Phase I, the concentration is upon the *well-being* and *skill* values. The concern with skill may be more than upon that which involves physical skill; it may also be social in nature. Parents and nurses, for instance, may be amused and delighted with signs of flirtatiousness or cuteness in the child, indicating positive social skills in relating to others. Since so much of the early months is focused on the biological drives, the concern with well-being is easily seen as being paramount.

In Phase II, concentration may now begin to shift to deal with the *affection* and *respect* values. At present, for instance, there is considerable questioning of whether the movement toward social interaction with a mothering person is to be interpreted as a sign of saliency of affection in the child's subjective system of perspectives or whether, indeed, the concern is primarily with the values of well-being and skill. There is growing reason to believe that affectionate feelings and moods are slower to develop than those relating to well-being and skill and we may have misread the affectionate value into the infant's early response patterns that characterize his social interactions. At this time, we would expect respect to be emerging also, since the socializer (the child's mother or surrogate) is being differentiated from other persons and the importance of the socializer as compared to others confers added prestige upon him or her.

In Phase III, another shift would occur toward increased attention toward *power* and *rectitude*. Once the socializer had become effective as a target for moods relating to affection and respect, we would expect the socializer to utilize such a base value position to put demands for responsibility upon the child and to buttress such demands by direct or threatened *intense* indulgences and deprivations. Hence, those aspects of mood anf feeling relating to rectitude and power would become more salient.

The last phase, Phase IV, would be a movement toward greater attention to *enlightenment* and *wealth*. We would expect a good deal of the early subjective life of the child to be characterized by confusion rather than illumination and by relatively isolated percepts rather than an integrated map of the whole. Moods of consciousness we would expect to appear last and be more difficult to sustain. The concept of wealth (money) had been discovered to be extremely difficult for a child to attain and probably depends upon having some large view *and experience* about how the family functions in relationship to the larger world. Hence, enlightenment and wealth may grow more or less simultaneously and moods crystallize with regard to both values during the last stages of socialization. It is interesting that it is precisely the last two values which we have found to have a relatively less elaborate set of terms to describe the life of mood and feeling related to them.

Needless to say, these hypotheses about phasing in the growth of mood and value during the socialization process are not to be taken as proven. The factual study of sequences in the life history is still very rudimentary and our statements about phasing are only to be taken as providing some general map for empirical value study. We would, furthermore, expect that the phasing would be slightly or seriously altered when the value systems of the socializer, and the child-rearing practices by which values are expressed, deviated much or greatly from conventions of culture. Nonetheless, we may utilize the phasing model to establish still further hypotheses which could be directly studied in the classroom. We would expect, for instance, that teacher appeals to moods and feelings of enlightenment would be much less effective in the early grades of schooling than during the later grades, while just the opposite pattern would hold well-being appeals. Wealth and respect appeals should also show a reversal of pattern with progressive years of schooling.

Whether teachers are aware of it or not, they are constantly making assumptions about what the moods and feelings of the students exposed to them are like and base much of their own classroom practices upon such inferences. These inferences should themselves be subjected to study. One rather interesting way by which the teacher may study the pattern of his inferences has been utilized rather successfully in some previous unpublished studies. The teacher asks herself to rate each child in his class for one or more of the moods or feelings associated with each value. He then examines these to see whether he tends to associate one mood or feeling with another. For instance, if a child is judged to be high in "feelings of warmth," he may also be judged to be low in "guilt feelings." When correlations like this are found which characterize the *whole* judgment system of the teacher, we can begin to see that certain "value stereotypes" are operating as a perspective for the teacher which conditions much of his classroom practices. When several teachers participate in such a self-survey, it is quickly found that what is a value stereotype for one may be present in another in a quite reverse way. For instance, some teachers may judge children who have high "feelings of warmth" as *also* having high "guilt feelings." When a nonparticipant observer trained in rating techniques observes, he is more likely to come up with results which will show little or no correlation between the various moods and feelings as he infers them from observations. This happens not because he does not find particular relationships among moods for any *one* child, but because he is relatively free from stereotypes that compel him to see *all* children as characterized by the same pattern.

Where value stereotypes operate and get into classroom practices, they may themselves *evoke* the mood patterns in the children exposed to them over time. The children may come to suppress or repress whatever moods or feelings do not seem very relevant to dealing effectively with the teacher, and which are difficult to get him to see in their patterned relationships. In this way, teachers are often engaged in building up cultures about feeling and value in ways of which they are not entirely conscious. It is not surprising that the general feeling the teacher has toward his role and occupation might be related to the particular "value stereotypes" which he develops. Thus, we do tend to find that teachers whose whole life is successfully satisfied in the role of educator of the young has quite different patterns of value inference about the patterning of mood and feeling than teachers who are discontented and unhappy in the teacher role. The latter tend more than the former to see high feelings relevant to power as associated with negative feelings with regard to rectitude, to mention only part of the configuration of differences. By no means is it to be taken that a stereotype with regard to value inferences (about the mood patterns of children) inevitably eventuates in something disastrous for education. The stereotype may be of such a nature that moods or feelings that are disruptive of education are minimized and overlooked, so that the child learns to suppress or repress them in making himself or herself relevant and effective in teacher-student relationships. An effective teacher will still wish to learn *why* he is effective and the exercise in examining his value inferences to determine what kind of patterns they make will not remove his skill but merely bring it under more articulate conscious control.

Most educationalists are now familiar with the projective techniques. The various devices center upon using some kind of stimuli in which there is highly reduced opportunity to interpret what is seen in any "right" or "wrong" way. Instead, the stimulus is of such an ambiguous nature that mood or feeling may be projected into it during the act of interpreting it. In short, images are asked to be given to stimuli which provide little direction as the form they are to take. Hence, the predominant mood of the personality may play an increased role in the production of the image. In this sense, merely asking children to make up a story of any sort is a form of administering a projective test. It is quite possible, when teachers solicit such stories by verbal or written means, to analyze these stories in terms of the degree to which they support or do not confirm the inferences about mood and feeling the teacher has been making about a child. In such a way, the teacher may go beyond discovering his value stereotypes toward actually confronting them with objective data about feeling and mood. It is not at all unusual, for instance, to find teachers who assumed a particular child struggled with "feelings of being unloved" actually produces projective story material which describes characters who are struggling with "feelings of being unimportant and disrespected." In our time, there appears to be difficulty in discriminating between the operation of the affection and respect values, and the teacher who sets out to help the child differentiate between the two sets of values in terms of their relevant feeling components may be performing a very useful cultural service.

We have stated (but not stressed) that moods and feeling can be collective (shared) rather than personalized and private. While it is much more difficult to do, the teacher may follow the rises and falls of mood and feelings for the class *as a whole* over time. Moods of respect, for instance, may be witnessed by increased attention about what the teacher has said and the use of his phrases subsequently. The injection of humor into the classroom in an effort to make the atmosphere more congenial often signifies the surge of feelings and moods of affection for the teacher and among the students. A rising tone of marked seriousness may indicate moods of growing responsibility. Tokens of the growing mood of fatigue may be contained within the slowness to start activities and the creeping pace by which they are carried out. For each mood, one may find *some* observation of the collectivity in terms of which one can judge what mood pattern has swept across the group as a whole. Once some practice at these mood inferences about groups has been acquired, it becomes quite interesting to put the skill to use and ask: *From* what mood *to* what mood? The time sampled can be one day, one week or an entire school year. When this kind of coding of collective mood is done on a small or large scale, a teacher will frequently find certain reoccurring patterns. An increased concern with affection, for instance, may usually presage a growing mood of fatigue. Often teachers are preconsciously aware of some of these mood patterns, but many times it is difficult to see how these change during the longer period of time (a year) in which the teacher may have made some impact upon the feeling life of the collectivity of which he is not really cognizant, since the change has occurred so gradually for him. By charting the major mood features of the entire sequence of events in the classroom for protracted periods of time, the larger sweep of mood movements can often be uncovered. If the teacher were to relate such mood charts to changes in his own policies toward the class (becoming more permissive or non-permissive at a certain point), he could gradually come up with a picture of educational processes that go rather deeply into the classroom management of moods and feelings, and the consequent impact produced by way of heightened or lowered learning.

In any event, it is clear that, once we have developed a systematic way of examining moods and feelings by extending the basic framework of this book to the new area, there is no end of interesting and important observations that can be made, the value of which will be to increase the deepening of our understanding of the educational process beyond mere surface description. As the teacher and educational specialist "zeros in" with increasing skill and precision upon the mood and feeling factors that operate in the classroom, he cannot help but become aware in simple day-to-day terms of how values are constantly being shaped and shared even during the most matter-of-fact stages of learning. The mood predispositions of the learner and the teacher condition how the learning will be presented and perceived and, hence, what type of enduring learning will be produced as a response. When we leave out of education the mood-feeling component of predispositions, we cannot be said to have placed ourselves in an intelligent position to understand how the self is or is not transformed through learning and, hence, what learning can be said to be significant or trivial in terms of modifying the state of affairs in which education is given an opportunity to effectively intervene.

Part III of this volume is devoted to giving form to value thinking in undertaking to deal with the problems of education. The next three chapters deal with systematic thinking with values, problem solving in the unit of instruction, and the organization of the decision seminar in the continuing study of school problems.

Part III

•

GIVING FORM TO VALUE THINKING

CHAPTER 9

•

Systematic Thinking with Values

In a continuing group, problems are constantly being both discovered and sharpened by thought brought to bear upon them. It is possible with five terms economically but comprehensively to exhaust all forms of thought brought into play in any such continuing group. These five forms of thought are interrelated. The sequence in which they are introduced and the ways in which they are interrelated become a matter of technique that can vary much for each group using them. Freedom is thus very high to allow the contingencies of specific kinds of group experience to dictate how the five forms of thought will be resorted to sequentially. Needless to say, it is not easy to exhaust any one of the five forms of thinking in regard to any particular problem or group of problems, but each or all may be used as far as one wishes to take them. One can reduce technicalization as much as possible and remain systematic or, instead, move in a highly technical direction if one wishes.

One component of technique we strongly advocate in order that the method be fully used, is that of using the walls of a seminar room as a visual reminder of where one has been, where one is now and where one wants to go.[1] The point is that such visual aids force one to be more contextual in regard to time and space, permitting constant effortless but insistent reminders of the configuration in which one is working, including both that which one has made and which has been made by others for one.

SYSTEMATIC PROBLEM SOLVING (COMPONENT OPERATIONS)

The outline of classroom operational indices presented in the Introduction to Part II of this volume suggests the systematic approach to analyzing and appraising classroom practices and personal strategies which are typical of any classroom under observation. It also suggests how through systematic thinking the teacher may be led to propose changes in classroom practices that are found to be detrimental to the realization of human dignity among pupils and teachers simply because values have not been shared on the basis of merit. Thus, new and

---

[1]See also Chapter 11, "Study of Emerging School Problems Through the Decision Seminar." See suggested form of wall chart on page 170.

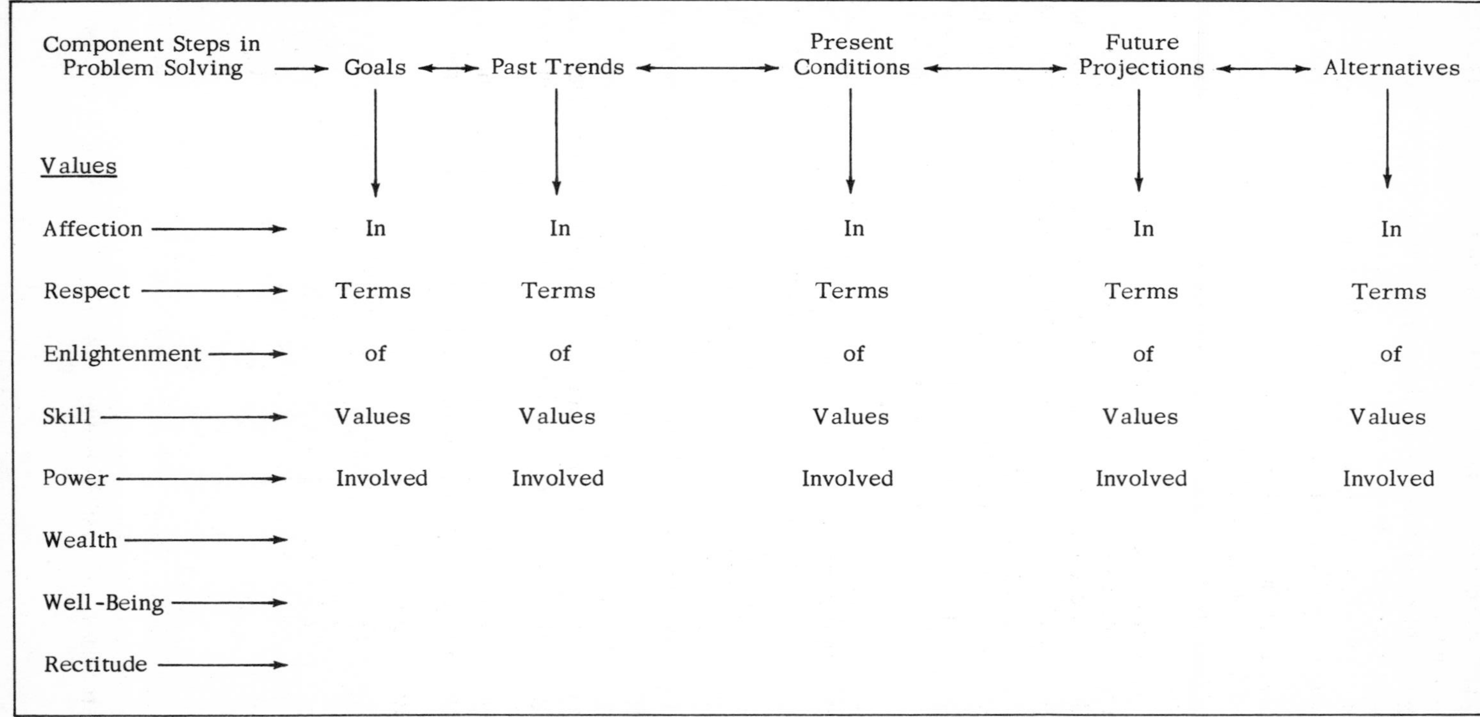

NOTE: Trend, condition, projective, and alternative data should be analyzed and appraised in terms of their relevance to the goal. One singular advantage of this chart is that it enables investigators to maintain orientation to the total process involved when moving in either direction from one intellectual task to another.

different practices should be created in order to insure the wider sharing of any or all of the values.

The approach to the solution of the problem may require the performance of systematic problem solving through the component operations of problem solving and value analysis. These include goal, trend, condition, projective, and alternative thinking. These ways of thinking are described briefly as follows:

Goal Thinking (Clarification of Goal)

Systematic thinking begins with the goal. The achievement of this goal involves problem solving. When we think of goal clarification, let us consider two necessary events in establishing the goal or stating the problem to be solved. First, the goal must be clearly specified and second, it must be justified. We say that when we have justified a goal we have established its validity. This raises a question that is so often asked and is often so difficult to answer if the goal is arrived at intuitively as are so many goals without regard to their compatibility with an overriding objective. This question is "How can the validity of a goal be determined?" As we have implied previously, the technique of validating a goal involves its analysis and appraisal in terms of the degree to which it contributes to the wider sharing of human values and thus to the realization of the overriding objective of the democratic society, the realization of human dignity. Let us take for example the goal of maximizing the well-being (mental and physical health) of pupils in a given school. The validity of this goal can be easily established because it will contribute to the increased sharing of one of the most important values which used as a base value will contribute markedly to the release of the child from crippling fears or physical disability which block his progress toward enlightenment and the development of his latent talents. It is obvious, therefore, that this goal is compatible with the overriding objective of a free society.

Goal thinking is one form of thought that is pivotal to all the rest. Until one has values or goals one wishes to actualize which are but imperfectly embodied in existing events that frequently fall far short, there is no problem. Goal thinking calls for systematic value analysis. It is specialized to clarify goals both conceptually and operationally, given the context to which they are being related. Only insofar as we have clear goals do we have clear problems.

Trend Thinking (Description of Past Trends)

Trend thinking involves the description of past events which are relative to the goal sought. The appraisal of past events is made in terms of the degree to which they have or have not facilitated movement toward the goal. The careful appraisal of events of the past requires a consistent use of the indices specific to each of the social values involved. Trend thinking is necessary to comprehensive insight. However, trend thinking alone will not make possible the shaping of the future. The events to be appraised are those which are relevant to the goal being sought. For example, all previous available physical examinations should be analyzed in terms of the degree to which attention has been given to the physical health of pupils in the past. This would require also a careful review of school policies regulating the control of physical health of pupils and the techniques and methods by which such policies were facilitated in the past.

Other data which reflect the impact of events of the past upon mental health will also need to be analyzed and appraised. Such questions as the following will need to be used as guides in the selection of data. What efforts were made in the past to determine the mental health status of the pupils of this school? What therapeutic measures have been employed to facilitate mental health? What has been the experience of the school with respect to the number of special cases requiring specialized treatment by the school psychologist or psychiatrist? What efforts have been made in the past to reduce the incidence of value deprivation occurring in the classroom or playgrounds of the school? What has been the extent of referrals of disciplinary problems to the principal during past years? What do available data reflect with respect to the extent of value deprivations suffered by pupils in this home and community environments? What efforts have been made to reduce environmental conditions which contribute to value deprivation among teachers? What efforts, if any, have been made to reduce the causes of conflict and tension in pupil-pupil and pupil-teacher relationships? Have the past administrative policies of the school tended to be coercive and restrictive or democratic and adaptable to changing conditions?

Trend thinking calls for looking at the flow of events in time relevant to goals. Events are always moving from one state to another state. Prices increase or decrease; populations grow or decline; the ratio of success to failure climbs or falls. One may find cycles at work involving rises and falls periodically occurring. When we ask how changes in tradition have affected values, we are engaged in trend thinking.

Condition Thinking (Analysis of Existing Conditions)

The next intellectual task to be performed is the appraisal of existing conditions relative to the goal sought. This requires the comprehensive analysis and appraisal of factors of the present in order to determine their bearing upon the achievement of the goal. Here again we ask many of the questions about the present that we asked previously in the course of trend thinking. The persisting inquiry is, what is the effect of present events upon the realization of the goal sought? This will involve the careful consideration of events which can be used as indices that point to the degree of mental and physical health of the pupils of the school.

Condition thinking directs our attention to factors that have shaped trends moving toward or away from goals. All conditions can be economically summarized as being cultural conditions, class conditions, interest group conditions, personality conditions and a fifth category called crisis conditions (such as wars, famine, riots, etc.). Cultural conditions are the crudest and most molar condition category. As we move from culture through class and interest group (religious groups, professional groups, etc.) to personality, we are progressively dealing with more refined conditions.

Projective Thinking (Projection of Future Developments)

The next intellectual task to be performed involves the estimate of probable events of the future. Projective thinking looks ahead to what one might realistically expect to happen, if past trends and conditions are likely to continue to operate or be naturally modified. A good deal of science fiction has introduced projective thinking into our everyday thought patterns. Projective thinking is not concerned with merely "extrapolating" the past into the future without taking account of self-corrective tendencies at work among the phenomena being studied. This form of thinking encourages us to create developmental constructs—some images of how new patterns will appear in the future (such as political patterns represented by the various racist regimes in Germany and Italy and elsewhere).

Alternative Thinking (Creation of Alternatives and their Scientific Appraisal)

In the light of past trends, present conditions, and estimates of probable trends of the future we undertake the next intellectual task in the search for our goal. Alternative thinking involves the creation of alternative ways of achieving the goal and the scientific determination of their effectiveness in contributing to maximizing the value well-being among pupils of the school.

It is in alternative thinking that the creative efforts of enlightened and sophisticated teachers, using all the facilities that can be made available to assist them in this undertaking, will be brought into action. The intellectual task to be performed here is clearly one of creating instructional techniques and methods which will contribute to the wider sharing of respect, affection, enlightenment, and skill as well as the other values which will have the important scope effect of reducing the tensions of school children that accompany fears and anxieties resulting from deprivation of these values. The teacher will, for example, probably decide to give considerable attention to the creation of practices which will encourage children to assume personal responsibility for their own behavior (rectitude). Any technique which is found to be effective in enhancing the rectitude status will contribute significantly toward the maximization of the mental health of children, for the enhancement of children's rectitude status will reduce the feelings of guilt which in the past have distorted their creative capacities to achieve the other human values.

Alternative thinking involves us in reconciling the product of the other various forms of thought. If our projections and our goals appear at odds, we need to consider how we can intervene to modify conditions so that in the immediate, mediate, or far future events will move more toward what we desire. The members of a deliberating group are themselves part of the conditions they are studying and, hence, can use themselves to modify the future, since they can "intervene" in the social process they are studying, in order to bring it closer to the heart's desire. On the other hand, it may be that goals will have to be reformulated, and made more "practical," in the sense that events are not easily amenable to change and formulating a lesser "step" toward a "greater" goal will allow for more success. Generally, alternative thinking calls for an exercise of imagination of how any alteration of conditions, including insight, will make things unwind differently than they would without each such alteration. We can study history this way. If certain leaders and collective events had not materialized when they did, the course of history might have been considerably changed. By such forms of thought, one becomes more aware of how much a product of history one is and how different one might have been had events in history been patterned in a quite diverse way than they were.

The "System" for Deliberating Is Important

As remarked previously, by following through any one form of thought, one is likely to have one's attention redirected to other forms of thought in new ways other than those previously explored. Frequently, for instance, it is necessary to go back to goal thinking again and again in the course of using the other four forms of thought to ask new and more detailed questions about value preferences, questions which had been previously not clearly envisaged.

No "magic" results from pursuing such systematic thinking, but the self-discipline imposed, while being relevant to a free flow of experience, tends to promote more creativity and productivity than just random discussions. Of course, many people intuitively are already exercising all of these forms of thought. Yet, it is important to give names to distinctive processes of thought so that they can be summoned more readily when they are needed—intuitive processes often fail us precisely because we have no way to name and identify what is missing or needed. Systematic thinking of this nature is, of course, uphill work. Many people who are disillusioned with "brain storming" and "T group" techniques, therefore, nonetheless resort to unsystematic thinking much like that embodied in such group technique, because the idea of having "a system" is also anathema to them. We cannot help but have a system, whether we acknowledge it or not. When we make what system we are using implicitly quite explicit, we will find it involves these five forms of thinking, often with one or more of the components highly underdeveloped and others too overdeveloped. The patterning among the five forms of thought has rigidified into one pattern, rather than allowing us, when all five are named and conscious, to experiment with fluid diverse forms of patterning.

THE PROCESS OF DECISION-MAKING

Any act of decision performed by a person or a group can be shown to have seven stages when it is completely analyzed. Consider, for instance, parents attempting to adopt a child-rearing "policy" with regard to their offspring. We would discover they engage in seven distinct kinds of activity in arriving at and carrying out an act of decision. These are: *intelligence, recommendation, prescription, invocation, application, appraisal* and *termination*. Any group or persons engaged in forming a policy can be analyzed in terms of these seven categories.

Intelligence phasing involves fact collection, processing of facts and consideration of alternative policies one can adopt, given the problem uncovered by the facts and processing. Recommendation phasing refers to selecting among one of the alternatives and actively working up enthusiasm for its adoption. Prescription phasing involves stating what practices will and will not be taken to be consistent with the policy adopted, and concerns under what conditions the rules do not hold and what conditions they do, as well as what consequences will follow from exemplary living up to or violating rules. Invocation phasing involves a preliminary judgment that an infraction of the rule has occurred when the circumstances do not justify it or that instead an exemplary compliance under the circumstances was a result. Application phasing involves a final judgment, after a complete investigation into the context, that the infraction or exemplary compliance has indeed taken place and the appropriate consequences are administered on the basis of that final judgment. Appraisal is any attempt to discover how well the policy is working, which involves fact collection, processing of it, and consideration of that policy's merits or demerits. Finally, the termination phase relates to any shift in the policy itself, as an example, to an alternative policy or with regard to a particular individual, who is presumed to have paid consequences and is restored to good graces or who is presumed to have received sufficient reward for exemplary conduct that no longer is expressed. With these seven categories by which to analyze decisions, it is possible even to watch the decision process in dreams, where often the phasing is unusual in the sense that some parts of it are altogether missing or endlessly elaborated. It is often found in a decision seminar that some people play one decision function role more than others and each person becomes more or less specialized to one function. Sometimes, no one arises to occupy a particular function or several people play multiple functions. Often when different value problems are under consideration, the person specializing in one function will shift to another as the value under focus shifts.

When we pointed out before that many times people take descriptions for evaluations, we often discover that they collapse the two decision functions of application and invocation. A preliminary judgment evoked by a description is immediately taken as a final judgment. This often happens because the prescriptive system of such individuals has not refined enough statements about the circumstances under which rules hold and do not hold. Hence, the pursuit of descriptive knowledge is not encouraged so much as movement into application.

It is possible to use these categories for both procedure (already indicated) as well as content. For instance, if we were to look at the policy of the United States toward the American Indian, it would be possible to analyze the decision-making process in terms of these seven categories over time. Changes of goals, trend shifts, conditions promoting these, projections and alternatives with regard to the decision-making process as a whole, could also be introduced. The two sets of categories—the five types of thinking and the seven decision functions—would supplement one another for this kind of value-content analysis.

SUMMARY

A point emphasized at the start, that the decision seminar being sketched here offers primarily a conceptual method to which many alternative technicalizations may be relevant, can now be reintroduced. It is clear that there is no one technical device by which to pursue this systematic thinking.

However, it is likely to speed up the decision group, if the product of each session can be economically visually summarized on the walls of the decision chamber. Cards can, for instance, be placed across the walls representing each value. Every value item and issue which appears can be classified under the appropriate value (or values) to which it is relevant. As time goes by, these items can be combined to give ever more quick economical visualization of what has already been a part of the pooled experience of the group in thinking through problems together.

People participating in such seminars who use these visual techniques, often without knowing it are being subliminally influenced to make connections between values, decision functions, or forms of thinking that appear quite "natural" and, yet, are highly creative and unusual. Many of us who have found highly creative ideas emerging in such decision groups have, through individual interviews, been able to get the person to trace the visual process which allowed him, quite without being fully conscious of it, to make unusual creative connections. Generally, there is some preference in such decision groups away from overtechnicalization. The categories help one *scan* each context, and the context as it shifts, to allow something of *significance* to appear that otherwise would not come to the fore. It is not necessary that any one-two-three steps be followed regularly in a way that "overmechanizes" the whole process—or even that the exact words be used as these are representing the conceptual categories. The idea is to promote the method or conceptual process of thinking, not to move into unthinking formalized rituals that become rigidified, either by word or deed.

Above all, the scanning process the categories provide assist one in raising significant but often overlooked questions about any content, and questions, too, which are often difficult to answer and, hence, help expose ignorance where there is supposed to be expertise. Without them, the tendency is to raise questions about problems to which one already has a good sense of the answers and, hence, makes a group move along very routine and conventional rails into well-worn grooves.

CHAPTER 10

•

Problem Solving in the Unit of Instruction

The component operations of problem solving have special application in considering classroom teaching methods. Problem solving gives to democracy greater precision for the deliberation of important questions and tends to guarantee decision making relatively free of compulsive, prejudiced, or hasty action. It provides a structuring of the deliberative process which, in effect, joins science and democracy in a most creative fashion.

Learning, thinking, goal clarification, and problem solving have great significance for the educative process. It is, therefore, of critical importance that educational methodology be so designed as to make sure the principal function of systematic schooling is to promote learning and thinking, goal clarification, and the other intellectual tasks in problem solving.

Do methods make a difference? Does the way a thing is learned have any effect on its quality and functional use? This entire volume and research in the behavioral sciences for a half century affirm that the methodological context is vitally important. Recently, the "discovery methods" in the new mathematics and sciences have given additional weight to this evidence.

It is becoming abundantly clear that science is not merely a collection of data but also a process of discovery, and that democracy is not merely a system of laws but also a process toward freedom in everyday living relationships. These developing insights give impetus to the creation of classroom methods which embody them.

The unit or problem project method has developed primarily as a result of John Dewey's influence on American education. It has had many different forms in practice, some of which do not really structure classroom activities to guarantee problem solving or group deliberation, but the original intention of such a classroom rationale was to provide (1) a group problem solving quest oriented around a general question (2) a breakdown or division of labor to investigate the several sub-problems within the general problem (3) individuation within sub-groups in terms of the goals, interests, and abilities of individual learners (4) whole group and subgroup decision making whereby learners determine with adult guidance what they are to learn, and (5) functional skill development to support the investigation.

The value-oriented conceptual framework presents a more comprehensive treatment of the Dewey inspired method with built-in value analysis and goal clarification. The process of goal clarification and problem solving are seen as critical processes of decision making and inquiry.

This framework has certain advantages over any previous prescription for problem solving. First, its *terms* communicate with greater clarity what the steps in problem solving are to accomplish over those usually attributed to John Dewey or, generally, the scientific method. Notice the old and new terms as presented in parallel fashion below. The arrows indicate the tasks of the old which are taken by the new. In addition "projections" add a new dimension to problem solving.

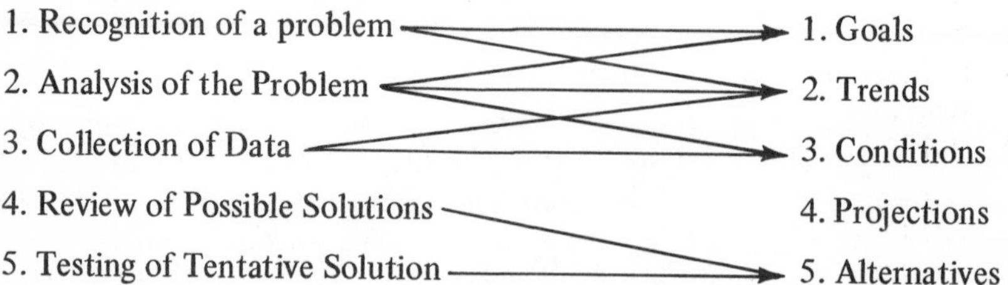

Second, the framework guarantees comprehensive inquiry in each step of problem solving by its insistence on value analysis in each investigative step. Of course, some value categories may have no relevance in some of the steps. However, the test for comprehensiveness, or depth of investigation, is the check on each value category, even if brief. Inevitably, this built-in check stimulates thinking in areas of the problem not likely to be considered otherwise. It points up ramifications which can lead to much creative discussion and research. It gives to the classroom an effective guide to controlled inquiry inherent in the everyday and usual curriculum. It does not, then, make inquiry the icing on the cake but, rather, the whole cake and the meat and potatoes as well.

Third, the framework provides a classroom rationale which makes at once for a community of the classroom–a miniature democracy–and a climate in which individual interest and ability can flourish. Since democracy is not alone a decision-making process, this comprehensive value analysis brings the true essence of democracy–value sharing–into the very core of the learning experience. Values are not only shared among the participants in the classroom but also with people living or dead, near or remote, who participated or now participate in the events studied.

The outline for the new instructional unit or problem project is as follows:

OUTLINE OF UNIT OR PROBLEM PROJECT METHOD[1]

I. GOAL THINKING (Clarification of Goal)

A. Identification of Goal.

1. Motivation by teacher.
2. Discussion of problem.
3. Goal defined in specific terms by teacher and pupils.

[1] This outline contributed by Ruth Holland.

B. Goal Justification.
   1. Teacher and pupils discuss and determine whether the study of this problem holds importance for the class in terms of values.
   2. Class discussion determines the appeal of the study to the class.
   3. Class discussion determines whether the realization of the goal will enhance the values of participants and/or society in living democratically.
   4. Extension of interests of class members in solving the problem.

II. TREND THINKING (Analysis and Appraisal of Relevant Past Events)
   A. What studies have been made in the area?
   B. Did these studies facilitate movements toward or away from the goal?
   C. Who made the studies?
   D. Did these studies present theoretical or factual alternative ways to achieve the goal.
   E. Are these studies outdated?
   F. Are these studies comprehensive?

   Resources and Institutions Used by Students in the Study of Trends:
      Books, Encyclopedias
      Resource persons, Discussion
      Reports
      Experiences of participants
      Historical films, Historical filmstrips

III. CONDITION THINKING (Analysis of Existing Conditions Relevant to the Goal)
   A. Do present conditions reveal the dimensions of and movements toward the goal?
   B. Does present-day thinking reveal intensive or extensive study?
   C. Are all sides of the issue presented?
   D. Have we drawn sufficiently from our own experiences?

   Resources and Institutions Used in Condition Thinking:
      Newspapers
      Television, Radio
      Magazines
      Resource persons
      Library
      Information gained by correspondence
      Experiences of participants

IV. PROJECTIVE THINKING (Estimate of Probable Future Developments)
   A. What will probably happen in the future if no new alternative ways of achieving the goal are created?
   B. Will outcome of past trends and present conditions enhance value distribution for participants? For society?
   C. What resources are available for future study?

D. Will this study lead participants to desire further research in related fields?
E. Will the learnings derived from this study extend to out-of-school situations?
F. Will the skills learned fit into the patterns for effective living?
G. What criteria should we set up to evaluate future developments?
H. Do we need new alternative ways of achieving the goal?

Resources and Institutions Used in Projective Thinking:
Written and oral reports of forecasts
Discussion
Resource persons
Experiments
Films, Filmstrips
Television
Magazines, Books

V. ALTERNATIVE THINKING (Creating Alternative Ways of Achieving the Goal and Appraising Alternatives)
A. Create alternative ways of achieving the goal (solving the problem).
B. Which alternatives appear to be the best in terms of our goal and our projected criteria?
C. How does the alternative give promise of contributing to the realization of the goal?
D. Is the method realistic in terms of the predisposition of people involved?
E. Is the method timely?
F. Is the method comprehensive?
G. Are all our questions answered?
H. Are our answers, or conclusions, consistent with the demands and expectations of society?

– – – – –

Evaluation of the Unit in Outcomes for the Student:

1. Have skills of thinking and communication been developed?
2. Have the students reflected their own personal views on the subject?
3. Has each student respected the opinions and works of others?
4. Have personal views and goals been broadened?
5. Have all participants benefited from the study in specific values gained.
6. Did each student have the opportunity to work at his own level of achievement?
7. Did each student have the opportunity to work to his full capacity?
8. Has each child acted individually as well as in the group?
9. Has each child matured in terms of directing his own activities?
10. Can the learners see that they are progressing?
11. Has this study aided in the development of the children's capacity for consciously and realistically making value choices?

12. Has this study aided the learner in knowing himself and better understanding the whys and wherefores of his activities and behavior?
13. Has this study aided the members of the class in understanding each other through group participation?
14. Has critical thinking and speech been encouraged?
15. Have potential talents been recognized and developed?
16. Have the students made progress in the basic study skills in all content areas?
17. Have the students made progress toward the assumption of personal responsibility for their own behavior (enhancement of rectitude status)?

– – – – –

Values Likely to be Enhanced by this Method:

A. POWER
   1. Making decisions about subject matter to be studied.
   2. Deciding on resource material to be used.
   3. Individuals practice democratic leadership.
   4. Freedom to challenge decisions of the group.
   5. Freedom to voice opinions.
   6. Freedom to offer constructive criticism.
   7. Participating in democratically held discussions.

B. SKILL
   1. Developing talents.
   2. Using sound logic instead of making hasty generalizations.
   3. Learning to think critically in sharing values.
   4. Learning to speak clearly and purposefully.
   5. Using basic study skills in research.
   6. Developing leadership ability.
   7. Developing followship ability.
   8. Taking part in group discussion.
   9. Recognizing potential skills in themselves including the aesthetic.

C. ENLIGHTENMENT
   1. Learning from each other.
   2. Use of resource material.
   3. Use of resource persons.
   4. Differentiating between sound logic and vague generalities.
   5. Clarification of goals.
   6. Developing creative abilities.
   7. Differentiating between fact and theory.
   8. Recognizing self as an individual of worth and dignity.

D. RESPECT
   1. Opportunities provided for developing individual talents.
   2. Choice of study is available to group with rights of all respected.

3. Clearer understanding of self as worthy individual.
4. Group respects individual's abilities and contributions.
5. Teacher respects thought processes of individuals.
6. Being an accepted working member of peer group.
7. Broadening views and goals as worthy individual.
8. Recognizing potential in self and others.

E. WELL-BEING
1. Aesthetic appreciations felt.
2. Freedom of bodily movement.
3. Feeling secure as worthy member of group.
4. Realizing potential talents.
5. Sympathy for peoples and nations.
6. Accepting praise or criticism gratefully.

F. AFFECTION
1. Recognizing the need for warm, friendly feelings among group.
2. Warm feelings teacher has for pupils.
3. Warm feelings pupils have for teacher.
4. Deliberate efforts made to build and maintain friendly relations in group, with class, and with teacher.
5. Outgoing warmth toward community, country, and other peoples.
6. Loyalty to family.

G. RECTITUDE
1. Responsibility of contributing to group study.
2. Abiding by rules and decisions of group.
3. Group and individual expectation of "fair play."
4. Evaluating contributions of others.
5. Offering praise with responsibility.
6. Fostering wide sharing of values.

H. WEALTH
1. Developing potential talents.
2. Learning how to provide for needs through service to others.
3. Development of resources.
4. Learning to be a constructive doer in making things.
5. Learning to work independently and to produce out of one's own initiative.

– – – – –

ILLUSTRATIVE UNIT ON SOLAR SYSTEM AND OUTER SPACE[2]

I. GOAL THINKING

A. Identification of Goal: To discover how man may exploit outer space in his own interest.

---

[2]This unit contributed by Lois Richardson, Mary Clinton, Inez Hamilton, Nola Warwich, Imogene Riggins, Helen Pinkham.

B. Instrumental Goals.
   1. To learn more about the forces and motions of heavenly bodies as well as possible resources that man may use.
   2. To learn the theories, nature and origin of the Solar System.
   3. To know more about space, space travel, and the space problems faced by the United States and other countries.
      a. Developing Interests.
         (1) Activities:
            (a) Show film, "Understanding Our Universe"
            (b) Arrange classroom environment in space theme:
                Bulletin board
                Pictures on wall
                Table displays: books, models, etc.
            (c) Visit an observatory or planetarium
         (2) Questions:
            (a) What is the Solar System?
            (b) How many planets are there?
            (c) Which planet is nearest the earth?
            (d) Do all planets move at different speeds?
            (e) Do all planets revolve around the sun in the same direction?
            (f) How do planets get their names?
            (g) Can any member of solar system be seen or observed without telescope?
            (h) Can all nine planets be seen on any one night?
            (i) Which planet gets most heat?
            (j) What causes rings around Saturn?
            (k) What is a star? What is a planet?
            (l) What is the difference between a star and a planet?
            (m) What is air?
            (n) Why is there a night and a day?
            (o) How far is the sun from us?
            (p) What is an eclipse?
            (q) What is the size of the sun?
            (r) How are planets held in the air?
            (s) What is the Milky Way?
            (t) What is the temperature of different planets?
            (u) Is there life on the Moon?
            (v) What are the canals on Mars?
   4. To organize the inquiry in terms of several sub-problems.
   5. To organize the class into committees to do work and research on each sub-problem.

C. Justification of Goal: The enhancement of man's opportunity to achieve values through adding to his resources from outer space.
   1. Reasons for colonization:
      a. Population growth may demand more resources than earth can provide.

b. Exhaustion of natural resources may become critical.
c. Economic security may be enhanced.

III. TREND THINKING
A. Early man did not understand nature.
B. Theories and beliefs of first scientists:
1. Aristotle.
2. Ptolemy.
3. Copernicus.
4. Tycha Brabe
5. Kepler.
6. Galileo.
C. Resulting Activities:
1. Reports on historical findings.
a. Use of rockets by Chinese in 13th century.
b. Use of missiles during World War II.
2. Draw Russian Space Orbit (first flight around earth).
3. Role playing depicting the planning of Wright Brothers' flight.

III. CONDITION THINKING
A. To enrich our knowledge of space and space vehicles.
B. Activities.
1. Have students compile scrapbook defining space terminology.
a. Acceleration.
b. Space.
c. Astronaut.
d. Astrophysics.
e. Blast-off.
f. Burn-out.
g. Centrifugal force.
h. Centripetal force.
i. Cosmic rays.
j. Gravity.
k. G Force.
l. Interplanetary.
m. Interstellar.
n. Inertia.
o. Motion.
p. Orbit.
q. Payload.
r. Propellant.
s. Revolution.
t. Rocket stage.
u. Satellite
v. Thrust.
x. Velocity.

2. Have classroom panel discuss these problems of space travel.
   a. Acceleration.
   b. Weightlessness.
   c. Meteors.
   d. Cosmic rays.
   e. Temperature.
   f. Fuel and speed.
   g. Navigation.
   h. Landing.
   i. Time and distance.
   j. Boredom.
   k. Isolation.
3. Show film of John Glenn's orbital flight.
4. Compile scrapbook of all findings of the astronauts as reported in the press.
5. Have someone demonstrate a space suit and equipment for space travel.
   a. Space suits.
   b. Space stations.
   c. Living in space.
6. Make a display on food for outer space.
7. Research and reporting.
   Pupil comparisons of problems of pioneers from old world to new as compared to the problems of traveling from earth to outer space for purposes of colonization.

IV. PROJECTIVE THINKING

A. Questions to be considered.

1. Shall we colonize the moon?
2. With all the space exploration going on, what may happen if we do not do something about it?
3 When are we likely to reach Mars?
4. How will our space exploration affect the national budget?
5. How will space exploration affect the food supply?
6. What if we do not have food preservative power?
7. What are our goals in the field of space?
8. Will we be able to communicate with our space neighbors?
9. Will our goals likely be compatible with our neighbors in space?
10. What training will be required by future space men?
11. What type suits will be worn?
12. What advantage will the country that first reaches the moon have?
13. Why should the United States continue the nuclear program?
14. On the basis of historical trends and present conditions, what are we likely to do about the exploitation of space?

B. Activities.

1. Bulletin boards showing collapsible tubes and how they are used for food for outer space.

2. Study of different types of food for outer space travel:
   a. Precooked.
   b. Dehydrated.
   c. Liquids.
   d. Semisolids.
   e. Snacks.
   f. Frozen foods.
3. Resource lecture.
4. Scrapbooks showing probable spacecrafts of future.
5. Reports on predictions of future.
6. Art:
   a. Drawings of future space ships.
   b. Drawings of pupils' ideas of life on other planets.
   c. Make scale mode of spacecraft.

V. ALTERNATIVE THINKING

A. Landings on the moon to be followed by study of resources available there.

B. Use space platforms possibly the moon itself, to extend mechanical controls over processes on earth. These may be of great value in weather observations and controls. They may add to our more effective use of devices of communication. (Our observations of bodies in space will become much more effective from space platforms where we shall not be hindered by the obstructive characteristics of the earth's atmosphere.)

C. Other possibilities to be considered in addition to securing resources from outer space:
1. Taking natural resources from ocean.
2. Exploiting energy resources from ocean movements.
3. Creation of more effective ways of capturing energy directly from sunlight.
4. More effective system of dams to control water resources.
5. Utilizing wasteland:
   a. Soil conservation.
   b. Better methods of using land.
   c. Teaching of birth control.

Evaluation of Unit

1. Unit involves systematic thinking in areas of:
   a. Language arts.
   b. Numerals.
   c. Social studies.
   d. Natural Sciences.
2. Interest created for further study of outer space.
3. Good use of lay resource people.
4. Democratic procedures used in all problem-solving activities.

5. The values were enhanced in the following ways:
   a. *Power*—pupils were permitted to participate in important decision making.
   b. *Respect*—all pupils were recognized before the entire class in their participation in developing the unit.
   c. *Affection*—the students gained a warm, friendly relation with many people as they worked together.
   d. *Well-being*—all pupils were encouraged to participate in satisfying ways.
   e. *Skill*—pupils were encouraged to learn new skills such as taking part in role-playing, art work, and other activities.
   f. *Enlightenment*—critical thinking was promoted by encouraging pupils to evaluate important events, books read, art work, and other studies made.
   g. *Wealth* (Economic Security)—pupils were introduced to many new and interesting occupations followed by people working in this area and were encouraged to build learning devices.
   h. *Rectitude*—by developing this unit the pupils learned responsibility and standards of right conduct as applied to problems of human behavior at the group level.

SUMMARY

The unit or problem project illustrated in this chapter demonstrates how definite procedural steps and goal clarification can become the principal rationale of the classroom for guiding learning into all areas of subject matter. When the teacher launches such a flexible process which gives way to almost infinite division of labor for subgroups and for individuals, individual differences in interest and ability, he is freed from mass teaching. This freedom gives him additional time also to help each learner move at his own best pace in basic sequential subject matter such as reading or arithmetic. But the curriculum process and the management and control of the class are governed by the science of values. Problems in either are taken up as the occasion demands. The teacher's job is complex and even exhaustive but under the control of definite intellectual tools. This concept of teaching cannot fit into the naive definition of teaching as a skill or a craft. Teaching within this context is a high professional calling: one which meets the criteria of worth and dignity.

CHAPTER 11

•

Study of Emerging School Problems Through the Decision Seminar

Building the school as a truly democratic institution demands more than intuitive procedures that may have their foundation in sentimental identification with the symbols of democracy. A school also should demand more than the employment of discrete practices selected from other school systems which under analysis could lay little claim to democratic aspirations. The American school system has long been recognized as an accumulation of practices, some of which had their origin in the schools of other nations whose claims to democracy were indeed tenuous, to say the least. However, during the past several decades, largely because of challenges to totalitarian governments, educational leaders of the free world have undertaken to alert citizens to the need for a continuing program of systematic, consistent, and timely classification of educational goals which are compatible with the goals of freedom. They have demanded, furthermore, that these goals be effectively implemented even though this means extensive revision, or in some cases, liquidation of many existing institutional policies, practices, and strategies which are in reality vestigial remains of the past in that they were transplanted from the educational programs of other nations and are in fact often incompatible with the democratic perspectives of the free world of the twentieth century.

Reference was made to the systematic employment of certain intellectual tasks in the analysis and appraisal of institutional practices in Chapter 9. These tasks were specified as the component operations of problem solving. The effort was made in Chapter 6 to demonstrate how teachers performed these intellectual tasks in the systematic thinking involved in the justification of teaching goals. The goals in the cases presented involved problems of handling interpersonal relationships. We shall now consider the systematic approach to the achievement of another goal of first priority in the democratic school. This goal is the creation of methods and techniques of classroom management which being compatible with the perspectives of a free society, contribute to the achievement and maintenance of the democratic classroom. It is proposed that full employment be made of the component operations of problem solving and all the other appropriate tools of thinking in the creation of these classroom practices.

It is furthermore proposed that these intellectual tools be employed in decision seminars organized and directed toward (1) the continuing clarification of the goals of the school and (2) toward the creation of classroom and other school practices designed to achieve these goals.

THE CHARTROOM

Still another proposal calls for the maintenance of a chartroom in which visual documentation can be provided in the form of records, reports, photographs, estimates, forecasts, and other data which are pertinent to all aspects of the work performed in the decision seminar, including the continuing clarification of goals, the analysis of past events, present conditions, estimates of the future, and the creation of alternative practices designed to achieve the goals with records of appraisal as these become available.[1]

The maintenance of a chartroom will first of all facilitate the *recall* function by reminding members of the decision seminar of the fundamental categories of the events under consideration. Such a chartroom would also serve to stimulate the *realistic imagination* of teachers in the creation of alternative classroom practices designed to achieve the goals of the project and would contribute to the development of *critical judgment* in the appraisal of such practices proposed in the process of alternative thinking.

Let us visualize, for example, the organization of decision seminars with chartrooms in *every educational building of the school system* and in the administrative offices of the superintendent of schools in accordance with the following principles of organization.

Each seminar would operate as a *continuing enterprise* that goes beyond the period of membership of any group of participants. This criterion of continuity serves to underline the advantages of cumulative research and would assist in the consolidation of progress through such research toward the realization of the goals and the overriding objective of democratic education.

Each seminar must provide *an environment in which the decision process involved is presented as a whole and as continued in time*. This principal emphasizes the importance of continuity in terms of the objective of the project, not simply in maintaining continuity of the act of decision making. Failure to maintain the focus of attention continuously on this objective may result in the making of decisions directed at goals which may be derived intuitively and which may not be valid in terms of compatibility with the overriding objective of the enterprise.

The point to be made here is that it is highly important to provide an environment which will perform the recall function of focusing the continuing attention of the members of the seminar upon the fundamental categories of the context under consideration. For this reason, it is suggested that each seminar, if possible, *conduct its deliberations in a room which may also serve as the chartroom*. One arrangement of the chartroom may be to reproduce on the walls

---

[1] The suggestions relative to the organization of the decision seminar are adapted from the manuscript by Harold D. Lasswell entitled *Technique of Decision Seminars Midwest Journal of Political Science* Vol. IV No. 3, August, 1960.

of the room the *Schema for Systematic Thinking with Values* shown in Chapter 9. The walls would thus be divided into segments representing the human value categories of the social process. One segment assigned to enlightenment, another to skill, another to mental and physical health, and so on, until all the value categories of the social process are represented. Information gathered about any event or series of events may be represented by a notation tacked to the surface of the wall under the appropriate component step in problem solving and in the section reserved for the value category reference. This device will serve as a continuing reminder of what has transpired in the work of the seminar. For example, any data referring to physical or mental health of school pupils five years before the decision seminar began would be placed in the section of the wall reserved for the *well-being* category and under the section of the chart reserved for the analysis of *past trends*.

As another example of the use of the chartroom, let us visualize a series of classroom practices designed to enhance the *rectitude* status (moral responsibility) of pupils which are planned to be put into effect the following semester, and that estimates of the future effects of these practices by years are to be made by the members of the decision seminar. Notation of the proposed classroom practices would be tacked to the wall under *alternatives* and in the rectitude category. Statements relative to the estimated effects of such practices at specific dates, would be noted also in the space reserved for the rectitude category and under *alternatives*.

It is obvious that by recording events of the past, conditions of the present, and estimates of the future, assuming no change of techniques or policy, and by recording each of these events in the appropriate section reserved for value categories, that we have in the chartroom technique a device which employs all types of audiovisual aids to assist the members of the seminar in the function of *recall* as well as to provide *stimulation for their creative imagination and the development of their critical judgment* in efforts to create alternative practices in programs of education which are in fact compatible with the goals of democracy.

We have referred repeatedly to the component operations of problem solving as important intellectual tools in the creation and appraisal of policies designed to achieve our clarified goals. We can see how these intellectual operations are adapted to the conduct of the decision seminar by providing classifications for reports of various types which will be found to be pertinent to the solution of the problems involved in the project.

1. *Goal Reports.* Such reports are intended to perform the function of clarifying the objectives of the project. They include statements relative to the specific goals to be achieved which tend to validate or justify such goals in terms of their contributions to the shaping and sharing of human values and thus to overriding objective of democracy.

2. *Trend Reports.* Such reports provide descriptions of past events in the history of education in general, and the school in particular, selected in terms of their relevance to the problem or problems to be solved. Careful attention is given to the correctness and adequacy of all data collected.

3. *Scientific Reports.* Scientific reports refer to those that undertake to explain conclusions to be drawn in the light of theory and data. The reports may be in the form of case studies of specific events in the ongoing operation of the school, as they may present the results of experimentation. The scientific report should be discussed in terms of the clarity of the generalizations it offers and the degree of their confirmation by the methods used and the findings obtained. Scientific reports are particularly pertinent to the analysis or relevant events of the present (condition thinking).

4. *Projection Reports.* Such reports are expected to provide estimates of probable future events, assuming that the participants in the seminar do not intervene effectively to influence them. The decision of the seminar is directed toward how such estimates were made and whether they are "high" or "low."

5. *Policy (Alternative) Reports.* Policy or alternative reports in connection with the problem under consideration include all statements of alternatives created by the seminar designed to achieve and maintain the democratic classroom (a minature model of a democratic community) and other institutional practices and strategies compatible with a society that aspires toward freedom. Such reports also offer appraisals of the proposed alternative solutions of the problem.

Seminar discussions may lead to the creation of additional alternatives or attention may be directed at criticisms of the proposed appraisals.

THE SEMINAR AGENDA

The agenda of the seminars are designed to contribute most effectively to the achievement of its goal or goals. Lasswell emphasizes that "The instructional purpose (of the agenda) is to provide skill in the use of all available aids to problem solving."

The preparation of the agenda should be a cooperative enterprise. One suggestion has been to ask all members to file individual proposals of items to be included in the seminar sessions from time to time. Later these items are discussed in open meetings and selections made in terms of the wishes of the group. Another method may be to rotate the chairmanship among the members of the group from time to time with the understanding that the chairman will be responsible for preparing the agenda for those meetings in which he serves as chairman. Following are some suggestions of operations to be performed and agenda items which may be included.

1. *The Filing of Independent Estimates.* This includes obtaining estimates by individual members of the seminar with respect to the probable future effect of strategies proposed. This independent estimate may be sealed and filed with the secretary of the seminar to be revealed later at the discretion of the member making the estimate. This process is valuable in that it will contribute to orienting the individual members toward the future.

2. *The Consideration of Estimates.* The seminar secretary may bring together all estimates made by individual members of the probable future effect of alternative practices which have been proposed and which are designed to

contribute to the solution of the problem (achievement of the goal). These estimates are to be considered in terms of the degree to which they may coincide (or contrast) with each other. At the end of the seminar, each member is encouraged to revise his own estimate in the light of his own experience in "tryouts" of alternative practices in his classroom or in whatever position he holds in the school system.

3. *The Reconsideration of Estimates.* After a seminar has been in operation long enough for certain events which were estimated for the future to recede into the past, attention may well be given to the reconsideration of the validity of the estimates made. For example, upon what assumptions were the estimates made? What sources of data were overlooked? What data were overemphasized, or de-emphasized? Such "autopsies" should be included as items on the agenda of the seminar and should provide valuable insight when considered in relation to the results of scientific studies which are made available from time to time.

4. *The Examination of New Information.* The agenda should provide for all new reports of trend, projections, and scientific factors being constantly produced in the field which are relevant to the achievement of the goal.

5. *The Clarification of Goals and the Appraisal of Alternatives.* The agenda should provide for the continuing process of goal clarification and the periodic appraisal of alternatives. The question to be constantly kept before the seminar is, *can alternative proposals of practice or strategy be justified in the light of the instrumental goals and overriding objective of democracy*?

The periodic appraisals of alternative practices designed to achieve the goals should be based specifically upon the determination of the degree to which such practices would likely contribute to the increase or decrease in value distribution.

The agenda can be adapted to serve many purposes of the seminar. For example, some seminar sessions may be limited to the exclusive consideration of trend studies, others to projections into the future, and still others to the creation and tentative appraisal of alternate practices and strategies designed to achieve the goals of the seminar.

SHARING THE WORK OF THE SEMINAR

1. *Individual and Team Projects.* Special projects may be assigned to individuals or to special teams who will assume responsibility for the performance of routine undertakings which facilitate the conduct of the seminar, for making analyses of special reports as they become available in the literature of the field, or for the more complex operations involving the creation of alternative practices under each of the value categories.

2. *Guests.* The problem of guests will often be brought before the seminar. It will likely be advantageous to recruit persons of high competence outside the regular members of the seminar to discuss problems and studies from their special fields. Their contributions should be analyzed and appropriately categorized within the intellectual framework of the seminar.

3. *Pretesting Alternative Proposals.* It will likely be found valuable to employ a pretest mechanism in order to gain information to be used in the further creation of alternatives by the seminar committees. These mechanisms will introduce a deliberate change in classroom or other school procedure which is small enough in scope as to avoid arousing latent opposition on a broad scale.

4. *Limited Innovation.* After the seminar is committed to a set of classroom or other school practices which represent innovations in policy, it may be found feasible to intervene in existing school situations on a scale appropriate to current predispositions and established practices in force in such situations. For example, (a) the intervention may be restricted to presenting before a limited audience of school officials an analysis of the alternatives which have been created by the seminars without indication of preference for any or all of the alternatives; (b) a limited audience of school officials may be given an analysis of the alternatives and a proposal; (c) several special audiences of teachers and other officials from the school system are presented with analyses and proposals; (d) general audiences from the community of the school are given an occasional report of analyses and recommendations; (e) vigorous favorable publicity is presented on behalf of the proposed innovations in policy and practice; (f) seminar participants seek the support of school officers in top positions of authority as well as selected members of the teaching staff in putting the recommendations into effect.

OTHER ADVANTAGES OF THE DECISION SEMINAR

The decision seminar technique can be employed in bringing out most effectively the talents of outside specialists who are brought to the school system for consultation and advice. Too often such talent is ineffectively employed either because no common insight is shared between the specialist and a large portion of his audience, or because the specialist uses terms which to his audience are ambiguous in reference. If such specialists can be exposed to the procedures outlined above and will agree to orient their contribution with these procedures, undoubtedly a great amount of loss motion which results from the making of unintelligible and quibbling statements that are not really pertinent to the current inquiry can be avoided.

Still another advantage of the seminar technique becomes obvious when reports or studies dealing with any or all of the problems with which the school is concerned are received. Such studies can quickly be "placed" in their appropriate categories and the probable consequences of their "findings" can be appraised in terms of the previous work of the seminar. This becomes possible because of the scope and depth of intellectual control which the seminar technique, with its intellectual frameworks and other mental and verbal tools, makes available to seminar participants.

The seminar technique can be employed with great effectiveness in the solution of problems involved in the construction and maintenance of the democratic classroom. Through its organization and operation it can become the center of a continuing process of analysis, creation, and appraisal from which can constantly emerge new and more effective classroom practices and strategies that are compatible with the emerging goals of a democratic society.

Not the least important consequence of the decision seminar is the opportunity it offers classroom teachers to practice the manipulation of categories of analysis and to employ many other intellectual tools not only in the solution of the problems of the school, but also in solving their own personal problems involving value deprivations they may suffer or may cause their colleagues to suffer through depriving them (often unknowingly) of values they hold dear.

The teacher in a free society must change his self-image from that of a police officer responsible for "making children conform to the rules" as his most important function, to that of the scientist responsible to his society for creating an environment which is most conducive to maximizing human values among the members of his classes.

In Chapters 2 and 3 we have seen how teachers have contributed to the classification of many existing classroom practices and to the creation of many others which are calculated to contribute to the wide sharing of values among children and teachers in their all-important interpersonal relationships. It may well be said that as the classroom goes, so goes the nation. This statement reflects the enormous responsibility a free society places upon the teacher. It also refers to the futility of assuming that somehow it is enough to want democracy, and that the handling of interpersonal relationships in the classroom can safely be left to intuitive judgments and decisions made by the teacher on the "spur of the moment." For in truth, action based upon a given "spur of the moment" decision may so damage a child's personality as seriously to distort his creative and productive capacity for a long period of time. This is human erosion which the free world can ill afford in the face of a most powerful and sinister intellectual invasion from the totalitarian world.

The free man should bring to bear upon his problems of manipulating his external environment, all the force of scientific technique and critical and creative thought. However, in handling his own internal problems and those involved in his interrelations with his fellows, he has been amazingly unsystematic in his fumbling and unrealistic efforts to relieve himself and his fellows of the tensions they suffer which accompany fears and anxieties that have their origin in actual or threatened deprivations of value goals.

The wide extent to which this is true is one of the persisting problems of the free world. The broad extension of the tendency toward unrealistic behavior is reflected widely in the creation of policies and strategies that often employs mechanisms of defense and escape that reflect a remarkable lack of insight and the failure to justify goals in terms of a free society's overriding objective.

It is indeed appropriate that the schools of our society take the lead in facing up realistically to the problem of clarifying our goals in terms of our postulated overriding objective, and in the creation and appraisal of alternative ways of achieving these goals. The organization and consistent operation of the decision seminar is suggested as an effective mechanism by which these purposes can be realized.

Part IV deals with the contextual reconstruction of education. The following three chapters devoted to the development of this concept are *Prototype Building for Educational Change, Transforming the Individual, and Multi-Valued Appraisal of Progress in Education.*

Part IV

•

CONTEXTUAL RECONSTRUCTION OF EDUCATION

CHAPTER 12

•

Prototype Building for Educational Change

CONSTRUCTING THE PROTOTYPE OF THE VALUE-ORIENTED SCHOOL

One of the most significant intellectual contributions which has been made to facilitate innovation and appraisal of the institutional practices of society has been the employment of the prototype. This technique can be employed for purposes of systematic research involving educational innovations either wholly or partly outside of the formal policy operations of the school. The prototype itself is a small-scale innovation which permits practices and strategies to be employed and to be systematically observed and appraised before being introduced as an innovation in the broader areas of the school system.

The aim of a value-shaping and -sharing prototype is to increase the sharing of human values on the basis of merit among pupils, teachers, administrators, supervisors and parents in all possible interpersonal relationships and in all institutional practices of the school. Each participant is a prototype and the process of prototype construction always begins and ends ultimately in one's social self. In the case of the value-shaping and -sharing prototype the past experiences of the participants and the institution should be analyzed and appraised. The convictions and principles of operation proposed by innovators should be presented to prospective participants in the prototype through consultation and persuasion. Any efforts to coerce teachers into accepting the innovation would be incompatible with the purposes of the innovation itself and would probably be rejected by them as an unjustified goal inasmuch as coercion deprives them of power and respect. In the initial stages of the project which involves direct communication with classroom teachers, the intellectual frame work, the value-oriented rationale, and the other tools of thinking including frameworks for special inquiry should be discussed and hypothetically applied with the hope that through free discussion and persuasion, the teachers themselves would be led to accept the overriding objective of the project and would agree quite generally that the instrumental goals offered realistic promise of achieving this objective, the realization of human dignity.

It must of course be recognized that classroom teachers enter into this type of experience with varying degrees of acceptance ranging from enthusiastic participation in the discussions along with many creative suggestions, to outright skepticism on the part of a small minority who may see the introduction of widespread value-sharing as threatening power and respect deprivation. It must be recognized, of course, that most of such individuals usually are almost wholly unconscious of the reasons for their skepticism.

On the other hand, some teachers honestly feel the teaching of children demands a strict autocratic disciplinary program. As some typical teachers have said in the past, "With as many children as we have to be responsible for in our classrooms, we simply have to prescribe many rules of behavior which must be accepted by the children." Later in the project teachers in conferences devoted to self-study will likely come to realize for themselves the origins of their resistances and the consequences for society of such an authoritarian approach to education.

CRITERIA FOR DEVELOPMENT OF PROTOTYPES

The proposed innovation should be introduced as a prototype when there is a clear majority of effective leaders who commit themselves to try out the innovation and who agree that the results sought through the innovation are likely to follow if it is given a fair trial. In a value-oriented prototype the effective leadership referred to in this criterion should include the chief administrator of the school system, the officer of the school who as director is to be immediately responsible for providing the environment in which the innovation is to be put into effect, the principal of the school, and the participating classroom teachers. This clearly accounts for the administrative leadership. Such leaders should be expected to cooperate with the innovators in providing the intellectual leadership largely responsible for the direction of the ongoing project in the classroom.

Still another criterion should obtain in the introduction of a prototype. *Early planning for the direction and operation of the project should include a clear statement of the power structure as it will operate in connection with the project, and specific allocation of responsibilities should be assigned and agreed upon by all participants including officers of the school and the consultant staff as primary innovators.*

The failure to specify in writing the lines of authority and responsibility for intellectual guidance often results in reducing the effectiveness of strategies which are created as the project develops.

No prototype can really be successful unless it has, first of all, central administrative support and sanction. Many prototypes in the educational world are supported by foundations or outside groups with financial resources as well as consultant help. It is therefore important to investigate the administrative relationships not only within the institution where the prototype is to be developed but the various administrative interrelationships between that institution and those attempting to assist it. It is obvious that the administrative relationships between the institution being affected directly and the supporting foundation or institution must be clarified in the very beginning. Foundations often work through colleges or universities in their support of prototypes for development in the public schools. The question of who has the power or who takes the initiative, then, is a key one in the development of any prototype.

An interesting question concerns how much influence on decision making is exerted by those who have furnished the financial support. Can any person or institution outside of the educational institution developing the prototype actually exercise direct power? Probably the answer to this question and the others above will be on the agenda for the instigating conferences between the various institutions involved.

In the development of the lines of authority and other interrelationships among the participants the problem of communication is crucial. It is extremely important that the channels of communication and the substance used in the channels of communication protect very carefully the respect status of the various participants. It is very easy for contempt to creep into the communicative substance of such projects. It is almost axiomatic that public school people will have a certain amount of contempt for the advice of "those college professors." It is also, on the other hand, very easy for college professors or consultants to develop the built-in state of mind that public school people are to be looked down upon and that they need rescuing from gross ignorance. The public school people often reply to attitudes imagined by teachers or expressed in the behavior of the college professors with the statement that the professors are lacking in experience in the problems of immediate concern to public schools and dwell in an ivory tower. The problem then of communication is a major one and a primary concern in the maintenance of respect by all parties concerned.

A person representing the consulting groups outside of the school system should be designated as well as a counterpart inside the system—a person on each side who can coordinate all the efforts and work out direct lines of communication between the groups who are to affect the prototyping function. It would be desirable for the chief executive officers and the sponsoring institutions to agree at a very early date on the coordinators for the out-group and the in-group functions. He also will want to know the nature of the consultant help to be provided and the specialists or consultants who will be employed. Policies and practices of the prototype should not be violently opposed to existing policies and practices within the school district unless the officers of the district deliberately wish to develop a prototype different from these policies for experimental purposes. Of course, a typical prototype does not attract enough attention to invite overwhelming criticism because it is small and relatively protected during its early development. The school officer should refrain from using his veto except for emergency situations. There should be a somewhat confidential publicity wall to be drawn around the prototype at least in the early stages to avoid any unfortunate prejudgments of the project by the public. These are matters that need to be carefully worked out between the coordinators.

Always it is pertinent to ask if the participants within an institution, even in a research situation, behave lawfully, that is, in terms of school policies, unless the head administrative officer declares that for purposes of study certain policies will be suspended. Such suspension must always be done very carefully and in writing. Special rules and special treatment lead to value conflicts.

Visitors who come into the institutional prototype situation should realize they are guests. Outside consultants have no built-in power to act. They are there at the request of the institution and can only participate in the role of presenting ideas or in persuading participants to respond in terms of certain value goals in ways that to their way of thinking will further the prototype situation.

Before the prototype can be said to be introduced, the participants in the program should be given an opportunity to master the intellectual framework for the program, and the definitions required in the intellectual manipulation of its categories. Another aspect of the training required is that all participants should have discussed the overriding objective and the conditions under which the overriding objective can be achieved as set forth in what has been called in this volume "the value-oriented rationale."

Prototypes are developed from within. They are built by the participants. Consultants can furnish a context of policy and technique ideas from which the participants may select. "Supersalesmanship" must be avoided to prevent respect deprivation. A prototype is successful if it works, if the participants feel successful in moving toward the goal, if its inventiveness is growing.

Nothing perhaps is more important for the successful launching of a prototype in an educational institution than to have a definite framework for creativity within which all participants including the visiting consultants can participate–not only from the standpoint of participation in enlightenment, but also from the standpoint of behavior in relation to each value in the universe of values and in problem solving. The entire process is continually one of problem solving. If all participants can address themselves in the same terminology and in terms of the same rationale for effecting the overriding objective of the project, there is a very definite potential established for unity as well as for clarified communication. Each participant within the framework of this prototype can better see how he can make a contribution and can feel that the way is open for him to make a creative contribution through his own performance. Even if the consultants are convinced that they know the ramifications of the framework within which all are to work, they should assume the humble position that every person, including themselves, should seek to learn because every prototyping experience is a new experience and should lead to the creation of innovations both in policy and its implementation.

Another aspect of the training required is that the broad outlines of the dynamic theory of personality development be understood. Experiences of the past indicate that actual practice in the value analysis and appraisal of individual behavior by teachers in regularly scheduled seminars is an important practice which appears to facilitate mastery of the information and skills which they will employ in the conduct of the project. Self-study by teachers in these seminars may be expected to contribute to the realization of the degree to which they personally have been affected by value deprivations and indulgences. A number of sessions given to the consideration of teachers' own problems which they submit to group thinking involving their own value deprivations appear to lead them to realize how extremely important it is for each to assume personal responsibility for contributing to the well-being of their colleagues through the wide sharing of values.

An important aspect of these group study sessions is that teachers come to recognize the debilitating effect of fear in their own personalities and to recognize how their own creative and productive thinking is inhibited in the state of fear which follows actual or threatened deprivation of such values as power, respect, affection, enlightenment, or skill. As one teacher remarked very significantly at one of such meetings, "For the first time, it has become very clear to me why my children sometimes will not undertake to answer a question when they really know the answer. They are afraid that unless the answer is perfect they will lose the respect of the group and become objects of derision." Teachers must come to recognize that children threatened with deprivation in one or more of the values are in a state of fear with its accompanying tensions and simply cannot be expected to do creative thinking although they may develop the routine skills which require only memorization for their mastery.

One of the most important contributions consultants can make to teacher growth in the skills necessary to promote the wise sharing of values is to cooperate with these teachers in analyzing the behavior of their children who appear to be working without fear as contrasted with the pitiable efforts of children in the grip of fears which originate with threatened value deprivation.

This leads to another point which should be made regarding the enhancement of enlightenment and skill of participants in the program. Consultants and teachers can with great profit analyze and appraise events of an antisocial nature exhibited in the behavior of children in the classroom. This study should be undertaken in the hope that the self-image of teachers may be changed gradually from that of the punitive officer appointed by society to enforce discipline in the classroom, to that of the scientist teacher whose major responsibility is to provide many opportunities for the shaping and sharing of human values among his pupils. For the teacher with an authoritative self-image, any antisocial act on the part of pupils offers the threat of power and respect deprivation. On the other hand the scientist teacher looks upon the antisocial behavior of the child as a cry for help. This is often the response of the child to a deprivational environment, which such a teacher can improve with overt efforts to enhance the child's value status where deprivation has occurred. The teacher whose self-image is characterized by this attitude is thus not threatened with deprivation of power and/or respect for he sees that the antisocial behavior of the child may not be directed at him personally, but against the child's image of the teacher as the symbol of a deprivational environment.

After it has been established that sympathetic support has developed among the participants of the prototype, the leadership should provide for the withdrawal without excessive embarrassment of participants in the program who for a number of reasons may prefer no longer to be identified with the project. To begin with, there may be those who simply do not believe that the educative process can be effectively implemented except in an environment characterized by externally imposed discipline. Some of these teachers may feel that they cannot operate with the innovation because it offers a constant threat to their achievement of status in those values which either consciously or unconsciously they sought when they entered the teaching profession. Still another reason why certain participants should be allowed to withdraw from the project is that they are not intellectually capable of dealing effectively with abstract categories of analysis to the extent required by active participation in the analysis and appraisal of human behavior and in the creation of classroom techniques and methods designed to implement the goals of the project. If such participants are permitted to remain in the project, much of their behavior is likely to be considered subversive by participants who have accepted the commitment to give every opportunity for a thoroughgoing tryout of the innovation.

A final important criterion is that *wide recognition should be given by all participants in the program to the need for continued clarification of the goals which are instrumental in the implementation of the innovation.*

It must be recognized that the actual introduction of the prototype cannot be held up until all participants have developed a high degree of skill in contributing to the creation of an environment which facilitates the sharing of values in the classroom, on the playground, and in the community. For this reason teachers should be provided with an environment in which they are encouraged to make creative contributions in the form of suggested classroom methods and techniques designed to promote wide value distribution. Shortly after preliminary instructions are given to participating teachers in the adaptation of the intellectual framework to the aims of the project, criteria for the creation of additional specific classroom practices should be listed as suggested guides to them in their efforts to create classroom practices to facilitate wide value-sharing among pupils.[1]

ORGANIZATION OF A SCHOOL PROTOTYPE

The Arena

When considering organization of the prototype situation within the educational institution, the arena for the educational intervention needs to be carefully spelled out. It may be possible that conferences and workshop situations can be arranged which provide a kind of pre-arena. This is where teachers and supervisors and principals think through what may happen in an imaginative sort of way, and anticipate the problems as well as the outcomes of certain activities. But the actual arena of activities, of course, would be in the situation where teachers, pupils, and other special service personnel of the school meet in an interaction situation to develop into institutional practices the new kinds of ideas being introduced. No prototype can be really experimental unless this arena for activity is carefully controlled. Such a prototype should be carefully planned as to the kinds of interventions that are to take place and also

[1] See Chapter 1 for such a representative list.

the kinds of evaluation that are to follow. Here it is important that, in the training of all staff and consultants, everyone understand carefully and thoroughly the ground rules which govern all activity in the arena. Again, these should be arrived at by mutual consent after much discussion and deliberation and, if possible, these should be placed in writing.

In a value-sharing project the prototype situation is one in which the everyday interrelationships of persons should be planned in terms of the value oriented rationale for achieving democracy. In other words, the prototype is expected to be a miniature democracy to demonstrate how interpersonal relationships can improve democracy in the everyday relationships of people. Since the value framework is comprehensive, involving in the global sense the entire educational program, the entire experience of the child may be involved. In the school situation, obviously, democracy is the all-embracing rationale including even the considerations of how he is to learn tool subjects like arithmetic. Again, it is significant that all understand how the general rationale and philosophy of a prototype affect all of the parts down to the most minute part, such as how to present to children the addition combinations in arithmetic.

Ultimately, the organization of the prototype in the educational institution is an attempt to organize cooperative research. This is a pattern of action involving participation of people in terms of the goals set down for the prototype, the evaluation of behavioral changes of the participants required if the goals are to be achieved, and the implications of these behavior changes for change in school operations. These changes should be valid not only in the prototype school but throughout the educational establishment of the nation which aspires to a democratic society. The action research pattern has, of course, the exploratory quality which takes the participants to goals that are beyond even their original expectations as held in the initial orientation periods. Action research, of course, is not the process of formal experimentation. There is a very definite place for both types of educational research. The prototyping situation in the educational institution of the type we are discussing is an applied research activity and is intended to lead people in their interrelationships to practice the desired behavioral changes which will in turn lead to social change on a larger scale. Action research, then, is designed primarily to change people in a desired direction, and that, ultimately, is the only change that makes much sense in the development of a society. It cannot be overemphasized that action research is a cooperative affair. Learning how to deal better with the learning situation, or how to help learners and their parents share values is not something that can be left to individual initiative of teachers, social workers, the police, or the church. It should be attacked in a systematic way by all concerned who follow problem-solving procedures in exploring all aspects of the social process.

The principal should take the lead in the development of school prototypes and carefully consider the responsible roles of supervisors, curriculum directors, and other officers of the school system who are in regular attendance in addition to the visiting personnel who may be furnished by the foundation or institution sponsoring the innovations. The principal is the key person in the intelligent guidance of genuine cooperation among teachers and special staff personnel, and he should always look upon his leadership role in these interactions as an opportunity to make the very best use of all the resources available to the school in the building of a high level educational program.

Role of the Decision Seminar in Prototyping

The rationale of prototyping is re-enforced and clarified in decision seminars scheduled for classroom teachers and other officers of the school system at periodic stages appropriate to the needs of the prototype development. The intellectual tasks involved in the decision seminar which include goal, trend, condition, projective and alternative thinking were presented in Chapter 11. The continuity of decision seminars is very important to the successful tryout of the prototype. The continuance of the decision seminar will contribute markedly to the development of common backgrounds of understanding and to the systematic use of terms of specific reference which will promote a common acceptance of goals because of their obvious contribution to the effectiveness of the innovation. While there may be wide agreement and acceptance of the broad principles and goals implied in the innovation, there may be many areas of disagreement in the specific strategies proposed by individual participants as important features of the innovation. There also may be intuitive disagreement on a specific criterion which is to be used in the appraisal of practices that are proposed. This involves goal thinking and may project the participants of the seminar into a full-scale effort to deal systematically with the solution of the problem involved by employing all the components of problem solving.

In the truest sense a value-sharing prototype may be said never to have achieved completion. Regardless of the degree to which classroom practices have been introduced and tried out, and regardless of the number of these practices which have received approval of scientific appraisers, the ingenuity of participants actively engaged in continuing efforts to facilitate the shaping and sharing of human values will lead to creations beyond the limits of anything that has yet been accomplished. It is certainly feasible to plan in the school system for a continuing scheduling of decision seminars in which teachers employing the intellectual framework used in this project may continue as a lifelong goal, the creation of ever new and different alternatives for still more extensions to the process of shaping and sharing of human values in education. The mature teacher who would accept this goal as a lifelong commitment could make innumerable contributions to the educative process which has as its aim the formation of mature personalities whose capabilities and predispositions are compatible with the ideals of the society that aspires toward freedom.

Procedures for Involving Participants from the Community

Some of the procedures which may be used to further the involvement of the participants from the community in the school prototype situation are: (1) general parent meetings, (2) grade level meetings, (3) homeroom meetings, (4) teacher-parent conferences, (5) teacher-parent-pupil conferences, (6) trips and tours involving children, parents, and teachers, (7) home visits by teachers, social workers, and guidance counselors, (8) the involvement of social agencies, public libraries, and other resources, (9) facilitation of communication by way of newsletter, greetings on special occasions like Christmas, demonstrations or communications about food preparation, nutrition, films, discussion of child development principles, by informed speakers or through newsletters, and programs providing for entertainment either produced locally or brought in at the expense of the Board of Education, and finally, (10) family dinners involving the children, parents, and the school core of teachers and administrators.

THE FANNINDEL PROTOTYPE[2]

Major Goals of the Project

The primary purpose of the project was to employ a broader frame of reference beyond the traditional for interns of the National Teacher Corps in their work with educationally deprived children and in promoting cooperative self-supervision by the entire professional staff. It was expected that improved climates for innovation would yield new curriculum and personnel strategies *in terms of a value-oriented conceptual framework.*

A second major goal of supervision in this project was to increase the interest of parents throughout the community in the education of their children in school and in the continuing process of community and family living.

The third major goal was to offer a realistic and demanding challenge to the entire staff of the Fannindel schools as professionals. This challenge consisted of providing motivational and intellectual frameworks enabling individual teachers and administrators to examine their own attitudes and techniques in ways that would bring about increasingly desirable modifications of their own self-images. Such a continuing program of self-examination and self-appraisal was seen as a way of releasing creativity for the invention of techniques compatible with the aspirations of our democratic society.

The fourth major goal was to mount a comprehensive attack on educational deprivation wherever it existed in the entire community. Stated positively, the improvement of instruction involved continuing efforts on the part of teachers to meet the needs and wants of all children on a broader conceptual spectrum than had been traditionally conceived. These needs and wants have been classified through previous empirical research in the social sciences over a period of more than thirty years under eight categories of human values including: respect, affection, skill, enlightenment, power, wealth, well-being, and rectitude. These needs and wants (human values) can be defined in terms of specific classroom activities, and are useful in analyzing and appraising teaching strategies designed to contribute to enhancing the value statuses of children at all grade levels as indicated on the following pages.

---

[2]Reports of the NCTEPS Demonstration Program in the Fannindel Independent School District, Ladonia, Texas–For the Year of the Non-Conference, 1966-67. Floyd C. Burnett, Superintendent of Schools; W. Ray Rucker, Project Director; W. Clyde Arnspiger, Chief Consultant; Barry M. Hawes, Research Assistant.

These value categories were employed also in diagnosing the value deprivations of children, in classifying their inherent potentials, in measuring the effectiveness of curriculum content and methods, and in appraising the strategies used by children and teachers in conscious and unconscious efforts to achieve their needs and wants.

Finally, the fifth major goal, cumulative with all these previously stated, was to develop a concept of education which truly assists American society to move more deliberately toward maximum realization of human dignity (optimum potential) for all citizens, according to merit. Stated as the overriding objective of a mature democracy, this goal is approached through the cumulative educational experiences of our people. Meritorious is defined, not in terms of traditional concepts of having "rights" or privileges but, rather, in the degree to which a person actively seeks to achieve more human dignity for others as well as for himself through the constantly enriching process of sharing human values.

Teachers and administrators, through in-service education and self-study, learned to recognize school techniques and community folkways which led to dignity or to indignity. They learned this way of perceiving through analysis of the value deprivations suffered or by the values enhanced in the shaping and sharing character of institutional practices or of personal strategies. Thus, human dignity (or optimum potential) as a broad, cumulative goal of education became specific and operational in the conscious activities of human value shaping and sharing. The teacher tended to become a specialist in the engineering of these value dynamics in the school situation and, with the cooperation of others, in those related situations which also affect vitally the educational development of children in the home and in the community.

Teacher Strategies and the Continuing Decision Seminar

In accordance with these strategies, teachers were encouraged to create specific practices in their everyday teaching which increased the sharing of all these values among all their children. Furthermore, plans were made for teachers to share their experiences with their fellow teachers and the parents, and to report the relative effectiveness of the techniques they have created and tried out in actual practice.

Regularly scheduled seminars involved the participation of the members of the teaching and administrative staffs. These seminars provided for the creation by teachers of classrooms strategies that were designed to achieve the goals of the project which were specified and justified or validated at the beginning of the project. This *clarification of goals* is one of the intellectual tasks to be performed in the process of systematic problem solving or policy making. Other intellectual tasks in addition to *goal thinking* include *trend* thinking (the analysis of events of the past relevant to the goal), *condition* thinking (the analysis of present conditions relevant to the goal), *projective* thinking (the estimate of probably future events unless human intervention occurs), and finally *alternative* thinking which involves the creation of classroom techniques designed to achieve the goals of the seminar followed by their hypothetical and finally their systematic appraisal.

The seminars were conducted in a chartroom. The chart, as organized, served the purpose of preserving the intellectual orientation of the seminar participants as well as providing a continuing reference to the progress toward the achievement of the goals of the project.

The seminar sessions began with several meetings in which the participants were introduced to the intellectual tools to be employed in the project and were given opportunities to employ these tools in undertaking to contribute personally to the realization of the project goals. These activities serve to encourage participants to exercise their creative and productive capacities in the solution of problems presented by individual categories. Classroom teachers used observational indices to identify the value deprivations suffered by pupils and then created classroom strategies to restore status in these values.

The project yielded scores of specific strategies which were employed by teachers in restoring respect, affection, rectitude, well-being, and the other value deprivations which observation had shown the children have suffered.

One of the most promising strategies was the periodic statements written by children regarding events of their lives in terms of the value consequences for them of these events. This process of value coding events of their own lives served to promote a more realistic study by pupils of their own experiences and resulted in their realization that many events which they had formerly considered to be deprivational were when placed in realistic context seen by them to have in reality been indulgent. For instance, many such pupils who formerly had been led by their unguided emotional responses to "feel" deprived by restrictive "rules" set by their parents and teachers, upon considering these events in their realistic context, realized that these "rules" had been established in an effort to enhance their statuses in respect, enlightenment, rectitude, well-being, and so on through the other value categories.

Here, one of the major goals of the project, the continuing enhancement of the self-esteem of pupils through the analysis of their own lives appeared to be in the process of realization. This has been evidenced by the release of pupils from many tensions of imagined deprivations and consequently has resulted in more creative and productive activities in their classrooms, on the playground, and in their home environments.

Project Resources

In the implementation of this program were employed all possible aids to instruction, including films, filmstrips, maps, globes, community resources, recordings, and original photography. Consultative services and additional augmentation of audiovisual aids were provided by East Texas State University, the cooperating institution of higher learning.

The school district comprises ninety square miles of agricultural land in northeast Texas, of which most is used for farming and ranching. Sixty-one percent of our students come from families with annual incomes of $3,000 or less, of which the majority are sharecroppers. However, wealth deprivation was not the main deprivation; the great deprivation was the failure to realize the untapped resources which lie in the human being which, up to this time, had been largely unrealized.

APPRAISING VALUE-SHARING PROJECT

Fannindel Independent School District
F.C. Burnett, Superintendent

The faculty of the Fannindel Independent School District has amended its philosophy of education to include a forward look into education which takes into account the development of the whole child. The many discussions and seminar meetings related to the final amendment of our school's philosophy led us to the conclusion that changes were needed in our teaching techniques. Also, the concensus of opinion was that we needed to define our overriding objective in the light of modern day aims of education.

My own thinking underwent revision. As a schoolman, I had looked for and had not found a philosophy of education that could be stated in simple terms and discussed with the man on the street. I recall the many, many times I have wondered how it was possible to transmit to youngsters an understanding of all the needs and wants of man which we call human values. In previous years I have wondered how we could involve children as learners until they could assist in the self-direction of their own activities toward growing up. Also, I have wondered about programs in schools that were designed to teach children to think. Now, I believe, I have encountered a framework designed to teach thinking that makes sense and one that can be transmitted to children. I have seen children in the actual process of thinking for and about themselves and their classmates.

Previously I have worried about human deprivation and about methods of overcoming the damage done to children who have been deprived of human values before they come to us in the schools. Nothing is more heartbreaking to the dedicated teacher than to try to teach the child who is seriously crippled by having been deprived of one or more of the values and at the same time realize that he does not have the intellectual tools to restore status in these values. We now believe that we have the techniques and methods of teaching necessary to overcome the tensions which accompany these serious deprivations which have distorted and inhibited the creative capacities of children. It has been most encouraging for me to watch my teachers grow in professional status as they have learned to help children achieve these all-important human values. Also, it has been most gratifying to me to see my teachers relieved of their own tensions. They can now divert more of their time and energies to the real task of teaching boys and girls in their classrooms to gain and share the real values which are the things human beings need and want.

The Faculty of Fannindel Independent School District believes (1) that a person is thought to have a well-established and integrated value system if that person is consciously trying to shape and share values in *all* categories, not withholding emphasis from any category, but maintaining a relative and flexible *balance*. (2) A person is less mature who gives a lopsided emphasis to only a few of the value categories. Such a person can be characterized as biased, prejudiced, inflexible, or even mentally ill. He tends to be autocratic and authoritative. The mature person who shares values on a wide scale can best choose among the various alternatives presented by any given social situation. His behavior is characterized by flexibility, congeniality, and wisdom. He has a balanced, multi-valued personality. He can thus be classified as a democratic person.

Some things we have in our school which we did not have before the project began in October, 1966.

1. A clear-cut statement of a democratic philosophy of education.
2. An intellectual tool in the form of a clear-cut definition of democracy as distinct from a society that is moving toward despotism.
3. A comprehensive statement of the needs and wants of children that we call human values.
4. A systematic approach to problem solving–one that operates in such a way that it can be transmitted to upper elementary grades as well as to high school pupils.
5. Tools for analyzing human behavior in the *Human Values Series*[3] plus daily opportunities for students to share human values with classmates and teachers. These tools also enable pupils to study the value consequences of the events in their own lives.

Results to date:

1. Teachers are more professional in their attitudes and practices. Their behavior reflects fewer tensions.
2. Fewer discipline problems.
3. Increased attendance is outstanding.
4. Higher grades in classwork.
5. Higher scores on standardized tests.
6. Enthusiastic cooperation of parents.

Appraisal Through Teacher Interviews

Interviews were held with all teachers who participated in the Fannindel value-sharing project. These interviews were structured in terms of the following items in the effort to get a fairly clear picture of the subjective judgements of these teachers relative to the effectiveness of the project.

I. Teacher's judgement of the change, if any, in pupils' status in each of the human values.
   A. Affection.
   B. Respect.
   C. Wealth.
   D. Enlightenment.
   E. Skill.
   F. Power.
   G. Rectitude.
   H. Well-being.

---

[3] N. Clyde Arnspiger, W. Ray Rucker, James A. Brill; *Human Values Series*; Steck-Vaughn Co.; Austin, Texas; 1967-1969.

II. Teacher's judgement of the degree of his own progress, if any, toward self-supervision during the project.
   A. General statement.
   B. Setting classroom goals.
   C. Creating classroom strategies designed to achieve goals.
   D. Methods of appraising pupils' work.

III. Effects, if any, upon teacher's status of well-being.

IV. Effects, if any, upon interpersonal and/or professional relations with colleagues on staff.

V. Effects, if any, upon relation with parents.

VI. Teacher's recall of most memorable experience during the project.

INTERVIEW: Mr. Conley, School Principal
Eighth-Grade Teacher
Date: March 28, 1968

I. A. Affection—I am sure that there was a general increase in the sharing of affection among our children during the project. There was definitely an increase in the sharing of affection among teachers and pupils.
   One evidence of the sharing of affection was the absence of conflicts among the children on the playground.
   B. Respect—The sharing of respect is one of the outstanding characteristics of our children. The semester following the project our school became completely integrated. I consider one outstanding index of the degree to which our children learned to share respect was the fact that this value has been widely shared by our children, not only toward other children but also in their relations with their teachers.
   C. Wealth—I had no difficulty in teaching my children the full concept of wealth. The evidence that this is true is given by our children who are able to trace the flow of wealth from services performed to money received which in turn is used as exchange in acquiring wealth both in goods and services.
   D. Enlightenment—The scores made by our children in the Metropolitan Achievement test indicated progress beyond what would normally have been expected of them during the period of the project. Our children learned the meaning of the values and they became more conscious of the needs and wants of others as well as themselves. This encouraged the wider sharing of all the values and was especially effective in raising the self-esteem of timid and fearful children. I feel that a most important contribution of the project was that we were able to secure the active participation of children who before the project had never really participated in the activities of the classroom.
   One of the techniques I used which I felt facilitated wide value sharing especially in respect and skill of communication was seating the group in

a semicircle. This enabled the children to communicate both verbally and non-verbally in a more effective manner. The children themselves said many times that this technique helped them to learn.

E. Skill—The skill in which my children gained higher status than most of the others was the skill of according values (social skills). This of course was one of our major goals and was given great attention by our entire staff. I feel that this contributed to the classroom environment which in itself tended to promote the development of the other skills. This was reflected in the Metropolitan test results.

F. Power—We tried to create every realistic opportunity to bring our children into decision-making situations. In doing this we felt we were able to increase not only the children's power status but also brought them into events which required them to assume important personal responsibilities for carrying out the decisions. This of course increased their standards of rectitude (acceptance of personal responsibility for own behavior).

G. Rectitude—I believe the concept of rectitude is the most difficult to impart to children. However, it must be taught and children must learn to live as value-sharing personalities, for in the absence of such citizens true democracy cannot be achieved and maintained.

H. Well-being—Our attendance records, which were very good, I feel indicated a high status of well-being among our children. After all, high status of well-being is in a very real sense the most important instrumental goal of educators for only in a relatively high state of well-being can the child be released to do the creative thinking and acting which is required in approaching his full potentials.

II. A. I find as a principal, it is easier to perform my job in a more democratic way. I find that power shared is more effective than power imposed. I am able to get more effective help in doing my job if all my staff participates in helping me make policy decisions. By according power and respect to my teachers I am confident that they in turn accord me respect by giving me the top level of their creative capacities.

B. My efforts in setting goals for my children and teachers has been broadened to go beyond the mastery of subject matter and the skills to include the achievement of the other six values which represent the needs and wants of the human being. In this I feel that I can most realistically contribute to the growth of the whole person. My belief is that the "whole person" is better able to guard himself against the damaging deprivations which tend to distort the personalities of those who are not given access to the whole range of human needs and wants.

C. This project demands continuing attention to creating techniques designed to encourage the wide sharing of values. The teacher must avoid many bad habits which really contribute to withholding values from children. The ill mental health of the teacher which is reflected in an unhappy critical attitude is as contagious as many germ diseases which may really be much less damaging to children.

I try to create situations which lead my children to help me restore the specific value deprivations suffered by any one of their group at any time. Sometimes the most highly privileged child may at a given moment be suffering a serious value deprivation which requires the help of all the children to overcome it.

D. In order to determine how near we have come to developing the well-rounded child which is a major goal, we must take into account how well this child has succeeded in gaining status in the wide range of the human values. This is a much more demanding type of appraisal of the child's growth and development than the more traditional methods but is one which must be used if we are really to measure our progress toward the democratic society.

III. I feel that since I have taken into account the value consequences of any decision I have made or action I have taken that I am relieved of the aftermath of worry and tension over whether I have done the wrong thing, for if I have taken all the value consequences into account I am confident that I can defend my actions without the feelings of guilt which contribute so often to the mental ill health of the school principal.

IV. Success in this project has been made possible largely because of the fine interpersonal relationships of our staff. I can truly say that the shaping and sharing of values among the members of our staff has really been one of their most important achievements.

V. I feel that the comprehensive set of values we now are trying to accord all of our children makes it possible for me to be very specific in telling our parents what our goals are in terms that they can understand and I am sure that this procedure has contributed to the outstanding cooperative assistance our parents have given to our program.

VI. The most memorable event in this project for me was to recognize for the first time the extent of the capacity of children to think when given the tools of thinking and after they had been relieved of the tensions of serious value deprivations.

INTERVIEW: Mrs. Yates
Seventh-Grade Teacher
Date: January 18, 1968

I. A. Affection—I now feel a closeness among all the children that I hadn't felt before the project started. I feel that there has been a fairly general dissolution of "exclusive cliques" and a recognition that such groups deprive other children of the affection and respect they all need and want.

I have been able at the seventh-grade level, to get the children to realize that their deprivation of affection and respect of other children in turn deprives them of rectitude since they have not assumed personal responsibility for sharing values with others. This is a cardinal principle of the democratic philosophy.

B. Respect–Many of my children have not been respected by their parents, so when they come to school they really are in another world. They know that in this project they are accorded respect. I feel that this is a most important factor in leading them to respect others as their teachers respect them. They have learned increasingly to respect their classmates. I have found that when a pupil makes an outstanding contribution, all the children show they are pleased. They tried to recognize the ability of pupils who make good grades by asking their help with problems they face in their own classwork. The brighter pupils in turn uniformly accord respect to children who seek their help by trying to give the assistance sought.

C. Wealth–I feel that I have been able to get over to my pupils the definition of wealth as goods and services and that money is only a claim against these.

   My children have come to realize that services they perform for other people is really according them wealth and that any service they perform in the classroom adds to the wealth of others in the group.

D. Enlightenment–This project has been very enlightening to my children. They see themselves in a new environment and in a new light. They have developed insights into the behavior of others and tend to seek the reasons why others act as they do. In their search for understanding the behavior of others, they employ the tools of systematic thinking in determining their goals (values sought by others).

   The children respond to the teacher's attitude toward education. The teacher must be able to lead children toward the mastery of subject matter in a realistic way (not by saying, "it's in the book and you must learn it"). The teacher should share her knowledge of the worth of education with her children by leading them to see the values involved in their studies for themselves and others.

E. Skill–I feel that the skill of communication is developing "normally" with my children.

   The value categories help the children specify and clarify for themselves what they are seeking. Most of my children want to "stand out" or gain respect in their outstanding development of one or more skills. This search for respect is therefore considered to be an important motivating force in the development of skills.

   I feel that my children have increasingly gained the social skills of learning how to share values with their classmates and with others outside of school. For example they have learned important ways of according respect to others on the basis of merit.

F. Power–I create situations in the classroom which contribute to the power statuses of my children. They really want to have power and they really want to exercise it in ways that contribute to the sharing of values. For example, each day I have a pupil who is responsible for my room while I'm absent for short periods for any reason. This has led the children to realize that they must accord respect and power to the pupil who is the current "student teacher" if he is to expect to be accorded these values when he becomes the "student teacher."

G. Rectitude–I feel that I was less adequate in the enhancement of status in this category than in any other. I had to face the fact that many children had been taught at home and in Sunday School that achieving rectitude was limited to what we are instructed to do by our religious beliefs. I was able, I think, to lead them to see that rectitude was in addition to religious beliefs, the practice of rectitude in their daily living which encompasses the wide sharing of human values.

H. Well-Being–I believe that my childrens' well-being statuses have been greatly enhanced by this project. The values they achieved which contributed to their high well-being statuses included all the categories, for I had set my major goal the enhancement of the child of his own status in each of the values. Thus, I believe this has added markedly to the enhancement of self-esteem by most of my pupils.
An index of the high status of well-being among my pupils is the absence of tensions brought on by value deprivation. They appear to be more happy and relaxed than before the project.

II. A. Education has been my heritage from my forefathers. My reading has become more meaningful to me than before the project. I am more aware of the techniques of systematic thinking in my work. I am better able to analyze my own work and if I see that I have neglected instruction in one or more of the value categories. I undertake to create activities to overcome these weaknesses. I have become accustomed to analyzing myself first to see if the weakness lies within me. I generally find that there is a lack of communication between myself and others and this realization places me on the proper road toward the solution of my problems.

B. I have become better able to see the total picture of human needs and wants. This has led me to the conslusion that my children have suffered deprivations in many of the human values which I must systematically take into account in setting my goals for the classroom.

C. We undertook to help the children analyze their own personalities in terms of the values in which they had achieved high status. This led the children to question themselves as to why they had high status in some values and "not so high" in others. This led the children to the self-realization that they needed to learn ways in which they may build toward higher statuses in those values in which they had come to see they were lacking. I believe this procedure is most successful at the upper elementary level.

D. I find that having learned and used the value categories, both directly and indirectly, I use them constantly in the appraisal of my children's activities. This process of evaluation has become often quite unconscious but on the other hand I use the values in conscious efforts of appraisal.

III. My mental well-being has been enhanced by a knowledge of the value categories. I have grown mentally in that I have learned not to be shocked by the realities of human living. I have learned to see that my deprivations are few compared with many other people and to face reality as it appears. This has enabled me to avoid many situations which would bring on the tensions of frustration. It has also enabled me to overcome temporary feelings of tension by analyzing and appraising the events that caused them.

IV. I feel that knowledge of the value system has broadened my ability to recognize that all my colleagues share values with each other. This contributes to a better school and a higher status of well-being for all teachers.

V. I am better able to understand the actions of parents because they too have been and are being deprived of many of their value goals. I believe I am better able directly to lead parents to see the value deprivations their children suffer and also indirectly to enlist them in assisting me to establish or restore status in these deprivations.

VI. My most memorable realization was that children respond creatively to a classroom environment which is free of tensions and therefore is conducive to the mastery of learning and the achievement of the other human values.

INTERVIEW: Mrs. Burleson
Sixth-Grade Teacher
Date: January 16 and 18, 1968

I. A. Affection–The children show much more concern or affection for each other. This results in much less friction and fewer conflicts of interest and of course fewer problems of discipline.

B. Respect–Children have much more respect for other children and the teachers of the staff. This results in a broader tendency to accord recognition to others in complimenting the work of other pupils and in offering to share information and skills with each other.

C. Wealth–The children have not developed as clear an understanding of the definition of wealth as "goods and services" as I have wished. They have memorized the definition but I'm afraid they do not have a complete understanding of the place of services in the formation or distribution of wealth. We must provide more opportunities for them to master this concept in actual practice.

D. Enlightenment–Children are more able to do creative work, including the research necessary to its foundation and especially their willingness to try to do their best in creative art and writing. They are able to define all the value categories. They have gained insights into the reasons for the behavior of others. They have made real progress toward understanding and analyzing their own actions. They have shown great progress toward eliminating racial prejudices and jealousies which have been common among children at this level. This has been one of the most important outcomes of the project in my opinion.

E. Skill–I feel that they have developed many social skills in their interpersonal relations and in their ability to recognize others for their contributions in the form of school work. They compliment each other for all good work they do. Their skill in memorizing poetry has increased. This has resulted in the development of taste in selecting good poetry to read and in appreciating its place in literature. The children's use of the value definitions as tools for thinking has been an outstanding achievement. They have often analyzed and appraised the behavior of children in class as well as that of other associates. They are outstanding in their ability to analyze and appraise events presented in stories they read and in the subject matter of other courses such as history and science. The stories they read were in the Human Value series.

F. Power–The opportunity to vote on all kinds of issues had led the children to deal more realistically with these issues in terms of their value consequences. There is disposition on the part of the children to want to take part in the power process (decision making) in a responsible manner. This disposition extends to the demand by children that decisions made by vote be lived up to in their everyday living.

G. Rectitude–Personal responsibility for behavior is much higher than that of other children in their age group in my experinece. This behavior also extends outside the classroom. Pupils have asked for assignments which would add to their mastery of certain subject areas, reflecting personal responsibility for their own growth. Pupils have been able and willing to analyze and appraise their own behavior in conflicts on the playground and have undertaken to restore value deprivations they have caused other children to suffer.

H. Well-Being–The high well-being status of my children is attested by the fact that they like to come to school and are absent only when they are physically ill. One little girl said that she felt so bad that she knew she should go home but that she didn't want to be away from her class. Of twenty-six students, I have ten with perfect attendance and five who have been absent only one day during the year. We are sure that the enhancement of their statuses in the other values named has contributed to their increased feelings of self-esteem which we believe has contributed to enhancing their well-being statuses.

II. A. I'm more conscious of the need for a systematic use of the value categories in educational literature. I use the value categories in analyzing proposed teaching methods and courses of study in terms of specific values that may be accorded to or withheld from children. I feel more confident of my ability to analyze events within and outside the classroom in terms of the values and whether they are being withheld or accorded.

B. I am better able to define my teaching goals in terms of the values I hope to accord my children as well as the values I hope to have them achieve for themselves. I also find that the value categories enable me systematically rather than intuitively to define my goals in my relationships with my children and other persons in the community.

C. I try to tie in the children's understanding of the values with their classwork. I try to show them how comprehensive the value categories are as they pertain to all the activities of human beings. I use this approach in poster work, in creative writing, art, and social studies. For example, any human incident can be classified under one or more of the values. I used the newspaper articles about the earthquake in Sicily to appraise its effects upon the people. They were for example deprived of wealth, and well-being but other values were involved in the victims' interpersonal relations with each other.

I make every effort to lead pupils toward creative thinking. For example, I try to get them to express their opinions of selected classroom practices and participation on field trips in terms of the sharing of values on the part of all members of the class. This approach encourages pupils directly to think about the value effects of any proposed activity.

I am constantly aware of how children, if given the tools of thinking in the form of value categories, and wide opportunities to use them, really develop their capacities for creative thinking. I know that such activities contribute to the enhancement of the self-esteem of my pupils as well as my own.

D. In appraising pupils' work I take into account, more than I did before, the project started, the evidence I get of their growth in the manipulation of human values in connection with their academic work and in their social activities inside and outside the classroom.

III. My own well-being has been greatly increased by my taking part in this project. My increasing self-confidence, which has come about through the development of my professional skills, has added to my self-respect status. My opportunity to demonstrate value-sharing techniques before visiting groups and other audiences led me to realize that I had skills which I have learned to use without the tensions of impending value deprivations.

This project has enabled me to overcome to a large degree, the great loss I sustained in the death of my husband which occurred shortly before the project started.

IV. My understanding of the value system and the human needs and wants it classifies has markedly added to the effectiveness of my personal interrelationships. I think I have been able to add to the self-esteem of my colleagues by my attempts to accord them the values they seemed to need.

V. The project has helped me to deal more realistically with the parents of my children in that I have been able to enlist them in helping me to accord their children the values I have found they need to raise their feeling of self-esteem. I have found that many values which have been withheld from children in the home can be restored if the matter is discussed with their parents. I feel that parents can be led to realize that value deprivations in the home can lead to tensions which retard the child's realization of his full potentials and that they are eager to help prevent this crippling effect.

VI. The outstanding events I experienced during the project were the demonstrations I gave before student and teacher audiences, especially those at the Teachers Institute at East Texas State University.
The most rewarding classroom experience I had during the project was to see the week-to-week growth of my pupils in their understanding and use of the value system in meeting their own needs as well as those of their classmates.
I have appreciated the opportunity to work with those responsible for the direction of the project. Through them I have learned to use techniques of solving school problems I have never before encountered.

INTERVIEW: Mrs. Flora Byers
Fifth-Grade Teacher
Date: January 30, 1968

I. A. Affection–There has been a lot of progress made in sharing affection in my classroom. This has led to a reassessment of the personalities of the children by each other. It's surprising to learn how many ways children can share affection. At first this was difficult until the children learned to express warm feelings toward each other. Creative growth toward the development of social skills begins possibly from one successful way of sharing affection that suggests still another way that should be tried out, etc.

B. Respect–I think my childen have grown in almost every aspect of sharing respect. They have grown markedly in their feeling that they are themselves persons who are respected because they deserve respect in that they accord others respect on the basis of merit. It is surprising the degree to which the vocabulary of the child grows with increasing understanding and use of the values. This all adds to the respect status of the child.
One important index of sharing respect is that my children are willing for others to have opinions which differ from their own. They no longer try to pick other children's efforts to pieces, by unjust criticism of their work.

C. Wealth–I have tried to teach my children that services are an important part of wealth and that children who have the services of a loving mother and teacher are really wealthy even though they may have little in the form of goods or money. My children eagerly seek ways of giving their services to others. I have learned for example that one of my children is exceptionally skilled as an "assistant teacher." She seems to express herself in the "language of children," concepts which are otherwise difficult to convey. My children realize that when they perform helpful services that they are adding to the wealth of the classroom.

Especially this year we have tried to lead our children to see that they are not so deprived in wealth simply because they have few "goods," so long as they share services of themselves and others.

D. Enlightenment–I feel that teaching the values and their use helped my children in the enhancement of their knowledge about subject matter studied. I also have the feeling that the lower the children are in achievement the more they are encouraged and can learn by according them the other values.

E. Skill–One of the most successful skill techniques we have created for our classroom is called the "sunshine box." If at any time during the week any child sees another child according values to others he may write a short note to that child commending him upon his "act of courtesy" in which he accorded respect to another and so on with all the other values. On Friday afternoon the appointed postman would deliver the notes that had been written to all the children. Obviously the child receiving the most letters had been seen most often in the process of sharing values. My children seemed to take great delight in discovering other children sharing values who had not formerly done so. Obviously this offered a real incentive for the child so recognized to continue to learn other ways to gain the respect of his classmates by according values.

F. Power–One of my children said, "What I like about the values is power." "Just making up my own mind about what I should do is using power." Many of my children have gained power status where formerly they had none. Some of them have become very good leaders with influence through this project. On the other hand, children who seemed to have all the power have learned that it is more democratic to share their power with others. They have become the kind of persons who are willing to take the opinion of others into account.

G. Rectitude–I find that it is difficult to lead children to realize in the face of some religious prescriptions (or behavior) that to gain high status in rectitude one must learn to share human needs and wants (or values) with others on the basis of merit. It is also a matter of rectitude for all of us to seek these values for ourselves, remembering that in doing so we do minimum damage to the freedom of choice and the value assets of others.

I see my children as growing more and more toward high rectitude status because as I have already said they are increasingly learning to share values with their classmates even as they seek these values for themselves.

H. Well-Being–Through widely sharing all the previously named values among themselves my children have generally established a rather high status of well-being for themselves.

Through congenial and happy associations with their classmates and teacher they demonstrate their feelings of well-being.

I can say that with the increasing status of well-being and the consequent general reduction of the tensions of frustration and anxiety, that my children are able to go beyond simple rote learning to more creative and original activity. Incidentally, most of my children have made higher grades on the standardized achievement tests than would normally have been expected of them.

II. A. The project has definitely affected my work. I feel that there have been many more times when I have been overtly aware of having to make important decisions that I consider to be in line with the philosophy of the project.

I think, now, first of the effect my decision will have upon the child. I therefore find myself refusing to "jump to conclusions." Rather I find myself thinking about what is best for the child in terms of the values he has been deprived of and how I can help restore these values to him.

B. Our children have made great progress in this project. They have come to understand the values as the teachers have. This sharing of values has become a part of the children and the first goal we have now in the study of stories is to analyze the events in terms of the value consequences of the events presented.

Almost any question you can ask the child now, he can interpret so as to give his answer in terms of the human values.

I feel that we have very few children now who are so predominantly self-centered that they cannot consider the goals sought by their classmates as also important. This fact enables me to set goals for children that are much more mature than before the project.

C. I find that in many of the teaching and strategies I have formerly created in my teaching, I, as well as my children, now see a much deeper significance because of the value indulgences which come from them.

Many of our classroom strategies have been created by my children who have learned the importance of value sharing.

I believe this study of the values has tended to raise the self-esteem of my children. I feel that the value analysis approach we used in the Human Value readers was most effective in our beginning history class.

D. The project has affected my methods of appraising pupils' work. I tend to look at my pupils activities for evidence that they are trying to behave morally. They try to share values and this I consider to be a measure of their rectitude status.

III. During the early weeks of the project my well-being was threatened. I lost sleep over what I was expected to do. I felt that every other member of the staff understood the goals of the project and how to proceed.

My well-being really began to be restored when I saw a teacher experienced in leading children in the study of values and how to code events appearing in their readers, at work in the classroom. I found after I came to realize what the project was expected to accomplish, that my well-being status quickly improved.

The project has been a wonderful experience for me. I'm sure all our teachers and our children have taken what they have learned about values to their homes, and to other places such as the Sunday Schools, where they have contact with other people.

IV. The project served to bring us all on the staff closer together in the way we feel toward each other. We have experienced the process of learning from each other and we have learned to share not only enlightenment and skills, but also the other values.

V. This project has led me to realize that many of our parents learned the value system from their children and I think that this led them to see that we have the value statuses of their children at heart. This has led our parents to give us more effective help in working for our goals.
My most serious problems with the parents of one family led me to gain important insight into the value deprivations suffered by their children. I found that I was able to use the techniques of value analysis in leading one of these parents to become very cooperative in the teaching of his child.
One statement made by a little girl this week was interesting. She said: "I wish they wouldn't throw the values at us. I wish we had to look for them as we used to." This meant of course that she had learned to value analyze the events in her texts with less effort as time went on and did not require definitions by others.

VI. I think the most important event to me was when I witnessed the reading demonstration from the Human Value readers and came to realize almost immediately that here was something I knew I could do and that I could do it correctly.

INTERVIEW: Mrs. Milligan
Fourth-Grade Teacher
Date: March 14, 1968

I. A. Affection–The project led the children to be more aware of opportunities to share affection and they were more conscious of the skill of sharing this value. They seemed to work harder at this effort as a result of the project.
   B. Respect–I found it became easier to get my children to respect the rights of others. I'm sure they came to respect the property of others more than before the project began. My children learned also to seek respect by displaying good work they had done. They also became anxious to accord respect to pupils in other classes which they visited by recognizing and praising creative work displayed. I try to accord the child respect by calling attention to the good qualities of his work and behavior in the classroom.
   C. Wealth–I think I was able to lead my children to understand that wealth was made up of goods and services. I gave them practice in dealing with

the concepts of wealth by asking them to list the services they performed at home and at school which added to the wealth of their communities.

D. Enlightenment–The project led my children to gain enlightenment in recognizing the needs and wants of all people, and they were given wide practice in how to gain these values for themselves and accord them to others.

The project led my children to be released from many of their tensions and this seemed to lead them to want to gain enlightenment from their studies and in reality to be more effective in their work.

E. Skill–I think we were able to develop social skills probably better than any others in this category. My children learned that I was anxious to aware recognition for any display of social skills they developed. Many times during the project some of my children would say to me, "We must do unto you as we would have you do unto us." This of course was evidence to me of their recognition of the significance of sharing values.

F. Power–My children gave evidence of their appreciation of the part I had given them in sharing power through making decisions about many aspects of classroom work. This led them to participate in making these decisions with more excitement and enjoyment.

G. Rectitude–My children felt that rectitude represented what their associates thought was right. They all seemed to want the assistance of their classmates in deciding what was right and what was wrong. I am convinced that they came to understand that it was right (moral) to share values with other children on the basis of merit, and that it was wrong (immoral) to deprive others of any of the values without merit.

H. Well-Being–My children gave evidence through their ease in pursuing classroom activities and their enjoyment of the program that their tensions had been greatly reduced and this of course was an important index I used in deciding that their well-being improved increasingly during the project.

II. A. I felt that the intellectual tools I got to use in the project made it possible for me to create the kind of classroom environment that made it easy to achieve the main goal of the project which was to provide a great deal of practice in widening the sharing of values.

B. In setting my goals I found that I could better take into account the values needed by individual children and I tried to provide them as they were merited.

C. I think my direction of pupil activity was pointed more in the direction of creative writing about themselves and telling what values they had gained as well as those in which they had suffered deprivation.

My assignments which involved the children's writing on cards events in their lives, and undertaking to specify the values involved, led them to be very realistic in telling about these experiences. For example, they wrote of many experiences about which they were ashamed and felt guilty. This way of facing reality, however, made it easier for me to lead them into a more realistic interpretation of the events that they had at first felt were deprivational, but afterward upon examination decided they were not. The values they seemed to gain in doing this were self-respect, enlightenment, affection for me, rectitude, skill, and of course well-being.

D. I appraise my children's work often in terms of their apparent high well-being status shown by the full use of their time, staying on the job until completed, and asking to make additions to their "Values Book" when other work is done. The additions to the "Values Book were creative sketches and written comments about the values represented.

III. The project has added to my well-being status by my understanding more clearly what my goals were, the ease with which my children worked without friction or conflicts, and the relaxed way in which they completed assignments.
Another important condition which contributed to my mental health was my ability to reduce many of the tensions my children had suffered. And I am sure that my lack of tension contributed to the enhancement of the children's well-being.

IV. We have all become more aware of how to get along with each other and the advantage of contributing specifically to each other's value needs. This I know has contributed to the enhancement of well-being for all of us.

V. My parents have cooperated very well in trying to learn the important aspects of value-oriented instruction. They asked their children to bring them the definitions of the values. They discussed with me how these values were shared in the home. Children reported that they were actively working with their parents in trying to bring about the wider sharing of certain of the values which they felt had been neglected before.
I can say that the common understanding of the values and our goal of widely sharing them makes it easier to tell the parents what we are actually trying to accomplish in their children's education. As I have said, this makes it easier to gain the full support of my children's parents.

VI. My most memorable event occurred in our first meeting when the full impact of the potential contribution to education which could be made through the values approach dawned upon me.

INTERVIEW: Mrs. Melton
Third-Grade Teacher
Date: March 7 and 12, 1968

I. A. Affection—It seemed to me that my children were more aware of being "nice" to each other during the project. We analyzed all our deprivations in affection that occurred. We talked about how to keep our tempers cool when arguments started. I tried to lead my children to share affection especially when disagreements arose.
My children never seemed to withhold affection from me.

B. Respect–After some of my children who were less able than the others began to show improvement, the other children would often applaud their efforts. I encouraged them to do this because it resulted in the gain of self-respect by the children who were thus recognized for their good work. This and other techniques of sharing respect I tried to develop, led the children to help each other in developing skills and in many other ways to share respect with each other.

C. Wealth–I feel that I was able to get my children to see that services as well as goods were an important part of wealth. I believe I was able to lead my children to see that luxuries in the form of goods do not mean happiness without affection, respect, rectitude, and the other preferred values.

D. Enlightenment–At the beginning of the year I regarded a number of my children as similar to retarded children in their low achievement and in their social skills. I drew this conclusion from observing their behavior and in appraising the low state of their work. It seemed that they had a definite mental block toward learning. As a result I became discouraged with the slow progress they made even though I gave extended intensive effort to help them improve their performance. However, as my children gained status in some of the other values that had been withheld from them they also began to gain in this value.

E. Skill–I believe my children progressed most in the social, communication, and thinking skills and that they came to realize their progress in this category. I think that this entire interview will indicate my belief that my children made important progress in the mastery of these skills.

F. Power–As a group, at the beginning of the project, my children tried to get me to make most of the decisions. However, as the project proceeded I insisted upon their making choices and decisions on their own whenever I could, depending of course on them. They then began to take part in making decisions which definitely resulted in the raising of their level of self-confidence or self-respect.

G. Rectitude–This, I believe, is the most difficult of the values for young children to learn. Of course, I tried to teach them the difference between right and wrong. I feel that I was successful in leading them to see that sharing values with others as well as gaining values for themselves increased their rectitude status. I tried also to lead them to despise immoral things people did but not the people themselves. I also concentrated upon trying to get my children to admit when they had done wrong and to do what they could to correct it.

H. Well-Being–The well-being of my children was much higher at the end of the project. They were able, therefore, to work with less tension of frustration and with more creativity as the project progressed.
The marked reduction of absences, I believe, reflected an improving level of well-being. (Additional comments pertinent to this section are given in Section III of Mrs. Melton's interview.)

II. A. I have learned to feel better about my work. I am sure I have gained in self-esteem during the project. The freedom we have had during the project has encouraged me as I gained in self-esteem, to undertake to create many new techniques of teaching designed to lead my children to become more conscious of their responsibilities for contributing to this process.

B. In all my work I tried to direct the thinking of my children toward the human values involved. I undertook to teach values in connection with every subject we studied and in the analysis of all really significant events which occurred. On special birthdays such as Lincoln's and Washington's I tried to lead the children to see that the high respect and affection accorded these great men were given on the basis of merit. Through this approach I tried to lead them to see that in order to expect others to accord values to them they in turn must accord these values to others, of course, as they merited them.

My goals came to be to try to get my children to share all these values with each other since my value analysis of their condition had led me to see the many needs and wants they had failed to achieve.

C. One classroom technique involved was an art project, in which the children painted pictures to depict specific events as they were related to given value categories; for example, they were asked to paint pictures related to power, respect, rectitude, and so on through all the values.

We also did creative writing about how we hoped to share or in fact how we had shared values with others at home and in the larger community.

I also assigned the children projects which required them to choose a community helper (milkman, custodian, doctor, etc.) and analyze the values they shared with us in performing their work.

At our milk period we undertook to talk about the human values involved in the production and distribution of the milk we were drinking.

We assigned the job of writing on cards the events from the lives of the children and asked them to code these events in terms of value deprivations or indulgences.

We tried to detect events from the playground and classroom of value deprivations and value indulgences experienced by children. In the case of deprivations we tried to analyze the events in terms of the values sought by those who deprived others of values, and joined in trying to restore the values in which such children had suffered deprivation. Results from this experience were uniformly good in raising the children's statuses in a number of the values including, of course, well-being.

D. I encouraged my children to participate with me in the appraisal of each other's work. Each child came to see that when he thought something another child had done was good, others, including the teachers, agreed with him.

I was always on the lookout for any events in the classroom that indicated progress on the part of the children in recognizing value deprivations or indulgences and in sharing these values with each other. I sometimes would think, "Today we shall spend more time on the specific skills in such subjects as spelling, reading, arithmetic, and perhaps not make explicit some of the other values." But usually something would occur that would lead me to see that certain children really needed to be given opportunities to gain status in other values than the skills and I believe my work came to be a better balanced educational offering as a result.

III. After our seminar which dealt with self-appraisal, in the face of my feeling of frustration and especially my feeling of guilt, I came to realize that in order to become a truly professional teacher I had to change my own self-image. This began to come about when I really faced some realities such as the following:

It wasn't my fault that my children had *suffered the specific value deprivations* that had reduced their well-being to the point where they simply could not live up to what I had come to think children at this level should accomplish.

I concentrated upon strategies I designed to restore status in the children's deprivations in affection, respect, and the other values in a more deliberate and relaxed manner.

As I began to see very positive results from this procedure I also began to recognize that my own feeling of well-being had become greatly improved. I found that at recess periods my children often came to me to talk on their own initiative and would tell me of the deprivations they were suffering; for example, they reported how they were disappointed by the way other people had treated them. One of my children this year reports nearly every day that her stomach hurts while she is eating lunch. My diagnosis of this case led me to think that this child believes a little brother five years younger, who has been very ill and has to be given a lot of attention, has deprived her of affection and respect. My procedure now is to lead this child to see that she really is loved and respected by her parents.

Good results are already beginning to appear in this case. She comes to me several times each week and tells me she loves me and that I'm the best teacher she ever had. This and other evidence points to the real improvement of her well-being status.

IV. We have always had one of the most congenial groups of teachers I ever lived and worked with.

The project, however, had led us to know each other better and to understand each other better because we have actually experienced the sharing of values with each other.

V. I can say that when I discussed this program with parents they have agreed that this project fills a long-felt need. I have the feeling that my parents have a higher regard for our educational offering because of the project.

VI. The most memorable event of the project to me was when I came to see how very much we could accomplish when I witnessed the first demonstration given by Mrs. Burleson in the use of the Human Values reading text.

INTERVIEW: Mrs. Reid
Second-Grade Teacher
Date: February 22, 1968

I. A. Affection–The children were very conscious of the value of affection. They sought affection in many ways. They also became very alert to children who needed affection. The discussions they had in class about the meaning of affection I feel contributed to the enhancement of their status in this value.

B. Respect–I think one of the most moticeable events in our class which reflected increase in the accordance of respect was the behavior of my boys at the water fountain. They courteously stood aside and invited the girls to drink first. This attitude carried over into other activities, such as passing through doors, and eating in the cafeteria.

C. Wealth–My children came to realize that wealth meant material possessions they had and they also realized that when they performed a service they were creating wealth but it was difficult to get them to really understand that money is only a claim against whatever goods and services are available. When my children learned that services are an important part of wealth, they came to see that with all the services performed for them by their mothers and fathers, their teachers, and others, they were indeed much wealthier than they had believed.

D. Enlightenment–The children showed that they were able to use the term enlightenment in a knowing way. One day a child said, "We are being enlightened as our parents are when they read the 'Big' newspaper, when we have our own little newspaper to read." When the children realize that they have learned anything new about the values they become more eager to gain additional knowledge.

E. Skill–The enhancement of the skills of thinking was easily recognized in my class. For example, one of our boys reported that cattlemen were shredding old newspapers, mixing them with heavy molasses and feeding them to their cattle. This led to an extended discussion of this practice and its possible worth. After a while another boy remarked that cows ate grain the same as human beings and that the practice of feeding them newspapers and molasses may be very important because this could mean more grain left for humans to eat. This, he said, would help us to feed the growing populations all over the world.

F. Power–I think it was significant that when any of the children wished to discontinue what the class was doing, for example reading a given story, they would say let us use our power and vote on whether we want to do something else. When this happened I always gave them a chance to decide what the majority of the group wanted. This leaving it to the will of the majority became a common occurrence in my class.

G. Rectitude–At first, going to church and Sunday School meant rectitude or morality to my children. I tried to get them to see, I think with success, that rectitude means assuming personal responsibility for sharing human values. I am sure that this teaching led my children increasingly to assume responsibility for their own behavior. One index of the status of rectitude of my children was that when left alone in the classrooms in my absence, they continued with the work to which they had been assigned without interruption. I believe this is now true of all the classrooms in our school.

H. Well-Being–My children were happy. They were not tense and afraid even when they individually realized that they had not done as well in their work as other children. There was a general attitude of "feeling safe" when they realized that none of the others would make fun of them, or otherwise withhold respect and affection from them. No one took an overbearing attitude toward anyone else in this class. I believe this was an important outcome of our value-sharing project.

II. A. All along during my teaching experience I have tried to share human values in my classes. The project has made me more alert to needs children have for achieving specific values in the classroom.
I tend to analyze the professional literature I read more in terms of values than before the project.

B. I've tried to get the children to assume responsibility for doing their classroom study even though I'm out of the room. This has enhanced their standards of rectitude. I think that in teaching my children definitions of all the values that they have learned to deal with people all around them. This is also true in their family relationships. They have learned how people are seeking certain values when they act as they do.

C. One technique I used was to have pupils tell of events in their lives and how these events had affected their lives either in depriving or in indulging them in specific values. For example, one of my boys went to his friend's home and returned with a ball belonging to his host. His mother insisted that he return the ball. The boy said that his mother had deprived him of respect because she had said he did wrong (deprived him of rectitude) and in insisting that he return the ball himself, the boy felt that he would be further deprived of respect. The boy said after he returned the ball and thought more about it he decided that his mother did what she should have done, and in returning the ball he had removed his feeling of guilt (rectitude deprivation) and that his feeling of well-being had also returned.

D. I know that the project added to my children's grade standings when they demonstrated growth in their ability to think in terms of human values. To me this is an important index of the child's growth toward maturity.

III. When I see how my children gain in their skills of dealing with human values I am conscious of the enhancement of my own self-esteem. This obviously involves the increase in my feelings of well-being. I'm sure that what I have done in this project will be a continuing practice in all my future teaching. I certainly don't intend to "let up" in trying to achieve the goals of this project.

IV. Our teachers have always enjoyed good relationships with each other. This program has intensified our appreciation of the importance of good relations in undertaking to create a project such as we have had. I can say that with the coming of full integration in our school these good relationships have continued to facilitate the sharing of human values.

V. My children have told me how their parents have appreciated their learning and being able to talk about human values in the home. I think this reflects an increasingly favorable attitude of parents toward our school.

VI. The most outstanding event I recall from the project was when one of my children came into the room during recess and reported that the children who were playing "jump the rope" were not taking their turns and were not showing respect for the other children. This was the first example I had of a second grader making a value analysis of a human interrelationship.

INTERVIEW: Mrs. Cooksie
First- and Second-Grade Teacher
Date: January 23, 1968

I. A. Affection–My children get along with each other in a more congenial way than before the project. Before the project, my boys often fought on the playground. During the project they became used to reporting conflicts they had. "He didn't like me" came to mean specifically that the child was deprived of affection. I would tell them "remember we're studying the values. Now did you withhold affection from your classmate?" If the answer was "yes" I'd bring both children together and lead them to see what it means to withhold affection from others and encourage them to make amends. This always improved their feelings of well-being and would greatly reduce the chances that these children would be drawn into conflicts again.

Learning to share affection, "being nice to each other," seemed to become the goal of more and more of my children.

B. Respect–I could see a growth during the project toward sharing respect, when they admired the work of others. I feel that these children who have been one year in the project accord me more respect. I felt that in coming into this new integrated school I may have "respect problems" but I have been happy to say that this is not true. On the other hand, my children go out of their way to accord me respect.

C. Wealth–My children commonly volunteer to perform services for me and for their classmates, such as helping each other in their work. I find that in their performance as "assistant teachers" they often do a better job of removing the fear of failure than I do.

I have found that the concept of services as wealth requires a great amount of repetition to master.

D. Enlightenment–I found that their knowledge becomes much more precise as they learn to value analyze stories in terms of the value consequences of events which are related. This gives children better insights into the real meaning of what they are studying.

E. Skill–I feel that my children did more work on their own and were more creative in art, in writing and telling stories, and in the skills of spelling and reading.

My children seemed to be encouraged to perform skill activities after I had been able to teach them that skills are "highly developed talents which we may not even know we have" until we try them out.

It is my opinion that to segregate children in terms of their achievement scores definitely leads them to feel that they are deprived of respect, enlightenment and skill, unless great care is made to show them that they are brought together in order that their special and individual needs may be better served by their teachers. They should be shown that this is really according respect as well as enlightenment and skill.

F. Power–We have a club called the citizenship club in which my children are given many opportunities to vote and otherwise to take part in decision making. This activity provides the children with opportunities to make decisions about their plans in a cooperative manner. This activity places a high premium upon the skills of thinking and communication. My children, after they have expressed themselves, and are out-voted do not become angry and seriously disturbed.

G. Rectitude–I know I must concentrate upon teaching my children that rectitude refers to the degree to which people accord values to others as well as themselves. I think I have been less successful in teaching this clear-cut concept than I have the other value categories. However, my children have in fact enhanced their rectitude status in their sharing of values in the classroom, on the playground and at home. It is most important that I in my teaching lead them to see that this is true.

H. Well-Being–My children seem to have mastered the concept of mental and physical well-being status as well or better than any other value category. They easily recognize that "to smile is to reflect a rather high state of well-being." The effort I have made to lead my children to share values with each other has enhanced their well-being status and has resulted in their increased happiness. In a high state of well-being they are free to learn more efficiently and to "think on their own" more skillfully.

II. A. I have been more conscious of what it means to assume responsibility for the growth of my children since the value-sharing project began. I believe this has been due to my better understanding of the real purposes of education. If I know better what I am to achieve, then I can check on my own work in terms of whether I'm performing as I can and should.

B. It's easier to set goals for my children that make sense, knowing the full scope of the needs and wants (values) of human beings. My present goals take into account not only the growth of children in the values, enlightenment and skill, but also the other six value categories that are often ignored as specific goals of teaching.

C. I try to do things myself in my relations with my children that accord them the values in which I think they are deprived. Concern for how the child feels accords him affection. Praise for good work he has done accords him respect, as does asking his opinion about aspects of the lesson and encouraging him to lead out in discussions.

I look for "signs" that the well-being of my children is high. Their smiles of pride after doing a good job and their enthusiastic cooperation in undertaking a project we have set for ourselves, their willingness to share values with their classmates and with me are all signs of good mental health.

We try to justify the goals we set by asking ourselves what values will be accorded ourselves and others if the goals are reached.

D. Appraising pupils' work should specifically take into account the way they try to achieve the values for themselves and avoid withholding them from others.

III. As I have indicated earlier in this interview, my well-being status has been improved by the way my children accord me the values. Also, I feel that I have been helped mentally by having a better understanding of all the values that underlie a good teaching program. When the teacher is happy, the well-being of the children is improved.

IV. I think my colleagues of the faculty have a fine understanding of what it means to us all to share values with each other and live up to the responsibility each has to meet this obligation. This adds to our rectitude status.

V. My relations with my parents have been improved by my ability to lead them to realize the specific values needed by their children with suggestions as to how they can help restore the values in which they have been deprived.

VI. I think the most important events for me in the project were the seminars we had which were given to the solution of our problems of teaching by applying our understanding of the value categories.

INTERVIEW: Mrs. Wanda D. Johnson
First-Grade Teacher
Date: April 11, 1968

I. A. Affection—I had no actual evidence that my children made any progress in sharing affection with each other during the project. I suppose we spent so much time on enlightenment and skill development that we did not give enough attention to the enhancement of the children's affection statuses.

We did stress the importance of kindness to parents more than to each other and I believe that to my children affection meant love of mother and father and the love their parents had for them.

B. Respect–To my first-grade children respect meant "looking up to someone," usually older people, or people with authority. In the classroom we discussed the ways in which respect could be accorded or withheld from others, and I tried to impress upon my children the importance of sharing respect; for example, if a child who himself wanted attention should interrupt a classmate's recitation or statement he was making, I would ask whether this child was withholding respect from the child who had the floor. In this way I called attention to the importance of sharing respect and stressed how improper it was to deny respect for others.

C. Wealth–We talked about wealth in terms of the children's wealth in their homes with the emphasis upon goods, such as beds to sleep in, food to eat, clothes to wear. I believe that my children looked upon money as the most important symbol of wealth.

D. Enlightenment–My children did very well in the mastery of the subject matter they were taught. I think my children certainly mastered the definitions of the values. My evidence that the children had learned the values was their ability to give verbal equivalents for each of the categories, for example, "liking, loving, and friendship" were equivalents for affection. "Looking up to" was respect. "Learning arithmetic" and other subjects including human values meant enlightenment. "Coloring, pasting, and reading" meant skills. "Voting and choosing" were power. "Doing right" was rectitude. "Being happy and healthy" meant well-being.

E. Skill–We stressed the importance of the school program as being greatly concerned with the development of the skills of children. The skills in which my children gained most were the rote skills of reading, writing, and numbers. We stressed some of the social skills; we taught that "girls are to go first"; "we do not take things of others without permission"; "we take turns at play and at work"; "we share in a reasonable manner our possessions with others."

F. Power–I gave my children many opportunities to vote in matters that fell within their capacities, always proceeding according to the vote. My children exercised their choices in the songs they wished to sing. They chose the class favorite and in other ways they participated in the power process.

G. Rectitude–My children's statuses in rectitude definitely increased during the project. To my children, "doing right" meant rectitude. I failed to get all my children to see that sharing values was a moral thing except in the deprivation of wealth (in taking things that belonged to others) or enlightenment, which meant cheating on tests. (I tried to discourage malicious gossip designed to deprive others of rectitude or respect unjustly.)

H. Well-Being–I think the status of well-being of my children was high. There seemed to be a minimum of carry-over effects upon my children of most value deprivations they had in the course of classroom activities. The main problem first-grade children feel they have is getting other children to play with them. I meet this situation by telling such children to join in with the play group without more ado. The real problem seems to be that some children want only one other child to play with them exclusively. When they fail in this objective they usually come crying to me with the statement that no one will play with them. I try to combat this attitude by getting the child to reinterpret the event more realistically and thus become able to see that if he wishes to join in the play of others he will be accepted.

II. A. We became more aware of the whole range of the children's needs and wants or values. We became more aware also of how we may help children achieve these values.

B. We presented all the value categories one at a time–one each day–and illustrated each of the values by pictures selected by the children. Our main goal here was to have the children learn the specific meaning of each value. I implemented this goal by posters I made and collected for classroom display.

C. I held sessions in which the children were asked to tell what the values meant in their own terms or in terms they had learned in discussions. To begin with, I introduced verbal equivalents for the value categories. For example, "liking" and "loving" was affection; "looking up to" referred to respect; "toys," "clothes," "homes," and "food" referred to wealth; "doing right," "not cheating in class," was rectitude. And the like through all the values. After about three months, however, the children had used the value categories often enough that they did not need to use the simpler verbal equivalents we taught at the beginning. They seemed to prefer to use the terms referring to the basic categories, affection, respect, power, rectitude, well-being, and so on.

D. I appraised my children's work by noting the degrees to which they could use the terms referring to the values correctly.

III. I feel that my well-being was enhanced during the project largely because of the more specific goals I had during the year.

IV. My relationships with all my colleagues have been characterized by mutual respect and affection. None of the staff has taken an arbitrary power position. I consider the rectitude status of the group to be high. The enlightenment and skill statuses of the staff are certainly higher than any other group with which I have been associated. I believe we all have a very high status of well-being. Our children won't let us be unhappy for any length of time.

V. My relationships with parents have been marked by mutual respect. I had no conflicts of any kind with my parents during the project.

VI. My most memorable experience during the project was to witness the demonstration by Mrs. Crook of the Human Values series of readers in the sixth-grade classroom, in which the children value analyzed the events of one of the stories.

INTERVIEW: Mrs. Linnie M. Wright
Special Education
Date: April 2, 1968

I. A. Affection—I think the children shared affection increasingly as they learned the real meaning of this term.
The children talked among themselves about sharing affection and how it was right to share wealth in the form of paper, pencils, etc., with their classmates. They decided that this was a "sign" of sharing affection.
One index of affection I saw repeatedly was the tendency for my children to rush to the aid of any other child who had been hurt physically. They would help each other to their feet and stay until the crisis was over.

B. Respect—At first respect was only a word but I was able to lead the children to an understanding of the terms discrimination and recognition which encompass respect, by illustrating how they could show respect for a speaker by paying attention as he speaks, and by waiting until one of their members has finished speaking before trying to speak themselves. I was able to show them that in showing deference to each other they were according respect.

C. Wealth—I taught my children that it was not money that represented wealth, but really goods and services. I did stress that a high state of well-being helped us in giving wealth to others in the form of our services. I tried to teach the simplest principles of economics by discussing the use the children made of the money they received for their services in the community. I believe the statuses of my children in this value were enhanced because I saw that they were more careful with their money and bought more things of lasting value such as clothing instead of too much candy and the like.

D. Enlightenment—I'm sure that my children came to master the meanings of the values and this led them to be on the lookout for chances to add to their enlightenment. The outside reading of newspapers and magazines contributed increasingly to their growth in this value.
I encouraged my children to read or tell stories to the class and then asked the members of the class to tell what values were involved in the events of the stories. I am convinced that this strategy contributed to the increase of my children's enlightenment. In fact, the scores made by my children in the Metropolitan tests were much higher than the scores they made the previous year.
Another index of increased enlightenment on the part of my children was the marked gains they made in vocabulary growth. The very fact

that they all were familiar with the terms and definitions of the values made it possible for them to gain a great amount of knowledge about human beings. This, of course, added generally to their enlightenment.

E. Skill–My children gained greatly in their skills of looking for information and skills in connection with their drawings in arts and crafts. They also learned to be more efficient in the skills of thinking in connection with organizing their work.

I noticed that my children increasingly began to develop social skills of according respect and affection with children who had been deprived of these values. I have in mind a little girl who at the beginning of the project held herself aloof from the other children. She would get very angry at any child who tried to have anything to do with her. She obviously refused to share affection and respect with the other children. Slowly but surely the other children gained skills in sharing respect and affection and used these skills in trying to get the little deprived girl to accept their kindness and consideration. Finally their efforts began to prove successful. Today this little girl, seriously deprived at the beginning of our project, is now a fully participating citizen of her class and is capable and willing to do her share in helping her classmates accord values to other children who like herself have been temporarily deprived of one or more of the values.

I found another index that pointed to the growth of my children in the mastery of skills was their ability to talk about the values as well as grownups who had also learned their meaning. My children repeatedly asked that they be given the opportunity to increase their skills in value analysis by discussing the events of everyday living in terms of the values involved.

F. Power–We practiced the exercise of power at every opportunity. One device we had was to organize the class at the beginning of the year with class officers being elected by the children. During the project, we asked the elected officers to appoint members of the class to act in their places beginning on Monday and ending on Friday. This served to be an effective way to share power among all members of the class.

The officers would sometimes assess fines against certain members of the class for breaking the rules they had all agreed upon. The highest fine was 5¢. This fine was willingly accepted by all the children as far as I could tell.

I made it a practice to have my children help in making decisions during the year until this practice came to be a generally accepted thing.

G. Rectitude–This was the most difficult word to learn and to spell but my children soon learned its true meaning and that their moral or rectitude status depended upon whether they shared the values with each other.

I tried to bring out of everyday ordinary events the real meaning of rectitude which was to assume responsibility for sharing values with others who deserved them.

H. Well-Being–All my children seemed to be happier and worked together better on the study of values than in any other aspect of their class work. They reflected increasing well-being by their attitude toward their classmates on the playground as well as in class.

My children were really conscious that they were gaining these values for themselves and this added to their own self-confidence or self-esteem.

The children seemed to gain in well-being as their specific value deprivations were restored and their tensions reduced.

One example of how this worked was shown by a little girl who entered school at the middle of the year. On being asked to read a book and review it before the class, she could at first only stand and cry. I was careful to show her respect and affection by telling her to select another story to read and to let me know when she had a story she'd like to tell about before the class. At the end of three weeks she reported that she was ready and in fact made what I felt was an almost perfect report.

II. A. I think the project has made me a better teacher. It has led me to learn to do things for my children as well as myself which I am confident meet real needs and wants. I became more aware of the need I had to supervise myself in teaching. Before the project, I had not been clear in my mind about what my strategies should be in the classroom. However, I now have become more precise in dealing with the values in terms of restoring them when needed and in analyzing children's behavior as well as my own feelings. I have become more enlightened about what really happens in class than before the project in terms of the value consequences of happenings in the classroom.

B. In setting up my goals I was more conscious of the specific value statuses we needed to achieve. I became quite conscious of my own growth in the ability to determine the specific values in which my children had suffered deprivation. I also tried to help restore statuses in these values. For example, one day my children were asked to draw pictures similar to that of a bird on the wall and to identify all the parts of the bird. One little boy seemed very shy and unable to communicate with the other children. He would not respond when asked to indicate the various parts of the bird.

C. I continued to ask this child questions about the bird on the wall, urging him to tell me more about this picture. In this conversation I tried to speak in ways that would accord the child respect and affection. Apparently this reduced his tension of threatened deprivation in these categories and released him to propose that he could make a bird like the one in the picture with a few chicken feathers and other materials he had at home. I saw immediately his self-respect status as well as the respect of his classmates would be increased if he could build a respectable model of the bird.

The next day the child brought in his bird. He had done a fine piece of work and was obviously proud of his effort and confident of his ability to communicate with his classmates about his project. This seemed to have a lasting effect upon the little boy. Again, for instance, he could not seem to learn to spell. He said he did not have anyone to help him by giving out the words and checking on his spelling. I volunteered to help him during one recess period each day and three weeks later we had a spelling bee and this child won the contest. I was certainly surprised at his progress but, of course, avoided showing this and praised and congratulated him before the entire class.

Following these successes this child never again withdrew into himself as the shy boy he was before the project. On the contrary, he seemed eager and thrilled at every opportunity to participate in classroom activities. To me this provided a real index to this child's growth in the values of respect, affection, skill, enlightenment, and of course well-being.

D. I often asked my children who would volunteer to lead our discussion for the day. If several children volunteered I asked them to vote on the first one to undertake the leader's place, then the second, and so on.

In these voting sessions when children were exercising their power positions, I watched closely for evidence of the degree to which they accorded other values to their classmates or whether there was evidence that anti-democratic practices were going on which contributed to the deprivation of values on the part of any pupil.

Specifically I tried to analyze the behavior of my children and gather indices that I used in appraising their activities in the classroom and on the playground.

III. I think the project contributed greatly to the enhancement of my well-being status. The reason, I believe, was that the tools I got enabled me to know very precisely what my goals were, and I no longer felt that I was floundering in a bewildered state of wondering why I was doing what I had been asked to do. I think this fact contributed more than any other to the enhancement of my well-being.

IV. I think this project gave us a background environment that enabled us as teachers to grow professionally as we shared values with each other. This was especially true when opportunities arose that called for the sharing of skills in the management of the classroom. The seminars led us to realize that respect and affection could really be shared by teachers of different ethnic and regional origins, thus overcoming many long-standing prejudices that would likely have prevented a mutually enjoyed experience as teachers in this school.

V. The fact that my children have discussed the values at home has contributed to the parents' increasing respect for the goals and work of our school. This is evidenced by an increasing willingness to cooperate in the affairs of the school by "pitching in" and helping with their goods and services when called upon to do so.

VI. I believe my most memorable event was the pride I took in being recognized and called upon by the leader of our first seminar to respond to comments which were being made by the group. In calling upon me he showed that he recognized I had been taking a great many notes on what was being said and I clearly felt that I was capable of responding. This feeling was accompanied by a complete release from the tension I seemed to have earlier in the meeting. I know now that what happened was that I had been accorded respect before all my colleagues.

INTERVIEW: Mr. Paul Bradford
Member National Teacher Corps
Date: March 21, 1968

I. A. Affection–At the beginning of the year I was a stranger to all the children at this school. As the project progressed there was certainly an increasing amount of value sharing. They were more relaxed in their relations with me, in their greetings, etc.

B. Respect–I was impressed by the way my children generally tended to respect each other. However, in one case, a boy whose home environment left much to be desired in promoting respect tended to withhold respect from his classmates. This led the other children to deprive him of respect and I tried to give him opportunities to gain respect by special attention in asking him to recite, etc. However, I could never be sure that his overt efforts in turn to accord respect were entirely sincere.

C. Wealth–My children tended to consider the value wealth as involving material goods more specifically than services. I detected a tendency of my boys especially to set as their goals the gaining of wealth in the form of material goods.

D. Enlightenment–My children were mainly low achievers at the beginning of the project. At the end of the project, however, the majority of these children have been advanced to their regular groups. Some of these children made notable gains in their achievement beyond what I could have expected of them.

E. Skill–I should say that the gains made by my children in skills were comparable with their gains in enlightenment.

F. Power–I made a continuing effort to share power with my children. They came to accept the fact that they should and could participate in decision making. I feel that this sharing of power tended to lead them to look for more opportunities to share in this process.

G. Rectitude–This is one area in which I felt I should stay away from church prescribed mores. I tried, however, to lead my children to see that morality consisted more in the shaping and sharing of the human values with their fellow students and other associates.

My problems of discipline were at a minimum. One of my boys, I detected cheating on a test. After talking with him my diagnosis was that he cheated in the face of fear that he could not live up to his family's expectations. I told him I honestly felt that he could do as well or even better than the other members of his group. This accordance of respect seemed to improve his attitude and after proving to himself that he didn't need to cheat, his self-respect improved and the remainder of the project he worked on his own and with consistent success.

H. Well-Being—I think that my efforts to reduce unrealistic and unfair competition on a "pupil against pupil" basis tended to increase their feelings of well-being, because the chances that they would suffer deprivation of respect, enlightenment, skill, and even rectitude were markedly reduced.

II. A. I find myself analyzing events in my own life in terms of the specific values involved.

B. My classroom goals became more relevant to the values sought by myself and my children.

C. I became more aware of the specific value deprivations of my children and as a consequence I tried to direct my activities toward restoring values in these categories.

D. I was influenced more toward leading my children to achieve up to the level of their capabilities. This obviously influenced my appraisal of their activities.

III. As the project proceeded I came to be more relaxed in my work. And while I came to realize that teaching was a much more complex function than I had suspected, I felt that the intellectual tools I was learning to use gave me a better insight into the goals of teaching and how to work toward them.

IV. I have had a fine relationship with all my colleagues in the project. I was accepted at the very start as an individual. All my colleagues took part actively in sharing values with me.

V. All my relationships with parents have been very congenial. Probably the outstanding value shared with my parents was respect.

VI. I think that the most memorable event of the project was my first exposure to the pupils' work in the various classrooms. This display reflected the growing understanding of these pupils and their teachers of the human value categories and their applications to the educational process.

Appraisal Through Parent Interviews

One of the most frequently stated references made by teachers to the shortcomings of the total educative process is the failure of the home to provide an environment favorable to the child's pattern of growth and development which the school undertakes to promote. According to the position often taken by those responsible for the education of children are the following observations.

The school undertakes to lead the child toward the mastery of reading and the other tool subjects while in the home the child often suffers deprivations that create anxieties and tensions which tend to block this process.

The school tries to promote and maintain ethical standards and moral practices while many of the practices of parents fail to support and in many cases counteract this effort.

The school undertakes to encourage the child to make decisions which are compatible with his rising maturity levels, while in many autocratic homes, he is often denied any opportunity whatever to make even the most casual choices without the express permission of the authoritative figure of the home who may be extremely jealous of his status of power. This condition also is seen often to render ineffective the efforts of the school to encourage the sharing of responsibility in democratic processes such as discussions of issues followed by voting in which all children are expected to participate.

An analysis of the value deprivations suffered in the home since early childhood as reported by some 200 freshman college students indicated that the most frequent deprivations were in the categories of respect and affection, followed by deprivations in power and rectitude.

It is interesting to note that the coding of children's reports at the Fannindel Elementary School of their home and family activities over a period of several months also indicated respect and affection as their most frequent deprivations followed by deprivations in power and rectitude.

From the viewpoint of the parent, however, he is largely uninformed about the goals of the school and consequently has few if any ideas of how he can contribute to what the school is trying to accomplish.

One of the important goals of the Fannindel project was to promote a closer relationship between the school and the parents of the community.

In undertaking to implement this goal the teachers encouraged the children to discuss with their parents the value-sharing program in as many of its aspects as they could as the project developed. At a minimum, they were asked (1) to define each of the values, (2) to discuss with their parents the importance of having every member of the family share these values with each other, and (3) to discuss events in the home in terms of the specific values involved and whether these values were accorded on the basis of merit, or whether they were withheld without merit, from one or more members of the family.

In order to appraise efforts to achieve this goal, interviews with parents of children at various grade levels were held. These interviews were structured in terms of the following points.

I. Number of children in the project-age and grade level.

II. Effects, if any, of the project upon the behavior of the children in family living.

III. Change, if any, in the self-esteem of children during the project.

IV. Effect, if any, in the attitudes of children toward the school and toward their teachers.

V. Parents' estimate of the worth of the value-sharing project.

VI. Change, if any, in relations of parents with teachers.

VII. Have you discussed the human values with your children? With what outcomes?

INTERVIEW: Mrs. T.A. Young
Parent
Date: January 23, 1968

I. Jill is the only child I have in school. We adopted her at the age of five in December, 1960. She was in the sixth grade.

II. The program I believe led her to a better understanding of how we loved and respected her. It definitely led her to show the other members of the family more respect and affection than before the program started.
She definitely came to be a more responsible child in doing her part toward improving the life of the home. This program led to a definite improvement in her well-being. She was more self-confident. She lost her fear of what would happen to her in the event of the death of Mr. Young and myself (her foster parents).

III. She definitely moved toward more maturity. Her gain in the statuses of affection, respect, power, rectitude, well-being, enlightenment and skill contributed toward her realization that she was somebody.(Enhancement of self-esteem.) Her strong feeling of general inferiority before the project began was replaced by growing confidence in herself.

IV. My child's attitude toward the school was greatly improved. This was shown by her love for her teachers and her classmates and in her increased eagerness to go to school.

V. My child did better in this project than she has ever before done in school. She learned more, had better skills in spelling and reading, and studied on her own more than ever before. I feel that in this project the teachers know better than ever before how to give children the things they needed to really grow as human beings. These things I think are the things children look for without ever knowing it. I think the teachers gave the children these values every day so that the effect of the program carried over into home life. This program in my opinion, is one that go completely through high school and should be before the children and teachers every day of the year. I think we would have had a better world to live in if this program had been in the schools years ago.

VII. When things came up in our living we talked about them in terms of the values that were being added to our home. My daughter has learned to appreciate what she had in specific terms.

INTERVIEW: Mrs. Carlton Grant
Parent
Date: January 29, 1968

I. We have one child, a daughter, in school. Charisse was in the sixth grade.

II. The project seemed to broaden our child's outlook on living. She often remarked that she was trying to share the eight values with me and my husband. I think we both found it easier to discuss any problems of behavior with her after the project started. My child's reasoning power seemed to grow and she was more objective in her discussion of problems of all kinds. She was more aware of sharing all the values in the home and felt that such sharing helped us as well as herself.

III. The project was a great challenge to Charisse and she enjoyed it greatly. This of course added to her consistent feeling of well-being. From the very first she tried to apply the values to herself in her behavior. The discussions we had with her about the values seemed to add to her own feeling of self-confidence and self-importance as a member of the family.

IV. This project led her to anticipate working at school with great pleasure. She looked forward to participating in all the demonstrations of the children's ability to use the values in their work. Her attitude toward her teachers seemed to involve her according them more respect and affection. She never wanted to miss any of her school work. Her increase in rectitude status was shown by her insistence upon doing her own work and depending less and less upon help from me.

V. I cannot think of anything in my child's experience that has helped her in the development of her personality more than this project.
I think this has added greatly to the effectiveness of the whole school program for all the children.
I got a great thrill in taking the children to and from the demonstrations they gave, in listening to them talk about the values and how they seek them in everything they do throughout their lives.
We took a trip to Carlsbad Caverns last summer and while we were in the Caverns, Charisse (who had to miss this one demonstration being given by the class) kept asking the time and finally said "right now my class is giving a demonstration in analyzing values at the University."

VI. The project gave me many opportunities to talk with the teachers about the specific aspects of the project and this led me to realize that we could talk about the children's progress and the other aspects of the program much more realistically and with more common understanding than ever before. This of course added to my respect for our teachers. They were able to discuss the children's problems so that I could get a clearer picture of the part I could play in the education of my child.

VII. At first I did not know what the project was all about and I asked my child to tell me. She seemed glad and able to give me the whole purpose of the program. She was anxious to tell me in detail what all the values were and to show me how anyone could use them. These terms of common understanding we had together made it possible for us to discuss all kinds of human problems without the meaningless arguments about issues in which we did not have a common understanding.

I thought it was wonderful to see how the children could apply their knowledge of these values in their everyday relations. Their discussion of what values were involved in everyday events seemed to be a very serious and important kind of intellectual exercise that they never tired of practicing.

My discussions with my child of the value-sharing program have added greatly to my own education and I don't think I've ever enjoyed any experience more than I have this project.

My husband also witnessed the good effects upon our child of this project and joins me in our enthusiastic approval of the program.

INTERVIEW: Mrs. Siebenhausen
Parent
Date: February 2, 1968

I. I have one child in the Fannindel project. Rickey was in the sixth grade.

II. I feel that the project had a definite effect upon the improved ability of my child to participate more effectively in the life of the family. My son had "tools" which enabled him to get at the real significance of what was going on in the family relations. For example, due to a serious accident to my husband from which he is still recovering, I suffered a great amount of fear and tension which I'm sure led me to unconsciously deprive my child of several values. However, with his understanding of the value system and recognition of my need, he was able to accord many values of which I had been deprived, thus restoring values I had lost in these categories. I can truly say that his efforts in this regard did more than any other thing to reduce my tensions and restore my feelings of well-being during this critical period.

III. I am sure my child has gained respect for himself beyond what could have been expected for a child of his age of twelve years. To illustrate his growth in self-esteem, I recall an event in which I said to him that it was his duty to respect me, his mother, and that I demanded this respect from him. His reply added to my enlightenment, or my insight into the thinking of children who have an understanding of the values sought by human beings. He said, "Mother, this is not the seventeenth century when respect was withheld from millions of people without merit. You must remember I, too, am a human being and that while I owe respect to you, I deserve respect from you when I earn the right to be accorded this value."

IV. I think this project enabled him to understand the significance of the work of teachers now more than ever before. I feel that he came to realize that during the value-sharing project, his teachers were undertaking to provide him with a much broader range of his needs than heretofore. This project also led him to a much more effective sharing of all the values with his teacher. I think the child who has a teacher who learns with him (as a student of human personality) as he learns, begins to assume responsibility for what he thinks and does in his relationships with the teacher. In this situation the teacher is "just one of the guys" who is also trying to learn.

V. I think the school program has been greatly improved. I have also received a great deal of education from my experiences with my child. I now realize that I have learned much more than ever before, the most important purposes of education and I feel that our school definitely moved toward these goals during the project.

VI. The growth made in the understanding of human values by my child, his teacher, and myself enabled me to communicate with my son's teacher in terms of all the needs and wants or values of my child and myself.

VII. While my child did most of the talking, I learned in my discussions with him the definitions of the values and how people go about getting them. We often have discussions around the table of family problems and our everyday environment in which we try to estimate the value results of things that happen to any members of the family. When we try to solve these problems in this way there seems to occur an inner feeling of peace and increased well-being for us all.

INTERVIEW: Mrs. Elvin Fisk
Parent
Date: February 29, 1968

I. We have one child in school. Junior is in the fifth grade.

II. I think the program has increased my child's tendency to respect others. I find that he is more alert to the possibility of helping others achieve the values they have had withheld from them.
I also believe he has learned better how to share affection with others and therefore knows better how to make and keep friends.
I think he is conscious of any events in which he is deprived of respect, but I feel that he responds well to my explanation, for example, when he is disciplined, of why I acted as I did.

III. This program has helped him gain in his achievement, for example in arithmetic, reading, and the other subjects. I believe that the program has added greatly to his self-confidence. Isn't this a part of self-esteem? I believe this is one of the most important functions of the school. I believe that my older son who did not have the advantage of this program was deprived of respect and other values in his classes and lost a great amount of self-esteem which he never recovered until after he completed his school career. He never made such high grades as my son in the value-sharing program.

IV. My son is more enthusiastic about his school work than before the project. He loves his teachers. I know of no conflicts he has had with his schoolmates.

V. I believe that if we are to teach our children how to live as free men and women they must be taught what human values are and how they can achieve them. I think that we should not put material values (wealth) above all others, but rather should teach how the children can achieve all the values which mature people need and want during their lives.
I feel that I also have gained an education through this program. I have learned that I must cooperate with the school by according my child more respect and affection, for example. In order for us to survive as a free society I feel that all our schools must teach how all these values can be gained by the individual in his search for self-esteem. I feel that the value-sharing program at Fannindel is achieving this goal.

VI. My relations with the teachers of the school have always been good. My important change in attitude has been in coming to know more precisely what our teachers are trying to do for our children and how I can help them do it.

VII. At the beginning of the project, Junior would discuss with me the meaning of all the values. He would tell us about the events of the school that involved the values.
I feel that this program has increased my son's understanding of the difference between what is right and what is wrong and that he is accepting more responsibility for his own actions.

INTERVIEW: Mr. Walter L. Zimmerman
Parent, Protestant Minister
Date: February 5, 1968

I. I have one child, a daughter Deborah, in the value-sharing project. She was in the third grade.

II. I noticed after the project started that there was a great amount of discussion of the values. I feel there was a significant difference in her attitude toward the values and what they meant. From time to time she identified events of family in terms of the values involved.
In my Boy Scout Troup I often heard them talking about the values they had learned at school and particularly when a problem would come up they would try to apply these values to its solution.

III. I feel that the project added to my daughter's self-esteem. She had a fuller understanding of herself and I'm sure a feeling of her increased capacity as a human being. I think this means that her self-esteem was enhanced.

IV. I'd say that the value project clarified and sharpened my daughter's awareness that other people had abilities and other values the same as she did. This indicated an improving attitude toward the school and led her to see that what she was learning in school helped her solve problems in her living.

V. I feel that the program has breached a broad gap in education. Our school has progressed from the job of simply teaching facts to assuming responsibility for demonstrating how what the children have learned in school will help them gain an understanding through actual practice, of how to add to their statuses in all the major values of the human being.
Our children learn how to apply the knowledge they gain to their personal situations.

VI. We have always made it a point to talk with our teachers about how we could assist in the educational process at home. In my discussions with teachers since the project began they have spoken about how the children get along better together and how they have learned more about sharing values with others. Our relation with my child's teachers continues to be very good.

VII. We have discussed the specific meanings of all the value categories with our child. We have also discussed the settings in life in which all the human values are involved.
To me it seems the purpose of the basic institutions, the family, the school, and the church is to equip the coming generations, creatively and adequately to take their places in society as people responsible to themselves and each other. This to me is the broad definition of what education really is. This value-sharing program has seemed to better achieve this on the part of the children than traditional formal programs of education that only teach unrelated facts.

INTERVIEW: Mr. Buel L. Moody
Parent, Member of School Board
Date: April 9, 1968

I. We have two children, a boy 11 years old in the fifth grade, and a girl 8 years old in the second grade, in school.

II. When the program first began my boy had the tendency to be sick and miss school on the slightest provocation, but since the program got well under way he hasn't been absent a single day. He actually insisted on going to school one day when he was actually ill. He simply said he didn't want to miss a day.
Since my wife and I both work, the children have been looked after by a lady from the neighborhood. They have had several conflicting situations between themselves that we wouldn't expect in normal children until my wife and I had to step in and "lay down the law." My children both seemed

to realize that important values such as respect, power, affection, and well-being were being withheld from each other and from us their parents, and following this discussion their behavior toward each other has been reversed in that they have ever since been sharing these values with each other and their parents.

Last Christmas the children came to us and asked whether they could be given responsibility for taking care of themselves without the extra care they had been given. My wife and I told them that in February when the girl reached the age of nine and the boy twelve in March, that we would try out this plan as they proposed it, increasing their allowance if they lived up to their responsibility. This gave them, in addition to wealth, rectitude, respect, and power.

The plan as set up by the children has been in operation for only a short period but to date it appears to be successful. However, we intend to check up on the effect of the plan again after two months and then in council with all four members of the family decide whether any changes should be made. Here we shall all share power with each other.

III. I can definitely say that there has been an increase in the self-esteem of both of my children. I feel sure that this increase in their self-esteem has been largely due to their increase in assuring personal responsibility for their own behavior (gain in rectitude status).

IV. I believe my children both increased in their well-being and general attitude toward wanting to go to school.

V. There is only one way I hope we go in human relations, and that is forward and I think the program will contribute toward solving some of these problems of human relations. I would say that the value-sharing program is really valuable.

VI. I have always had the highest respect for our teachers. As a member of the school board I realize the increasing time and effort our teachers have to give with the coming of integration and this adds to the respect I have for them.

VII. The fact is our children learned during the project to use all the values and could name and define each of them. I'd say that they were able to decide what they were doing to others and to themselves in terms of values.

INTERVIEW: Mr. and Mrs. W.H. Wilson, Jr.
Parents
Date: April 30, 1968

I. We have one child in the project, Betty Sue, 11 years old, in the fourth grade.

II. The project resulted in a great amount of discussion about the values in the home. I think that my child tended to keep in mind the specific values and consciously tried to share them with us in our home. I think that the project led her to a continuing effort to share values also with associates outside the home.

III. Our child has increased in her self-confidence (self-esteem). We think that this has been largely due to her growing ability to deal with human values. We think the most remarkable result of the project upon our child was her growing ability to deal realistically with apparent deprivations from other people. Her tendency now is to "consider the source' in such cases and avoid tensions of frustration caused by such happenings.

IV. Our child was more interested in her school work during and since the project started. We say this because the first thing she does on arriving at home from school is to talk about what went on in school with one or both of us and to discuss with her mother the work she plans to do the following day. Another reason we know what her work meant was that she allowed nothing to interfere with her going to school. She has been absent from school only one day since the project began eighteen months ago.

V. Mr. Wilson: I think it has been very helpful for the whole family for Betty to have gone through the project. She has learned important things she wouldn't have otherwise learned and so have we (her parents).
We think Betty in her growing maturity has done a great deal to "make things smoother" in the home and thus has added to the happiness of all of us.
Mr. Wilson: The mastery of the values simply is never brought about in the ordinary school because it has never been a part of the course of study except incidentally and in a haphazard way.

VI. We think the project makes it easier for parents to talk to teachers because we both know more precisely what the schools are trying to do for our children.

VII. Our child discussed the values in our home. She was interested in why people acted as they did in trying to get the values. She seemed always to be able to lead the family in important discussions because she knew how to talk about human values. We often saw how she used the values in getting at the meaning of articles in magazines. She could tell from the article what values the writer was trying to get.
We agree that to learn what the human values are and what they mean to all of us is the most important thing to be learned in the school.

RESULTS OF METROPOLITAN ACHIEVEMENT TESTS

It was expected that an environment which provided for the enhancement of value statuses of pupils would release them from tensions of value deprivations they had suffered which not only would free them for more creative individual work but should also enable them to make more progress in the "tool subjects" including reading, arithmetic, and others as measured by the Metropolitan Achievement Test.

Results of the Metropolitan Achievement Tests were available for only 108 pupils of the school who had taken the test the year before the value-sharing project began. The median scores of these pupils reflected a gain of 13 months during the 9 months period of the project. This indicates a gain of 4 months beyond normal expectations for the project period.

The median gains beyond the norms for specific school levels including grades 3, 4, 5, 6, and 7 were as follows: (Metropolitan Achievement Test scores for grades 1, 2, and 8 were not available.)

The scores of the third-grade pupils showed a gain of 14 months during the 9 months of the project.

The scores of two groups of the fourth-grade pupils reflected a gain of 14 months during the 9-month period of the project. It seems significant to report that scores of 10 Negro children at the fourth-grade level reflected median gains ranging from 8 months to 25 months with a median gain of 18 months during the 9 months of the project. The scores of only one of these children reflected a gain of less than 9 months during this period and this was by one month.

The scores of fifth-grade pupils reflected a median gain of 13 months during the 9-month period of the project. With this group, scores were available also for the Metropolitan Achievement Test given at the beginning and end of the entire year before the project began. The median score of this group for the year of 1965-66 reflected a growth of only 6 months, or 3 months below the normal growth during that 9-month period. At the end of the value-sharing project year, however, the scores of this group reflected a growth of 13 months or a score reflecting 16 months above the growth during the year before the project.

The median score for the sixth-grade pupils during the 9 months of the project reflected a gain of 12 months.

The test scores given above from the pilot project on value-sharing probably represent too few cases to establish statistical significance. It is assumed that this project will be followed by another in a school system or a combination of two or more schools enrolling a minimum of 700 pupils in grades 1 through 7 in order to meet the most demanding statistical requirements.

SUMMARY

The imperative need for curriculum change to reduce the cultural lag in our society today should not need to be argued as justification for the dedicated and cooperative participation of school administrators and teachers. This task will require a prodigious effort if the educational establishment is to realize the recognized goals of American society and a compatible educational system. Indifference, pettiness, egocentricity, resentment, and intolerance always seem to impede progress in attempts to develop democratic prototypes. There is need to build among teachers and administrators greater interest and enthusiasm in democratic participation in situations which demonstrate that each person has a contribution to make and to foster the predisposition among teachers that sharing ideas is best when there is need for solution of common problems.

Democracy depends for its existence upon systematic group and individual thinking. Teachers, especially, should develop skill in the use of democratic process and consciously practice skills in all of their relationships.

Cooperative action research is a promising process in any effort to institute a value-shaping and -sharing curriculum. It involves the participation of the very people who should be led to change their own behavior. There is an exploratory quality to action research which motivates activity and goal clarifications beyond initial expectations or commitments. While many citizens are aware of the need for curriculum and social change to help humanity grow up psychologically and socially, they have lacked an effective prototyping design for achieving such a goal. Formal experimentation has limited applicability to behavioral changes in teachers, parents, pupils, and administrators. Action research with a planned prototype arena leads people to change themselves. Ultimately, this is the only change with lasting consequences for a safe, ordered, and peaceful world.

CHAPTER 13

•

Transforming the Individual

The child who enters school at the age of six has had thousands of experiences which have contributed to the shaping of his personality. He has enjoyed indulgencies and has suffered deprivations during the formation of his personality. He has probably been indulged by his parents with love which he may feel they also often deprive him of without merit. He has been indulged by his environment with many of the things he needs and wants (values). On the other hand he has been deprived of many of the things he feels he needs and wants.

The consequence of these experiences have been favorable and unfavorable. He has many important assets. He has accepted in varying degree, the practice of mutually sharing values with those about him. He has become accustomed to according respect to those who have achieved goals that he has learned to consider valuable. He "returns" the love of those who love him. He participates in the give and take of making choices in his actions which have their origin in his innate drives in the form of desires, wishes, and needs (the id) which have contributed to his happiness and well-being.

On the other hand he has come to realize that many of these drives have to be controlled if he is to be accepted as a citizen by his fellows. This process of being judged by his associates contributes powerfully to the formation of his conscience (superego). By the time he enters school this conscience conditions his behavior in all his relations with his environment. He has had many cravings which because of his conscience he would never undertake to satisfy. There were many things he would have enjoyed doing and saying but his conscience intervened. This produced conflicts within him which manifested themselves in many ways, some quite painful while some produced tensions which he accepts as "natural" and perhaps will continue to do all his life. On the other hand his conscience often rewards him with feelings of self-adulation following behavior that conforms with what he has "learned" to be "right and proper."

The child's conscience has contributed to the structure of his own internalized predispositions to behave as he has been urged to behave by precept and example of people in his environment, beginning with his parents, and later with others. The "blocking" or "approval" effect of the conscience, depending upon the behavior stimulation involved, often operates regardless of the conscious desires of the child. When it prevents his acting in ways that would provide satisfaction he is faced with a conflict that threatens his well-being.

Still another aspect of the personality referred to usually as the ego, performs mainly the function of consciously weighing the probable consequences of the individual's actions. He is thereby enabled often to determine whether the dictates of his conscience are justified in the light of the reality of the situation. For example, his conscience tells him that it is wrong to tell a lie, but his experience has led him to realize that to tell the exact truth in all situations often injures people unnecessarily. So his ego, often assessing the reality of the situation may lead him to tell his grandmother that her hair is not gray, or his father that he is enjoying a trip which thrills his father but which produces only boredom for himself. By the time he starts to school, therefore, his ego has contributed to his ability to appraise reality and to question the validity of some of the things he has been taught. He has acquired a great deal of self-knowledge. There are many things he knows from experience that he can and cannot do. He therefore, has a self-image or an inner picture of himself.

Quite apart from the child's self-image or concept of what he *is* stands the ideal image of himself, the concept of what he *ought* to be. This ego ideal as it is technically referred to may influence the individual toward the achievement of many goals. These depending upon his individual preferences may be classified, of course, under one or more of the social values.

A systematic inventory of the personality of the child would reveal not only the value assets to which he has aspired and thus his ego ideal, but also, it would through an analysis of what he has actually achieved, provide a picture of what he is. Further analysis would reveal actual or threatened value deprivations which have contributed to his fears and/or anxieties with their accompanying tensions that seriously block his progress toward becoming a creative and productive person.

In this chapter some additional value deprivations suffered by the preschool child are discussed with an analysis of the environmental events which contribute to these deprivations. It is a mistake to assume that only children living in economically deprived sections of the population are subjected to serious value deprivations. The eroding tensions of frustration can be widely observed at all socioeconomic levels of society. The analysis of the consequences of personality damage resulting from typical value deprivations will include a consideration of how the school contributes to personality damage. The teacher may see himself as the punitive officer of the school rather than as a scientist teacher responsible for providing an environment which promotes the maximization of values among children and thus contributing to the realease of their tensions. These consequences of value deprivations are extremely serious not only for the child, but also for the teacher, the administrative officer of the school, the parent and others with whom the child comes in significant contact.

Since the time of Freud the insights of psychoanalysis have influenced the thinking and actions of many people who work with children, such as psychotherapists, psychoanalytically oriented teachers, parents, counselors, social workers, principals, and supervisors. The growing insights of such people have led more and more to the realization that the threat of value deprivations confronts all members of the population at every period of life. Thus, it would seem that the effort to maximize values in the classroom and to reduce value conflicts will require many new approaches in all functions and relationships in the child's social milieu along with the traditional conceptions suggested by psychotherapy.

The tools of thinking with values, when applied to the value conflicts of children, will illumine the impact of actual or threatened value deprivations upon the emerging personalities of children. This approach can give increased precision to the skills and enlightenment of the scientist teacher. Incapacitating value deprivations can just as seriously blight the learning process as the existence of a debilitating disease or other disabling threat to the well-being of the child.

THE SIGNIFICANCE OF VALUE PREFERENCES AMONG TEACHERS

Another factor must also be considered in dealing with unrealistic behavior. The teacher who deals with the child must take into account his own value preferences. For the teacher to deny that he, himself, has a value orientation is to reveal that he is simply unconscious of many of his own predispositions which appear in many forms in every conversation he may have with a child. This means that he tends to pass on his own value preferences to the child. Any logical approach to this situation demands that any teacher who deals with children should, therefore, strive to achieve increasingly clear insights into his own value preferences, deprivations, and tensions. Self-knowledge is a prerequisite to the teacher's achievement of maturity, and, of course, intellectual and emotional maturity is required in dealing effectively with the anxieties of children. [1]

ANXIETIES AND TENSIONS OF PARENTS

Many of the anxieties and tensions which the children bring with them when they start to school have their origins in the home. For this reason, therefore, it becomes necessary for us to explore all promising techniques which have been developed to lead the mothers, and wherever possible, the fathers, of children to clearer understandings of the major contributions they can make to the maturation of the personalities of their children. It is suggested that the school consider every possibility for coming in contact with the parents of the very young children, and to lead them through open and free discussions to important insights which will enable them to contribute to the facilitation of value goals of their own children. It is a shocking realization to come face to face

---

[1] For a fuller statement of this problem read L.S. Kubie, "The Forgotten Man in Education." *Harvard Alumni Bulletin* LVI (1954) (349-53).

with the fact that many thousands of parents love their children, but are ignorant of children's real needs and wants (values), and thus have great difficulty in dealing effectively with them.

It is suggested that the school undertake the enlightenment of parents to the limit of facilities available in the school system. The provision of opportunities for parents to practice the important social skills may take place in free discussion situations, in which several parents and teachers participate, or in situations in which the teacher confers with the parent or parents of a single child. It is well to point out here that advice given by teachers is not always accepted by parents because such advice may interfere with the unconscious value goals of parents in connection with the situation involved. In other words, the teacher must realize that some advice which they give to certain parents may indeed be threatening to them and thus will be rejected by them.

This demands, of course, that the teacher undertake insofar as possible to discover in the parent-child relationship, whether children have parents who themselves are suffering serious value deprivations and are transferring their tensions to their children in ways that result in serious psychological damage to the children. Many anxieties of children originate with and are reflections of the tensions of their parents. The point has been made that many of these tensions and consequent unrealistic behavior patterns can be traced to value deprivations, such as lost respect and affection suffered by the parents themselves. It is suggested that one of the objectives of the school, therefore, should be to contribute when possible to the enhancement of respect, affection, and other value statuses among parents. It would appear that parent discussion groups at P.T.A. meetings and the like will provide many opportunities to apply techniques designed to achieve these ends.

EMOTIONAL DISTURBANCES DURING THE FIRST YEAR OF LIFE

A brief look at the origins of some of the most characteristic anxieties of children at various age levels along with their consequences in unrealistic behavior will point the way along which much of the effort at value enhancement must proceed. It seems clear that these anxieties can be traced to frustrating experiences, and that frustrations can be categorized as deprivations under one or more of the human values. It is through the use of such categories that we may hope to think more critically and to deal more precisely and systematically with the problem of avoiding unrealistic behavior among children at all age levels. Let us examine very briefly some of the beginnings of such behavior among preadolescent children.

Not so long ago all diseases of the young child were blamed upon his constitution. As knowledge about the human being grew, however, knowledge about the diseases of the respiratory system, the circulatory system, and mental diseases, the tendency came to be to avoid hiding behind the cloak of ignorance in blaming everything upon the child's constitution. With this knowledge came increasing ability to diagnose many human diseases as growing out of the experiences of the child in his interrelationships with other people.

Certainly a great preponderance of the anxieties of the child in the first year of life grow out of his experiences with others in feeding and the feeding process. The satisfactions he derives from the process of nursing include the flow of milk into his mouth and into his stomach. He enjoys the act of sucking and the rhythms dependent upon breathing and digestion. He enjoys the warmth of his mother's body, and the feeling of security which her nearness gives.

For a long time pediatricians have been able to demonstrate that the babies "left alone on their resources" simply do not "get along" as well as babies who are loved and who are given numerous demonstrations of the mother's loving care. Such babies being denied these satisfactions develop tensions. These symptoms reflect a low status of well-being resulting from being deprived of the certainty of mother's love. For the child to be left in a state of uncertainty is to encourage the feeling of anxiety. This uncertainty in the first year of life is likely to involve uncertainties about feeding, about attention from the mother, about his own natural rhythms which are likely to develop anxieties that may tend to persist throughout his life. This feeling of inadequacy which the individual may have toward his ability to manipulate his environment may, in fact, be considered one of the greatest deterrents to the development of the creative and productive personality. Any analysis of these feelings will certainly reveal that value deprivations and thus value conflicts have contributed to the unrealistic behavior of children during the first year of life. Such behavior may often become so pronounced as to be definitely neurotic.

EMOTIONAL DISTURBANCES DURING THE AGES OF TWO AND THREE

The emotional disturbances during this period may be said to grow mainly from the conflict between the child's instinctual desires and needs, and the demands of his society in its efforts to make an acceptable citizen of him. Anxiety at this age seems to center with extreme frequency around the period of toilet training where the child has the drive to seek the love and respect of his mother and yet fears that he cannot live up to what she expects of him in the matter of the processes of elimination. This internalized fear that he will lose the love of his mother increases in intensity to the degree to which his mother's toilet training procedures are very early and very strict. If this toilet training has been inordinately strict and demanding, then the child may revert to the feeling of hatred of his mother in which he does all in his power to avoid living up to the demands she places upon him. This feeling that he must not meet the demands of his mother in order to "get even with her" often results in many unnecessary constipated periods so that his physical health as well as his mental health may be seriously threatened. It seems clear that unless the proper balance in parental instruction is exercised, the child may come out of this period with personality characteristics in the form of tensions that definitely restrict his development. Such characteristics may include extremes in neatness, in being on time, in doing everything just exactly as he has always done it before, so that any deviation whatever from his accustomed way of doing things may be rejected as extremely painful to him. Such responses from the point of view of a totalitarian society may be very desirable but certainly he is not well equipped to develop the capacities necessary to perform the functions of a creative citizen in a society that aspires toward freedom.

THE PERIOD FROM THREE TO SIX

It is at this period that the child experiences infantile sexuality and his relationships with his mother and father are largely dominated by this emerging personality characteristic. The boy loves his mother and the girl loves her father. This situation may give rise to extreme feelings of jealousy on the part of the child which, unless accepted by the parents as a part of his normal development may result in their exercising extremely harsh and critical measures in dealing with him that may damage him for life. This situation, of course, places a heavy burden upon the school in its efforts to lead such a child into creative and productive living.

Another phenomenon that occurs during this period is masturbation. Masturbation is a universal and natural phenomenon of human growth and development and must be recognized as such by parents. While masturbation in its elementary stages may appear during the first year of life, it tends to increase in intensity during two important periods, the first, the period from three to six, and the second, at the onset of puberty. For the parent to reject any recognition of the child's practices in masturbation is simply to reject reality, and for the mother to say that her child has never masturbated is to resort to self-deception in the face of this reality. Whether masturbation becomes excessive and thus a pathological manifestation depends almost entirely upon the attitude of the parents at this time toward this normal function. Many children whose parents love them masturbate occasionally, but they do not worry about it. They have no excessive mental conflicts about this matter. It does them no physical harm and, therefore, is in no sense pathological in its effect.

It is during this period also that children quite often become curious about the problems of sexuality and reproduction, and unless parents meet this need for sex information, when it appears in ways that satisfy the child, this again may be the cause of many persisting anxieties and value conflicts which will require extreme caution and care on the part of the school in dealing with such children.

Anything that occurs during the child's life that results in actual or threatened value deprivations will increase his fears with their accompanying tensions. Such events may include the loss of the mother or the father or both, the birth of other children in the family, painful or crippling illnesses, the conscious and unconscious deprivation of love and respect on the part of the parents, excessive exposure to sexual stimulation or many other deprivational experiences.

It may be well to introduce at this point the consideration of two important disorders which occur most frequently during this period of the child's life, namely, unrealistic fears or phobias, and temper tantrums. It should be stated here that an important aspect of prevention and relief of these disorders would be the enlightenment of parents as well as teachers as to the origin and nature of such behavior as mental mechanisms which the child resorts to in his efforts to release his tensions that have their origin in value deprivations that he should never have had to suffer. This is one of the major goals of this volume.

THE PERIOD FROM SIX TO ELEVEN

This period, often called the period of sexual latency, begins at about the same age level at which the child enters school. His contacts with society have led him to accept many of the mores of that society as prescriptions of behavior which he agrees with himself to accept and live up to. Such a child has developed into a better understanding of himself as a person. During the period he was spending practically all of his time at home he was developing an understanding of himself as "I." This we have referred to as the ego, and during this period he saw himself as himself with certain definite wants and needs, and he consequently made every effort to satisfy them. However, in undertaking to satisfy his needs and wants he comes later to recognize that he does have responsibilities for other people and for the demands they place upon him. This effort to live as a responsible person has led him in varying degrees, depending upon the individual, to a conscious recognition of this responsibility. This we have called his conscience, a part of which we have referred to as the superego. The superego has both conscious and unconscious aspects. The superego acts as a censor of his actions, and may be called the agent of his morality. The superego which begins to appear at the latter part of the previous period, sometimes called the genital period, also results in a number of value conflicts arising in the course of his interpersonal relationships with his father and mother. It acts as a tabu agent in forbidding his actually acting out any hatred he may feel toward his parents. Another important aspect of the superego results in his acceptance of the attitudes which his parents and teachers have toward the things he needs and wants. A third aspect of the superego appears as a result of the customs of the society in which the child lives. Here the parent's attitude toward the child, the attitude of neighbors, the attitude of his playmates all contribute their share in the organization of personal strategies which reflect the ways in which the child accepts his role as a young citizen.

At the onset of this period, it must be recognized, therefore, that the child's personality has three important parts. (1) The instinctual characteristics which he inherited, which may be referred to as the id, (2) the ego, or his understanding of himself, the aspect of his personality in which he tries to face reality and actually measure realistically the consequences of his actions, and (3) the superego, in which he has incorporated as part of himself, the prescriptions and dictations of society. These three components of his personality he carries with him the remainder of his life.

THE CHILD'S ENTRANCE INTO SCHOOL

The first three levels in the development of the child's personality are extremely critical in terms of the responsibility of the school for his further growth and development. A great many events have contributed to the formation of his personality as we have seen. He brings with him whatever heritage he has been given during these periods when he starts to school. Thus the school can be said to inherit all the emotional problems that go with the frustrations (value deprivations) the child has experienced in his life up to this time. For this reason, it is extremely important that the school give full consideration to the importance of dealing with his parents and, in fact, with all other agencies that contribute to the conditioning of the child's personality before he starts to school. It is extremely significant, also, for the teacher in dealing with the child when he starts to school to recognize that these tensions and conflicts which he brings with him really exist within his inner being, and that he is often quite unconscious of some of the most serious of these. Experience has led to the conclusion that most of these emotional disturbances have resulted from real or imagined deprivations of love and respect. Here the wise teacher will undertake to act as the surrogate parent whose most important duty may be to restore the lost love and respect which the child needs so badly. Just as it can be said that the most important contribution the parent can make to his child's personality is to love and respect him as a person, so too, the teacher, if she really loves and respects the child for what he is, can provide the kind of social environment which will contribute most to the resolution of his conflicts and anxieties, and will smooth the way for his releasing himself from the resulting tensions which inhibit his creative and productive activity.

It is at this critical point in the life of the child that society has placed the greatest responsibility upon the teacher. This is a very critical period also for the future of a free society, for if the teacher through sympathetic understanding and expert guidance can lead the child to his release from these crippling fears and anxieties he will have contributed to the maturation of one more citizen whose great potentials for creative activity are thus made available for the achievement and maintenance of such a society.

The teacher must bear in mind that both the classroom and the playground contribute to the maximization of values among children. Value deprivations and conflicts of the child must be recognized by the teacher. The child at this period wants to satisfy his teacher, he wants the hand of supervision over him, and yet he wants to rebel. In this dichotomy of his being he is no different from the rest of us in our response to the molding effect of social forces. He consciously and unconsciously fears what he may do that will bring down punishment upon himself and will result in his loss of respect and affection, and of other values.

The period when the child is on the playground is also extremely important in the development of his personality. As a consequence of the inner conflicts which he may have been accumulating since his days in the nursery, the child can be very brutal in his relations with other children. He hates his rivals, he fights verbally and often with teeth and fists. In these antisocial practices he may really be seeking to enhance his respect status. The wise teacher, therefore, will create ways and means of providing realistically for the enhancement of this value and thus will reduce the unrealistic need for fighting and other antisocial expressions. It is during this period that the scientist teacher must recognize the problems the child faces in entering into an almost wholly new world. He has to meet and to learn about many new people. He begins to extend his environment through reading, through observation, and actual experience. He must learn what this broadening environment will demand of him in the way of moral behavior. He looks for and welcomes guide posts that point this way for him.

The sensitive teacher will detect evidences that the child's ambitions for the future begin to appear at this time. He has great need to work at classroom problems which contribute to the welfare of his group. For this he can achieve high status in respect and affection. This, of course, means both self-respect and the respect of his associates. These needs and wants (values) will be recognized by the teacher who is trying to build the kind of environment both in the classroom and on the playground which will contribute most to the child's development as a healthy, a creative, and a productive personality. This is a difficult task for the uninitiated teacher, but it is one which he will find to be well worthwhile to undertake.

The process of shaping and sharing values is essentially an act of communication between the teacher and his pupils. The skill involved is essentially a communication skill. The scientist teacher will have compiled an ever-growing inventory of the characteristics of his pupils in terms of their value preferences and value statuses achieved. He will seriously take these characteristics into account in undertaking to perform the act of communication involved in the shaping and sharing of values. This approach is essentially a persuasive act in which the teacher and the pupil both face reality in undertaking to share values each with the other.

Coercion has been resorted to extensively in the disciplinary approach employed by the school. This process of coercion has been resorted to probably because of the lack of communication skill in the educational system. The external enforcement of rules and regulations upon children with little regard for their internal responses to such coercive tactics in itself provides a prime example of serious value deprivation. The deprivations suffered here include not only respect and affection but also deprivation in rectitude, power, and in most of the other values. Deprivation in one or more of these human values has almost immediate repercussions in an impaired status of well-being. The child in a state or well-being impairment is simply blocked in most of his creative and productive undertakings. He is in a state of fear. Just as the trainer can use coercion in training dogs and many other of the lower animals to perform routine acts such as counting and performing other such tricks, so, too, in the presence of coercion and its accompanying state of fear the teacher can lead the child to master certain routine tasks in the school, such as learning the multiplication table, memorizing many of the various rules of grammar, dates in history, names of places on the map, but in this state of fear he cannot expect to lead youngsters to think systematically and creatively toward the solution of their problems. For this reason alone, if for no other, it can be seen that the coercive approach to the management of the classroom is incompatible with the ideals and goals of the democratic society.

THE CONSEQUENCES OF GUILT FEELINGS

We have considered in the previous paragraph, the crippling effect of fear growing out of actual or threatened deprivation in the values such as occurs in the process of coercive disciplinary controls of children. Guilt feelings among children as well as other participants in the social process have their origins in rectitude deprivation. Now, the feeling of guilt creates other enormous fears in children which in turn create other tensions so greatly feared by scientist teachers. It must be recognized here that there are those in education and in many other institutions who look upon the transmission of the feeling of guilt to youngsters as an important mechanism in education. They feel that this transmission of guilt to children is necessary in the process of forcing them into becoming socialized citizens. There are those who believe that unless a child is forced into the persistent feeling to guilt for antisocial action that there will be a great increase in juvenile delinquency. Many in fact trace juvenile delinquency, divorce, and other antisocial behavior behavior to the absence of the feelings of guilt on the part of the individual. Many parents seem to concur in this attitude. An example of such agreement is shown by the mother who may resort to the mechanism of becoming very ill after every act of misbehavior by one of her children. This creates an extreme feeling of guilt on the part of the child and, of course, this feeling of guilt projects him into a state of fear and/or anxiety which seriously impairs the development of the child toward maturity.

The present state of research tends to persuade us that the person in the grip of guilt feelings will not follow any consistent rules of behavior. His personality thus becomes disorganized rather than organized toward any overriding objective. The feeling of guilt is especially effective in blocking creative and productive thinking and promotoes extensive repetitional errors. Furthermore, it must be recognized that the feeling of guilt does not produce a greater concern for achieving a high status of rectitude. These conclusions deny the validity of the theory that feelings of guilt will reduce delinquency and other antisocial behaviors.

On the other hand there are those who believe human nature is essentially good and that it is only because this good is not allowed to have expression that children are projected into antisocial acts. The central theme of the argument in this chapter has been that the maximization of social values among children will contribute to the reduction of the effects of value deprivations they have suffered in the past and to the enhancement of their status in these values in the present and in the future. The effect of these processes will be to increase the probability that the overriding objective of democracy can be achieved in the classroom, for in such classrooms the environment which is most productive in the realization of the full potentials of children can be created. This is a long-range goal of the school which contributes to the realization of human dignity.

INTERVIEWING FOR SELF-DISCLOSURE

The teacher should provide as many opportunities as possible for the child to communicate directly and personally with him. This "talking with my teacher" under conditions of mutual respect and love can be one of the most significant experiences of the pupil. If the proper relationship can be provided it can lead to self-disclosure by the pupil. Without the disclosure by the pupil of his own thoughts, feelings, wants, beliefs, identifications, demands and expectations, what he worries about, facts about his past life, the things the teacher would otherwise never know, the educative process is greatly hindered and, of course, pupil counseling is ineffective.

This process of self-disclosure is beneficial both from the teacher's viewpoint and also from the pupil's. Self-disclosure is the most effective way of making ones self known to another person, but in this process the pupil comes through self-discovery to a knowledge of himself and thus takes the first long steps toward his own maturity.

Jourard asks:

> **Now, what is the connection between self-disclosure and healthy personality? Self-disclosure, or should I say "real' self-disclosure, is both a symptom of personality health and at the same time a means of ultimately achieving a healthy personality. The disclosure of self is an animated "real self be-er." This, of course, takes courage—the "courage to be." I have known people who would rather die than become known, and in fact some did die when it appeared that the chances were great that they would become known. When I say that self-disclosure is a symptom of personality health, what I really mean is that a person who displays many of the other characteristics that betoken healthy personality will also display the ability to make himself fully known to at least one other significant human being. When I say that self-disclosure is a means by which one achieves personality health, I mean something like the following: It is not until I *am* my real self and I *act* my real self that my real self is in a position to grow. One's self grows from the consequences of being. People's selves stop growing when they repress them. This growth-arrest in the self is what helps to account for the surprising paradox of finding an infant inside the skin of someone who is playing the role of an adult.[2]**

Careful planning for the interview in which the pupil's self-disclosure is sought is one of the most important responsibilities of the teacher. He should make every effort to establish a realistic feeling of mutual respect and affection between himself and the child. Anything that the teacher may do during the interview that does not appear to be genuine or that may be interpreted by the child as "phony" will destroy any good that may come from the interview. This characteristic of "phonyness" can be avoided only if the teacher is realistic in expressing his own feelings to the child. If the child feels that the teacher accepts him as a person of worth and dignity, if he feels that his teacher has accorded him status in respect and affection, and if he feels his mental and physical safety

---

[2]Sidney M. Jourard, "Healthy Personality and Self-Disclosure,' MENTAL HYGIENE, October, 1959, Journal of the National Association for Mental Health, New York, N.Y., pp. 55-56.

is assured regardless of what he has done or said previously, then he will be helpful in the process of revealing himself both to himself and to his teacher.

Here, again, it should be emphasized that any realistic progress toward the achievement of status in the values and thus a healthy personality must be made by the child himself. However, this process can be greatly facilitated by the kind of environment which the teacher provides. If he really comes to understand the child and is, therefore, not "horrified" by the child's behavior the teacher can contribute to the freedom with which the child searches for the precise self-knowledge so necessary to the maximization of status in the values.

If the teacher enters into this kind of relationship with the child, positive results can almost certainly be expected, unless the case is one of mental illness of long standing and definitely requires professional psychiatric treatment.

It should be mentioned here that the experience of many teachers who have undertaken the systematic use of the value framework many times develop the ability to face up to their own unreal perspectives and internalized predispositions with a salutary reduction in anxiety which may have led to self-deception and unrealistic behavior.

As we see in the following chart, the course of value deprivation moves from the deprivation itself whether in one or more of the value categories, to fear and/or anxiety with accompanying tensions which point to personality damage (low status of well-being) which provokes the individual to responses which may be classified as realistic or unrealistic behavior.

Let us examine a case of value deprivation in the classroom which will illustrate the premise we have just stated. James S. is a third-grade pupil. He is a bright child. His teacher recognizes that he is also a very sensitive child and from observation of James' behavior, she concluded that one of the major values James seeks in his relations with his teacher and with his peers is respect. Because of this concern for maintaining his respect status in the classroom, James seems always very anxious to give correct responses in answer to questions by his teacher and makes every effort to fulfill the assignments which he is called on to perform. On the day in question, however, in answer to a request by his teacher that he sketch on the blackboard a picture of an antelope which the group had discussed as a member of the deer family, he produced a sketch that appeared to be a moose rather than the slender, speedy antelope the class had been discussing. Several of the members of the class made rather sarcastic remarks about how James had never "even seen a picture of an antelope," that the picture he had drawn was that of a moose and one boy asked, "How stupid can you get?" in the characteristically cruel way in which some children can criticize the actions of other pupils. The teacher noticed that James became very confused, his face became quite flushed, he looked upon his tormentors as though he were ready to strike back at them, then dropped his head and, without a word, returned to his seat. The teacher undertook to point out to the other children that James had done a good job in drawing the moose but had not understood that the antelope is a much smaller, more slender, speedy animal with small antlers. As the teacher talked she observed James' reaction and decided that she had done much to relieve the tension brought on by the

THE COURSE OF VALUE DEPRIVATION
(Frustration)

Categories of Value Goal Deprivations

Respect
Skill
Enlightenment
Wealth
Well-being
Rectitude
Affection
Power

LEAD TO - - - - Fear and/or anxiety with accompanying tensions which provoke individual pupil responses that may be

realistic or unrealistic

Realistic efforts to relieve tensions, include achievement of denied value goals by;

- Retrial,
- Reinterpretation,
- Substitution of goals more in line with capabilities of individual

Realistic efforts to overcome the tensions of frustration lead to maturity which is the major aim of the school.

The mature person's efforts are self-actualizing and are directed toward the achievement of goals which are compatible with the overriding objective of democracy, the realization of human dignity. The creative facilities of the school, therefore, must be employed in the restoration of status in value goals denied (or never achieved) which contribute to the tensions of fear, and lead to unrealistic behavior and immaturity.

Unrealistic efforts to relieve tensions through mental mechanisms of defense or escape are;

- Substitution of unrealistic goals
  - Compensation
  - Sublimation
  - Conformity
  - Regression
  - Daydreaming
  - Phobias
- Self-deception
  - Rationalization
  - Perceptual rigidity
  - Displaced hostility
  - Projection
  - Reaction formation
  - Repression
- Retreat or withdrawal
  - Shyness
  - Depression
  - Hyperactivity
  - Drugs and alcohol
  - Psychosis
  - Suicide

These mechanisms lead to *immaturity and the distortion of creative and productive effort.*

heartless criticism of his fellow pupils, so she dropped the matter altogether, thinking that the damage had been only temporary. However, in the days following, James did not volunteer to respond to questions that were raised during the class period. In fact, he appeared to completely withdraw from participation in the activities of the group and spent most of his time at individual activities which the teacher interpreted as attention-seeking efforts to impress her with his enlightenment and skill. He appeared to be acting under the compulsion to be constantly busy at other interests unrelated to the work of the class. Here was a child who had obviously been deprived of respect and, also, as he appeared to interpret the behavior of his classmates, affection. His response to the deprivation of respect and affection was defensive behavior which we have classified as hyperactivity. This was a symptom of unrealistic withdrawal or retreat from his real problem.

Later, in discussing the incident in a seminar, his teacher reported that his withdrawal symptoms continued to persist. He seemed unwilling to participate again before the class, apparently in fear of further deprivation of respect and affection which he felt he had suffered earlier. He seemed to be very successfully repressing his feelings, however, and would smile in a rather shy manner when approached by the other members of his class. In the discussion by the participants in the seminar which followed, it was suggested to James' teacher that she make every effort to get him to face up to his problem and thus try to provide realistic relief from the tension into which he had been projected by the deprivations he had suffered. The participants observed that the goal to be set by the teacher should be to restore James' respect and affection status with the group. In a review of James' previous experiences and talents which he had displayed, she recalled that his mother reported he had been taking piano lessons for the past three years. She decided to provide him with an opportunity to enhance his respect status. She thought that this might be a successful performance on the piano before his classmates (assuming as she did, that James' most serious deprivation had been loss of respect). Soon after, at a recess period, she asked James if he would go with her to the school auditorium and play for her. After some coaxing James agreed. His mastery of the piano quite amazed his teacher. She was delighted to learn that he could execute many musical passages that were quite beyond the virtuosity of most children his age. She complimented him warmly and thanked him for providing her with the pleasure of hearing him play. She noticed that as James played the piano he seemed to recover much of his former self-confidence and noted, also, that he was greatly pleased by her compliments after his performance.

The next day at the "music period" the teacher announced that James had taken piano lessons for a long time and asked whether the members of the class would like to hear him play. The enthusiasm with which several pupils greeted the suggestion seemed to be very surprising to James, who, however, was greatly pleased by what he apparently interpreted as a friendly response toward him by these pupils. He went to the piano without a word, sat down and played the same number he had played for his teacher, but as the teacher recalled later, with even more self-confidence than he had displayed the day before when he had played for her. After his performance, the pupils applauded with enthusiasm and many of them remarked that they were greatly surprised that a member of their class could play as well as James.

In relating this incident later to her colleagues, the teacher reported that at the end of the period several of the pupils gathered around James and asked him when and how he had learned to play so well. James responded to their interest in a very positive manner. Still another boost to his self-confidence (respect) occurred when James overheard one of the pupils ask his teacher if James could play for them again the next music period. The teacher reported that James' tensions seemed to be greatly reduced following this incident and that he was once more taking an active part in the activities of the class. She reported that her plans included a very definite effort to provide James with further opportunities to restore his status of respect and affection which he obviously felt he had lost in the unfortunate incident in which he had unsuccessfully tried to sketch the picture of an antelope.

As we review this critical incident, we see here a good example of the intelligent efforts a scientist-teacher can make who is sensitive to the personality needs of children and who is quick to detect any incident which may result in unmerited value deprivation among pupils. We have seen, also, how the teacher by acting promptly in this situation, did restore value deprivations which unrelieved may have led this child into other types of unrealistic behavior which we have classified as defense mechanisms and which may have seriously obstructed his progress toward maturity.

TRAITS OF THE MULTI-VALUED PERSONALITY

While conscientious and creative teachers will make use of symptoms of personality damage in estimating the needs of children, the achievement of the major goal of education demands that a positive approach be made toward the development of healthy (multi-valued) personalities. This approach is based upon the assumption that the healthy personality exhibits certain observable traits and characteristics which distinguish him from people with impaired personalities. It is proposed, therefore, that a list of these personality traits be compiled for the use of the teacher. There are at least two important uses which can be made of such a list. First, the specific traits can be used in the formulation of objectives sought in counseling and in other work with children, and, second, these specific traits can be used in the creation of indices to be employed in measuring the health status of individual children as well as of their parents. (Here it should be emphasized that teachers will find such a list of indices very useful also in their own efforts to achieve self-knowledge).

Such a list of traits can be compiled from sources that are readily available in the fields of psychology, psychiatry, sociology, anthropology, and physiology. A tentative beginning has been made in the compilation of this list in the following pages.

Incidentally, it will be seen that an effort has been made to correlate traits of the healthy child (indices of well-being) with the indices of the other values. It should, of course, be recognized that one of the conditions of mental health is the achievement of status in several of the other values. For example, if a child has achieved high status in affection, respect, wealth, and other values, he will most likely have achieved mental and physical health (well-being). On the other hand, if he has been deprived of adequate food, shelter and clothing (wealth) or has not been loved and respected he cannot be expected to develop as a healthy, mature personality.

Indices of the healthy multi-valued personality have been abstracted with some modifications from Adler, Fromm, Blatz, Horney, Rank, Sullivan, Rogers, Maslow, Allport and Jourard. Healthy persons have the following characteristics.

1. They acknowledge personal responsibility for their own actions (high rectitude status).
2. They are self-reliant (high status of self-respect). They are more independent in the solution of their problems than average or ill persons.
3. They deal with their environment in a creative manner (enlightenment and skill). They use their own skills and understanding to do the things they need for health and happiness.
4. Their concepts about other people are realistic; and are not distorted by past experiences (Sullivan describes this trait as non-parataxic interpersonal relations). He says that such people are aware of these relationships and that their beliefs about themselves and other people are accurate (enlightenment and skill).
5. They have "social feeling" (love and respect). Alfred Adler says such persons are identified with mankind. He says that the unhealthy person spends all of his time competing for power in order to escape from his feelings of insecurity while the healthy person is free to love and respect others.
6. They tend to realize their latent potentials in everyday activities (skills). They are not afraid to try out new ways of doing things for fear of failure (with consequent loss of respect).
7. They tend to see reality as it is and to be comfortable in relationship with it. Such persons can more easily distinguish between the truth and the false, the honest and dishonest person. They do less "wishful" thinking than emotionally ill persons. They have less fear of the unknown and thus are relatively free to create new ways of doing things and to try them out with confidence (self-respect and skill).
8. They think and often act spontaneously. They will often accept the conventional in order to avoid hurting people while inwardly despising it. Such persons can thus be said to think more than to act unconventionally (rectitude).
9. They are concerned with problems outside themselves rather than with self as are insecure people (rectitude, enlightenment and skill). Such people, when they grow up, are concerned with the basic issues of life and work in the broadest frame of reference in thinking about values and their achievement.

10. They can be alone without discomfort (self-respect). Such people even have need of solitude or privacy more than the "average" or ill person who is usually uncomfortable when alone.

11. They continue to get pleasure from the beauty of their environment throughout life. They respond aesthetically and with pleasure to a beautiful flower even though they have seen one almost exactly like it many times before (high status of aesthetic skill). This attitude of continuing appreciation is an index of good mental health.

12. They have democratic personalities. They demand that all values be shared. This is an index of high rectitude status. They will learn from the experiences of any person of good character regardless of political belief, class, religious persuasion, or nationality (respect and affection). They treat people courteously, have respect for people on the basis of merit rather than on the basis of family or other unearned status. They are ethical in their interpersonal relationships. They demand that others have the same access to values that they demand for themselves (rectitude).

13. They are able to distinguish between means and ends (enlightenment) and skill). They always place the goals they seek above the means by which they seek to achieve them. This trait may often be displayed in the judicious management of personal finances.

14. They have an unhostile sense of humor (respect), do not laugh at misfortunes of others, and do not attempt to make people laugh by hurting others. Such people, however, are quick to see the humor in the errors of human beings in general, such as trying to feel important when this feeling is not justified. They can laugh at their own mistakes. Their humor is spontaneous rather than planned (well-being).

15. They offer intelligent and responsible resistance to many aspects of the cultural mold (rectitude). They conform with many of the observable symbols of conventionality but are really not conventional in the dependent sense. They accept conventional practices in their inner feelings toward them only to the degree to which they think they are good.

While it must not be inferred that the list of personality traits given above is comprehensive, such a list will be found helpful in that it suggests many excellent and precise indices of status in many of the social values which contribute to good mental health. The teacher can use these and other indices in appraising personalities of children and parents. He can also employ them in the estimate of his own status in the values. This overt effort may be seen as a beginning step in the achievement of self-knowledge.

SUMMARY

The experience of the young child upon entering school for the first time has been characterized by many deprivations and indulgences in the valuing process. The ability of such an individual to function fully as a person is dependent upon how these ups and downs of human existence have shaped his values. Is he open to love, to use power without guilt feelings, or skilled in those ways which make social living increasingly a success?

Teachers come to the classroom with past patterns of value deprivations and indulgences. Their ability to function fully as persons and as professionals depend upon the way these patterns have developed in the valuing process. The assumption is that teachers can understand their students only if they can understand themselves. They can deal with value deprivations if they are skilled in spotting them in the profiles of their students. They can lead students to self-disclosure if they know how to conduct themselves thither.

Transformation of the individual depends primarily on the ability of the individual to transcend frustrations and other blocks, increasingly through applying value analysis both to the self and to the social context.

Guilt feelings, particularly, inhibit transcendence and, although guilt is sometimes a necessary and realistic feeling when merited, unrealistic guilt feelings can be eliminated through self-study. All frustrations represent some kind of value deprivation. Even the fear of being deprived in one or more of the value categories becomes, for all intents purposes, a frustration that can lead to a damaged personality. Processes of self-study and of group consideration of common problems furnish the basis for the creation of techniques. Variations of these individual-group activities can be employed to promote continuous analyses.

The multi-valued personality is what others have described as the fully functioning person, social-self-realization, and the mature personality. Such personalities are richly endowed and function healthfully in all of the major value categories. Access to the values needs to remain open to achieve value maximization in all the categories. This is a major responsibility of the democratic school.

CHAPTER 14

•

Multi-Valued Appraisal of Progress in Education

Newer methods of evaluation and reporting progress are presented in this chapter against a backdrop of value shaping and sharing in all aspects of the educational program. Sharing in the evaluation and reporting procedure provides a significant role for the learner to play in his own evaluation and the further direction of his learning.

The study of young people is one of the primary tasks of the professional teacher. The assumption is that a better understanding of the unique way an individual looks out upon his world helps the teacher better to teach and to evaluate.

Perhaps the most fundamental technique involves analysis of the value profiles of students. A value profile is made on each student from the data a teacher gathers. It is necessary to make an inventory of the value statuses of children systematically by posting data under each value category. The kinds and quality of these data in each category give an indication of the status of the child with respect to that value. A line graph may then be drawn on a scale from low to high. This profile reflects the extent of value deprivations and indulgences experienced by the individual. An imbalance in the profile is a sign that the individual needs more than casual attention; indeed, it is a call to arms for the teacher.

The teacher also is interested in how young people accord values to others. For this purpose the teacher applies value sociometrics to the group. These data from the value sociogram help the teacher to better plan intervention in the social process of the classroom toward a wider distribution of value sharing among students. This kind of intervention is highly significant in the development of the classroom as a democratic community. Learning of all kinds and growth toward psychological maturity especially, depends upon a healthy multi-valued person. Teachers hold an important key to the development of mature and creative persons through knowledge of their value profiles.

Self-evaluation in the activities of the learner provides a systematic rationale for developing individual planning for teaching and learning and yields a much desired outcome of increasing self-direction for the learner.

Therefore, this chapter seeks to contribute to value theory and to the improvement of evaluation techniques through the introduction of (1) concepts of measurement in the context of value theory, (2) the making and use of value profiles of individuals, (3) techniques of value-sociometry, and (4) innovations in reporting pupil progress to parents.

EDUCATIONAL MEASUREMENT IN THE CONTEXT OF THE FRAMEWORK

Value Theory and Measurement

Why should psychological measurement be concerned with an operational theory of values? The answer lies in the challenge and opportunity it provides to stretch existing measurements toward new frontiers and pioneer in improvising more creative quantitative techniques that may be required. While doing so, measurement should become increasingly relevant to what social behavior is ultimately about–the attainment of values. Measurement is itself a value–the attainment of more precision in skill. When that attainment is purchased without regard to other values, it becomes skill for skill's sake alone–a policy that requires the neglect of other goals. Such kinds of precision often prove false, and can be maintained only by curtailing rigorous study of all other values. Research piles up selectively, however unwittingly, around what is most *readily* measured–matters of comfort and security that constitute well-being come, along with wealth, in for the heaviest share of quantification–instead of what most *needs* to be more rigorously measured, areas like insight and rectitude and affection. The practices of the measurement profession as a *whole* thus give selective inattention and selective overattention to different areas of valuation. Since society is increasingly being guided by scientific information, there are wider social ramifications stemming from selective measurement practices. Quantitative skill is developed to permit some values to move ahead (as far as increments in human insight and understanding are actually produced by such skill applications) while allowing others to lag behind. Thus, measurement experts can speak in favor of democracy in general but subtly subvert it by collective practices that are allowed to remain in inbalance. Such a pattern of word and deed is one example of unrealistic thinking in contrast to *effective* or critical intelligence.

Value thinking has been suffused with certain rather widely shared assumptions that have acted as handicaps. The tendency is to see facts not as instances of value, nor of acts of valuing as themselves facts. Instead, because values involve "prescriptions" or "norms" of various sorts, they are divorced from factual matters, the latter being reserved for what *is* rather than what *ought* to be. In this way, fact and value have become bifurcated until it seems hopeless to "patch" them together again, but the difficulty is only one that is of a thinker's own making. It permeates and obscures even the best intentions in social science today.

Contrary to traditional points of view, values can be described as facts. To say that X values Y is to assert a factual proposition that can be tested quite apart from who makes the statement. We simply observe X's practices in relationship to Y and employ all the available and devisable measurements of goal seeking. So too, all facts about social practices and behavior patterns can be examined in terms of the goals or objectives sought and/or realized through them. When we discover regularities in goal seeking, we can speak of "norms"; and we can pay attention to the "ought" statements of those engaged in the practice. Although people may tell us what their norms are, they are not supplying us with any kind of data that is in principle of a different order than their other behavior. Their statements, while data, can be tested apart from their mere utterance. Frequently, their "ought" and their other statements or practices conflict. How each specific goal is to be classified is to be dealt with like any other empirical problem of coding, although the most important thing about the descriptive framework described in Chapter 4 is that it compels any personality or group in any situation, however concrete, to clarify conflict and choice of goals by both (1) analytical coding of the specific issues that are under concern, as well as (2) seeing these issues in terms that transcend, while they are *exemplified* in, the ongoing situation.

Science is an attempt to learn from experience, to acquire insight, understanding and, as a result, a greater creativity and innovation. When we can see that this value conflict here before us is similar to others around us (and to still others that have occurred in the past), we are liberated from resolving each situation we come to in *ad hoc* overpersonalized terms. We are also forced to become more self-consistent, since when we see our situation as not too different from those in which others have been, we are less likely to prescribe in *one* way for others and in *another* way for ourselves. In short, thinking abstractly about goals allows us to see our particular situations of value conflict and choice with the breadth characteristic of science, since we are required to see it more generally and comprehensively, not only in immediate personal and emotional terms. We might speak of this as "putting the self in social context and process," in the wider stream of valuing coming out of the past, going on in the present, and to which we can contribute in the future by choices of goals we make now. We are, therefore, unlikely to be "alienated" from our society, by seeing our own capacity for intelligently intervening in it. The same value problems are being faced all over the social map, although their details may differ in each instance. No one is quite alone or unique no matter what his special value problems are.

Part of the answer, then, to the question: "Education for What?" is that there is now a descriptive science of values which may be taught and is being taught from the primary grades to graduate school levels. The aim is to use education primarily to help pre-adults master more scientific ways of thinking about value problems. Needless to say, the teaching job and the learning task is not merely a matter of learning how to use words. It is also, and primarily, one of *learning how to apply them to learning itself* and to all the interpersonal relations into which the school enters.

Nonetheless, mere description, however edifying if done systematically and comprehensively, does not by itself provide one with a necessarily intelligent prescription. There is probably no institution that has listened and talked so repetitiously about itself as being part of a democratic order, especially in

America, than the school. The concept of democracy among educators has been a bit fuzzy and unfocused; the attempts to apply it to day-to-day procedure, consequently, have often resulted in the same kind of rigid unthinking rituals, however permissive, that the talk was meant to supplant.

The authors aspire to build upon the movement that John Dewey instigated, but give it a new clarity. The overriding objective that democracy prescribes is realization of "human worth and dignity." This prescription, this "ought," is now related to the descriptive value categories so that it can be operationally used in concrete circumstances in descriptive ways. Human dignity is defined as a state where no participant pursues his value goal in such a way as to seriously and severely overdeprive or overindulge the pursuit of the value objectives of others in the process. The teacher who showers one child in the class with indulgences denied the others because that child has a father who might be in a position to get her a salary raise is engaged in a practice not conducive to human dignity. The teacher who continually nags and humiliates one child in the class, which she characteristically does not do to the others, because the father of that child voted against a raise of salary for her is engaged in a practice not conducive to human dignity.

While the concept of human dignity is, therefore, an "ought," a prescription, a norm, and all of these at a very abstract level, there is no difficulty in principle in operationalizing it through examining classroom practices (or any practices merely "discussed" in the classroom) in terms of what objectives such practices actuate as outcomes with what gains or costs to the values of whom, using all the eight value categories. Each is given the essential defining characteristics. It is the interplay of all, of any part of these, in the interpersonal acts occurring in the school that gives us a description of imbalance, slight or severe, that allows us to make a factual statement about the degree to which the democratic prescription has been realized or abrogated. Hard analytical uphill work is involved, not snap judgments, quick impressions or elegant literary intuitions about how to achieve democracy.

There is one feature of this general theoretical model which deserves marked emphasis. We have often heard of "democratic values"–uttered, one may add, not always without sentimental and pious overtones. *Democracy has to do with a balance or equilibrium among values*, not with one set of values considered in absolute terms apart from the relationships into which they enter with the rest in a special instance or a class of instances. The freedom to pursue *any* value is part and parcel of a democracy, no matter how "new" or "strange" the strategy or goal may seem. Democracy does enter in, and then descriptively as well as prescriptively in terms of relationships among values, when we consider at what costs to the self and others value objectives are attained in terms of other values. There may be undemocratic personalities not *only* in the sense of those who prove costly or disruptive to *others* to have around, but in the sense that they pursue one value at great costs to other values for *themselves*. The pursuit of power is consistent with democracy in the sense that a wish to play a larger share in setting or applying norms to govern the actions of others is the goal, but *only* when it is not pursued at great costs of imbalances to the self and to others in terms of all other values. Once such power is attained, it may be used democratically as long as it is employed to "right" imbalance rather than contribute further to it in total outcome.

The scientific study of values cannot be confined merely to laws about content. These laws about content have also to be applied to our procedures. The Robinson Crusoe image that the scientist has tended to have of himself might have been an excusable delusion in the days when it was not yet glaringly apparent how much science, as a pursuit of enlightenment, could modify the value of the conditions in which it arose. The power of enlightenment is at last staggeringly apparent, and although social science still has a long way to go until it produces the equivalence of an atom bomb or a rocket to the moon, there is no doubt such equivalent discoveries are before us and the seeds of them have already been intellectually planted among us. The sooner the expert on psychological measurement and the expert of values come to an effective working relationship, the sooner we can get on to the major discoveries ahead. It is not enough to study "achievement" as a skill. Let us ask "achievement of what objective?' And follow it by: "Achievement with what costs or gain to other achievements affected by it?" The intelligent guidance of value dynamics will help us enlarge and not constrict our map so that the norms of what we *do* may become the norms we most *profess*.

The Value Profile as a Measure of Deprivations

Ann was shy and withdrawing. She appeared especially to fear all adult males. Her teacher wondered what deprivations she had suffered to stunt her normal social development.

Alice had a sparkling gregarious disposition, was everybody's friend, had youthful parents who loved her. Any deprivation she might suffer would likely be temporary and slight.

Jack wanted a black leather jacket and a bicycle. Then other boys would look up to him; now they only laughed at the exaggerated stories he told of his exploits. His teacher realized this kind of behavior revealed a low self-esteem and a frantic attempt to gain the respect of his peers.

Jan hovered near the teacher and appeared to need constant attention and reassurance. She was from a broken home where love was shattered and the future uncertain. How could a teacher make up for such deprivation of affection?

The teacher mused over the personality patterns of other members of the class. If young people tended to show a pattern of value deprivations and indulgences in their daily behavior, she wanted to know more about them. There was sad-eyed Dick. He exuded an air of melancholy in most of his days. He was easily defeated or discouraged. He seldom tried anymore. Who or what had taken away his power to act? Was it as simple as that? Had someone systematically stripped him of his will and usurped his power to decide? Or was his problem multi-valued deprivation? She wanted to find out. She would study him in all the value categories, that is, make a value inventory, find his *status* in each, and then make a *value profile* on him. This could be a first step she would take in helping him to gather his courage and to work more in line with his real capacity.

Value Profile of Dick

Dick was a member of a family of five children. He had a sister who was living at home with her third husband. His mother was expecting another baby in the early spring. His mother worked as a waitress in an all-night restaurant. Her job kept her at work from twleve o'clock midnight until eight o'clock in the morning. She seemed tired and not well physically. During the conference, she revealed that there were three teenage brothers who cared for Dick most of the time. One of the boys had already dropped out of school. Dick went with them everywhere and was exposed to terrible language from this association with his older brothers. He apparently had no children his age to play with and had not learned how to play.

At a later conference, Dick's mother reported that her husband was drunk most of the time. She reported that many times the father would come home drunk and beat little Dick. Many times Dick would sleep on the floor all night fully clothed. He was not fed properly nor kept clean. He would wear the same clothes to school all week. The only shoes he had in the winter were sneakers that had worn out. He had no coat nor wraps of any kind to keep him warm when it was cold.

Dick's mother realized his lack of skills and his emotional insecurity. She was a mother who insisted that she was interested in her son and loved him, but evidently she had little time for him. She was filled with frustrations and anxieties which grew out of conditions in the home. Dick's welfare apparently was thought to be of little significance in comparison with the other problems which threatened her.

Dick's value statuses were qualitatively described as follows:

Power–Dick showed inability to make decisions for himself. He acted as though he expected others to tell him exactly what to do. He was not able to take on a responsible job and carry it out. Classroom and playground rules meant very little to him.

Enlightenment–Dick did not have access to printed materials at home except for undesirable magazines purchased by older, teenage brothers. His parents offered no encouragement for him to learn. Dick's understanding of the games of the playground were very limited. He had not had the opportunity to play or interact with children of his own age. Dick had no knowledge of nursery rhymes or any of the readiness attitudes which children bring from home. He had not been furnished with colorbooks, crayons or water paints. His social conduct was uninhibited and reflected low quality of parental guidance. Consequently this child reflected extreme deprivations in the status of enlightenment.

Respect–Dick showed respect for the other children to a limited degree. He tried to like the children and wanted them to like him, but due to his antisocial behavior, he did not receive much respect from his peers.

Wealth–Dick was deprived of this value. He did not have adequate clothing. His appearance was usually much below the standards of the other children.

Money in his pocket was a thing he had not experienced. He could not furnish his own materials needed in the classroom nor money for his lunches.

Skill—Dick rated very low in the reading readiness test at the beginning of the year. He was unable to talk clearly and many times the children laughed at him because of his being inarticulate. His co-ordination was poor and his motor abilities were very generally low. Much of this was due to his lack of opportunity to practice many of the skills of childhood. He had not had the pleasure of a coloring book or picture books in the home nor had he been given the opportunity to speak for himself. He started out the year lacking in all the skills necessary for formal reading. He was definitely not ready to read. Much of the deprivations of skills could be due to the fact that he was not strong physically. He did not always get the proper food or rest he needed.

Well-being—Dick was not strong physically. The nurses reported undernourishment after his physical checkup. He did not have a toothbrush, and he was seldom given a bath. His mental well-being reflected even more deprivations. He felt insecure, unwanted, and definitely longed for love and affection. He had experienced little success in any undertaking before coming to school. His low respect status with the peer group definitely inhibited his feeling of well-being.

Rectitude—Dick had not been properly taught about right or wrong. He did not hesitate to take things from other children. He had not been taught to be responsible for his behavior. Church school attendance was something that Dick had heard about but had never experienced.

Affection—Dick was very insecure. He was unable to get the children to like him because he tried to get their attention through methods that were distasteful. He did not know what it was to share affection with others. He would break rules made by the class in order to get attention. This child needed affection and respect. He needed to realize that he belonged and that there was a place for him.

Action Taken on Basis of Dick's Value Profile

It was very important to show this child that he could be loved and wanted. He had to have a feeling of security before any progress could be made. In the beginning, Dick had to learn that rules are made for the protection of all and had to be obeyed by all. The teacher attempted to help him realize that others would like him more if he would not take their things, and that misbehavior to get attention was not really rewarding conduct. He needed to be taught responsibility and was assigned errands and specific jobs to do.

Background and readiness skills were worked on independently. When he began formal reading, he was accorded respect by being encouraged and praised by the teacher. It was not long until the group began to show some respect for Dick. Many children offered to help him with problems that were difficult for him.

One day Dick was sent out of the room on an errand and the children were asked by the teacher to help him learn how to play. The children were told that Dick did not want to hurt anyone, but this was his way to get them to respect him. All should help him realize that everyone would be happier and would like

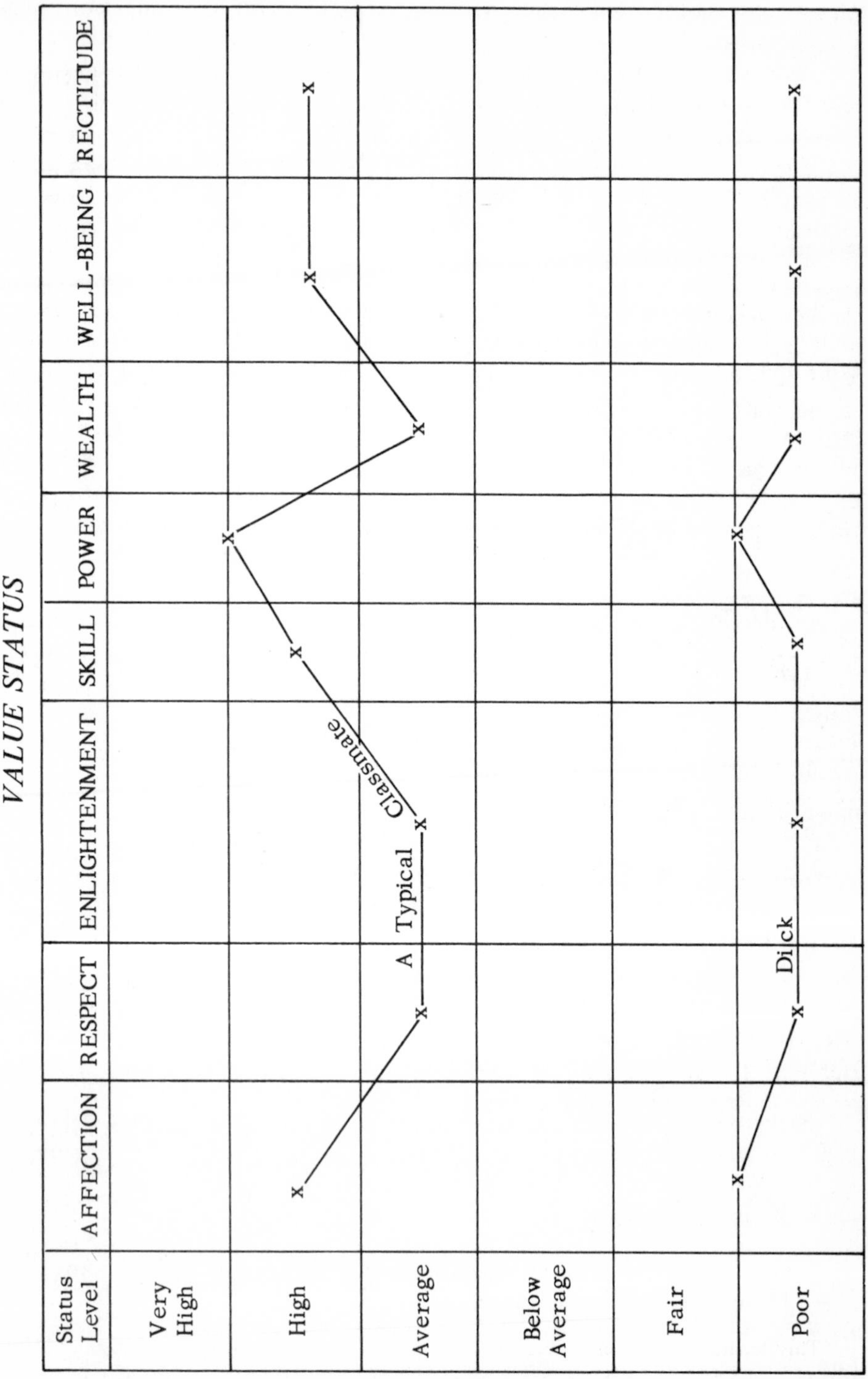

VALUE STATUS

Status Level	AFFECTION	RESPECT	ENLIGHTENMENT	SKILL	POWER	WEALTH	WELL-BEING	RECTITUDE
Very High					x			
High	x			x			x	x
Average		x A	Typical x Classmate			x		
Below Average								
Fair								
Poor	x	x Di	ck x	x	x	x	x	x

him more if he followed class rules. Dick began to realize that rules were made for the welfare of the whole group. He was always given a place in group functions and received respect when he carried out his part. He began to gain confidence and self-respect and tried to function with the group and do what was expected of each member of the group.

Due to the deprivation of his physical well-being, it became necessary to make special arrangements for his food. He was encouraged to keep his hands clean and to care for himself. Clothes were supplied for him through the school. All of this was acceptable to the parents. He was very proud of his new clothes. As a result, he really tried to improve his appearance.

He was given merited praise when he began to show progress in his reading ability. The children no longer laughed at him when he told a story. Quantitative skills and motor skills were slow to advance. Praise and encouragement (respect enhancement) seemed to be the key to his efforts to improve. Dick had tasted success in his reading ability. He found a place in the group and gained respect of his peers as well as their affection. He began to show self-respect and more interest in what he was doing. That he was definitely making progress became obvious.

The Sociogram

The sociogram is a diagram of the social status of the children in a group. The data for it is secured by asking individuals in the group to write on a slip of paper the names of those most liked. The first and second choices are recorded in such a fashion as to picture the social relationships of the population of the group. The boys may be represented by a rectangle and the girls by a circle. Lines drawn between these symbols marked with a code for the names indicate who chooses whom. Choices are recorded on a separate tally sheet. Those chosen most often are placed in the center. Those chosen less are seen in outer circles. If an individual is not chosen the teacher lists him as a tentative isolate who may need special help.

Value-Sociometry[1]

The teacher's observation of children may not turn up all the value information needed. He should collect information about the value statuses of each pupil throughout the school year, the better to guide behavior. However, the children themselves can throw much light on the value statuses of other children. To get this kind of information the traditional sociogram has been revised for purposes of value analysis.

Instead of asking children merely to name children they "most like" or "like to work with," the teacher uses the sociometric instrument to get comprehensive value information. Not only does this instrument "locate" the chosen and the isolated, but it also helps the teacher to spot specific value deprivations and indulgences. The teacher is interested in how he can promote value sharing among the members of the class. He can intervene in class activities and

---

[1]This technique first employed in the Chicago Value-Sharing Project, Chicago Public Schools, sponsored by National College of Education with the authors as consultants.

relationships with more success if he knows how children accord or withhold values among themselves. It is rewarding to the teacher to relate values accorded individual children. The leaders in the group tend to receive multi-valued nominations. This often belies the naive assumption that high intellect or strong physique alone may account for leadership. The teacher is likewise interested in whether values are "widely" rather than "narrowly" distributed among the class population. Repeated use of this questionnaire at regular intervals will enable the teacher to chart the progress the class is making in developing a "democratic community." These data, also, will undoubtedly sharpen the perceptions of the teacher in making value profiles on each child in the class and in keeping these up to date. It is very important to remember that such data is very confidential and should be revealed only to persons directly responsible for assisting with the progress of the learner.

The following questionnaire is an example of how necessary data are collected in making the value-oriented sociogram.

After the questionnaires have been completed by the students, the teacher will need to tablulate the results for analysis. The information will be initially brought together in a general table on graph paper (or any paper with both horizontal and vertical ruling). The names or numbers of the students are listed vertically and horizontally. The total number of choices in all value categories (although value categories are not listed) will tend to give the teacher the kind of data furnished by the traditional sociogram. The table would show the number of choices an individual received and who chose him. No rank order of choice need be assumed. If desired, the blanks on the questionnaire for names could be given in rank order. A speciman of this general table follows (pages 282-283).

To record the choices according to value categories, a table would have the names or numbers of students listed vertically on graph paper and the eight value categories listed horizontally. The teacher will be interested to know not only who has the highest status (number of choices) in each value category, but also who are accorded statuses in several categories; that is, who are considered multi-valued persons. A speciman of this chart follows (page 284).

To ascertain in the more intensive sense who accords whom which value, tables should be made on each value with student numbers listed both horizontally and vertically like the general table as in this speciman (page 285).

Over a period of one semester, the teacher would likely be able to redistribute values that tend to cluster deeply around the names of certain children. For instance, it is the normal tendency for a few children in a group to enjoy a high-power status; however, the teacher can "engineer" the process of decision making in such a way as to give other members of the group a chance to help lead. Children who have exceptionally high-power status should be helped to improve their affection and rectitude statuses by deliberately sharing more of the power activities (decision making) with others.

Children who have low statuses in any value category should, of course, be the object of intensive study, for ways which might be indicated for both teacher and peer intervention in events to turn hidden assets into value enhancements. It is sometimes a simple matter for a teacher to point up to the

Name________________________

WHO'S WHO?

Write the names of two members of your class after each question. Do not write your own name after any question; write your name at the top of this sheet. You may use a name several times if you think the person deserves it.

Well Being

1. (a) Who are happy most of the time and do not hold a grudge or have a "chip on their shoulder"?

   ________________ ________________

   (b) Who are hardly ever sick and have the best physical health?

   ________________ ________________

Affection

2. (a) Whom do you like most in the class?

   ________________ ________________

   (b) Who are liked most by the group?

   ________________ ________________

Power

3. (a) Who are usually chosen to lead the class?

   ________________ ________________

   (b) Who have the most influence when the group is trying to make a decision?

   ________________ ________________

Skill

4. (a) Who are good in such things as reading, spelling, writing, drawing, mechanics, or sports?

   ________________ ________________

   (b) Who are good at making speeches, making reports, or acting (dramatizing)?

   ________________ ________________

Enlightenment

5. (a) Who are best in answering hard thought questions asked in class?

   ________________ ________________

   (b) Who are best at bringing in new ideas of inventing something?

   ________________ ________________

Wealth

6. (a) Who have the best things to play and work with?

   ________________ ________________

   (b) Whom do you think have the most spending money?

   ________________ ________________

Respect

7. (a) Who are the best all-around persons among your classmates?

   ________________ ________________

   (b) Who in this class would you most want to be like other than yourself?

   ________________ ________________

Rectitude

8. (a) Who are the most dependable and will keep their word in your class?

   ________________ ________________

   (b) Who are most likely to be fair and do right no matter what?

   ________________ ________________

VALUE-SOCIOGRAM TABULATION

NUMBER OF CHOICES IN ALL VALUE CATEGORIES

Student No.	1	2	3	4	5	6	7	8	9	10	11	12	13	14
1														
2														
3														
4														
5														
6														
7														
8														
9														
10														
11														
12														
13														
14														
15														
16														
17														
18														
19														
20														
21														
22														
23														
24														
25														
26														
27														
28														
29														
30														

VALUE-SOCIOGRAM TABULATION (continued)

NUMBER OF CHOICES IN ALL VALUE CATEGORIES

15	16	17	18	19	20	21	22	23	24	25	26	27	28	29	30

STATUSES IN EIGHT VALUE CATEGORIES

Student No.	Affection	Respect	Skill	Enlightenment	Power	Wealth	Well-Being	Rectitude
1								
2								
3								
4								
5								
6								
7								
8								
9								
10								
11								
12								
13								
14								
15								
16								
17								
18								
19								
20								
21								
22								
23								
24								
25								
26								
27								
28								
29								
30								

AFFECTION

Student No.	1	2	3	4	5	6	7	8	9	etc.
1										
2										
3										
4										
5										
6										
7										
8										
9										
etc.										

class something which a child can do fairly well, thus helping him to earn additional respect. A lonely, friendless child could be the target for another child (whom the teacher might be helping) to develop more outgoing affection or rectitude. It is axiomatic that children who are overindulged in some values need help in sharing with those who are deprived. Balance is a goal in the value enhancement process. When children realize this along with the teacher, values are more readily distributed in the classroom.

Evaluation of the democratic behavior of the teacher can be made in the long run. For example, after several periodic sociometric value charts have been made over time, if the distribution pattern of his class has moved from dense clusters to widespread distribution among the class as a whole he can be confident that his personal behavior has tended to be democratic. Autocratic, rigid teachers who show little respect for their children and who are bent only on teaching the subject matter prescribed tend to have the opposite effect on the value statuses of children in the classroom.

INNOVATIONS IN REPORTING TO PARENTS

The increasing emphasis upon curricula to meet individual differences and to promote more self-direction in the learning process lead inevitably to new emphases on self-evaluation and the learner's participation in reporting his progress to parents. All of these related developments throw in bold relief some of the misconceptions of traditional practice.

Reporting Practices

While the child or parents may think they know what the "A" or "C" means on the typical report card, there is overwhelming evidence to indicate that it is really next to impossible to know exactly what these marks mean. The comparative A, B, C's on the report card are particularly misleading for the less able pupil and the superior pupil. Superior learners can meet the requirements for a typical "A" without the kind of effort that would challenge their full abilities. On the other hand, the inferior student may be doomed to monotonous failure, a loss of self-respect, and a cumulate loss of well-being.

Lindquist says:

> **The plan of reporting to parents percentage marks or letter grades is not consistent with the policy of meeting the needs of the individual pupils. Likewise the practice of simply marking of a pupil satisfactory or unsatisfactory, in terms of his general capacity, is inadequate. The weakness of the reporting methods is not that they tell too much about the pupil, but rather that they tell too little and their meaning is ambiguous.**[2]

To overcome the shortcomings of the letter grade reports a number of schools have discarded the usual report card and have adopted a letter to parents. The letter may call attention to (1) outstanding features of his work, (2) phases of the school program in which he is making satisfactory progress, and (3) those phases in which he will need special help and can make improvement.

It is difficult for a teacher to write a helpful letter to parents unless he has acquired skill in interpreting individual behavior, has time to go over all available information, and applies value analysis to the data. The letter report can reflect the individual point of view of a teacher better than marks. Letters are very time-consuming for the teacher and if poorly written create unfavorable attitudes instead of improving public relations. Another weakness of the written report is that it allows little give and take.

Like the graded school, the traditional report card is a foreign import conceived in Europe and designed to measure academic progress for a few, not the many. Hence, when applied to mass education, it is inappropriate.

The goal of making available to parents and teachers information that will enable them to work more constructively for the best growth of the child was not realized in the traditional report cards or the letter. One-way communication does not give the teacher information from the home situation or give the teacher the opportunity to understand the emotional climate which the parents provide, nor does it help the parent to help the child with his problems. It seems vitally necessary that the teacher and parent work together for the child's best interest. A promising solution to the problem of communication between the home and school is the personal, face-to-face conference.

Although personal conferences have had favorable results in almost all cases reported, the child may not feel sufficiently informed on his progress. Failure of the teacher to be diplomatic and skilled in human relations, and the failure on

---

[2]E.F. Lindquist, *Educational Measurement,* American Council on Education Co., 1951, p. 30. Used by permission.

the part of the parent in understanding the purpose of the conference, can achieve unfavorable results. It must be remembered that each conference is unique and confidential. Further, it should be remembered that in each conference values are being shared or withheld and that the teacher must make sure his own actions and words enhance the value statuses of the other participants.

Preplanning on the part of both the teacher and parent has been found to be a necessity in successful parent-teacher conferences. The teacher must be prepared to give an objective, anecdotal report and have achievement records at hand, as well as a well-thought-out approach to any existing problems, after finding out as much as possible about the child.

Where so many conferences fall short is in the teacher's neglect of basic areas of parent's interest and concern. What parents want to know varies with problems, values, experience and background. In Texas a study was conducted under the sponsorship of the Texas Congress of Parents and Teachers: it revealed several areas of general interest. The parents wanted to know where the child stood in the mastery of basic skills, specific information on subject matter the child was expected to cover and how it was being taught, the child's weaknesses, and the teacher's observations of his strengths and talents, the rate of progress in line with the teacher's expectations, "Is he working to capacity?", how the parents may help, effectiveness of the child's study habits, degree of participation in class activities, how well he expresses himself, and the child's degree of dependability, co-operation, initiative and attentiveness. The parents usually wanted frank answers.

Pupil Participation in Evaluating and Reporting

The significant factors in the suggested reporting practices revolve around parent-teacher planning, child-parent-teacher planning, teacher planning for the purpose of improving the experiences that the child encounters in his school living, so that the whole child, as a unique individual, will be encouraged to develop to the maximum his potential in all aspects of growth and learning.

The child is considered the person who must be most involved in the discussion of his school progress, since he is the one who will be making further educational developments. Of course, the teacher and parent sometimes confer alone. However, when the conference is planned to discuss and report pupil progress, the child undoubtedly should be included in the conference.

The Teacher-Parent-Pupil Conference

Rucker[3] has suggested how the teacher-pupil-parent type of evaluating conference may be planned. He indicated that the learner should be asked to develop a folder for a conference with parents and the teacher which can be organized to present the following:

His current goals and plans ("What I am trying to do").
His spelling lists for the previous evaluation period.

[3]W. Ray Rucker, *Curriculum Development in the Elementary School* (New York: Harper and Row, Publishers, 1960) pp. 165-66.

His arithmetic papers.
His book reports.
His drawing maps, etc.
His poems and stories.
His reports of field trips, projects, or films.
His write-ups of science experiments.
His progress estimate ("What I have done").
The teacher's evaluation-reaction.
His goals for next period.
The parents evaluation or reaction.

From this folder, the learner will present evidence of his own progress. The folder will furnish some resources for making plans cooperatively with the teacher and parents for the next learning period. This conference method enables all participants to focus realistically on meeting the individual's needs. The goal is the individual's optimum development through a maximum of self-direction by the learner. He, his teacher, and his parents cooperatively evaluate, gain new insights for subsequent application to the problems revealed in the reports, and explore more productive ways to shape and share values in terms of the uniqueness of this student and his background. A more confidential teacher's folder on each learner may include the following:

Scholastic aptitude profile.
Achievement battery profile.
Value-sociogram.
Anecdotal records.
Citizenship check list.
Records of daily achievement in basic skills and subjects.

This more confidential information may be shared with the parent when pertinent in that part of the conference after the student has made his report and has left the teacher alone with his parents. Interpretation and planning should feature this phase of the conference and lead to new strategies or confirmation of old ones for the teacher or parent to use in promoting the value enhancements of the learner where his special needs have come to be recognized.

Rucker suggests an agenda by which to conduct the teacher-pupil-parent conference although he feels experienced teachers often will vary the agenda to advantage by knowing the learner and his problems intimately. His suggested agenda follows:

1. Get warmly acquainted with all parties. Steer the discussion to points about the family so as to give the parents something about which they can talk with confidence. Find something favorable you can say about the parents or the child in the beginning.

2. Begin the reporting session by asking the child to tell about or show something he has done well during the previous evaluation period. Then ask the child to open his folder and read his goals and plans ("What I am trying to do") formulated at the last conference. Help him to specify his progress toward these goals as he turns through his spelling lists, arithmetic papers, book reports, etc.;

when appropriate ask him to supplement his folder with scientific apparatus, maps, construction products, and the like.

3. When the child has presented a representative sample of his work during the reporting period and has in an informal way indicated his attention to the goals and plans formulated at the last conference and elaborated upon continuously during the period, ask the child to read his progress estimate ("What I have done"). This progress estimate of the pupil must be composed by himself without help (except in the primary grades). It should be a short summary rather than a lengthy report of all activities in which the child may have been engaged.

4. Hand the pupil your short written evaluation-reaction prepared previously after studying the pupil folder and referring to the teacher folder for pertinent information.

5. Encourage a discussion of the differences in the pupil's and the teacher's evaluations. Make any necessary corrections in either report and place both back in the pupil folder. Ask the parent to write an evaluation for the folder like that of the pupil and teacher when the parent returns home. Review quickly the evaluations that were written by all three parties at the last reporting period to note the progress made by the child and to note any change of opinion held previously by either party.

6. Lead a discussion on goals for the next period by first asking the pupil to read his prepared list. Encourage the parent to enter the discussion freely by asking such questions as: "Do you think he can do this much?" "Does he have enough time at home to do this?" "Is there a place at home where he can lay this out?" Get tentative agreement by all on what the goals should be, subject to any changes indicated as the learning activities occur.

7. Dismiss the child from the conference. Have a plan for where he is to go and what he is to do during the time when the teacher and the parent have confidential discussion.

8. Review any points you or the parent may wish to discuss concerning the pupil's report.

9. Share information as needed from the teacher folder to account for any aspect of the pupil's progres or lack of it. Give the parent an indication of whether the child is working up to his capacity or potential. If not, try to account for the deficiency or ask the parent for any light he can throw on the problem.

10. Interpret standardized test scores either in percentile ranks or in grade equivalents. Avoid giving the IQ or mental age of the child but interpret his academic intelligence by referring to the profile and his percentile rank on the national norm. Avoid comparing the pupil with other pupils in his group.

11. Map plans to help the child with his problems or to facilitate his development in any way: physical, social, emotional, intellectual.

12. Express appreciation for the opportunity to visit with the parent and mention the probable time of the next conference.[4]

---

[4] *Ibid.*, pp. 67-68.

VALUE SHAPING AND VALUE SHARING IN THE TEACHER-PARENT-PUPIL CONFERENCE

The very existence of a teacher-parent-pupil conference indicates a willingness to participate in value shaping and value sharing. The most convenient means of analyzing the teacher-parent-pupil conference is through the familiar framework of analysis.

1. Values are shared and shaped when there is a mutual *respect*. When parent, teacher and pupil are willing to listen, if not always to agree, to one another, respect lends itself to real value sharing and shaping. Without respect for all concerned, there is no basis for a three-way conference. Respect can increase and develop, however, as relationships progress. Respect will always increase when individuals come together in common concern.

2. Values are shaped through *enlightenment*. Understanding between participants and exchange of ideas provides the climate in which enlightenment can flourish. Where there is freedom to participate in democratic problem-solving, pupils may build a "backlog of success." With each success, learning is expanded.

3. *Power* is a scope value extended through enlightenment. In a three-way conference, there should be free exercise of choice and judgment. Values are shaped and shared to the extent that the parent, pupil and teacher suggest and evaluate in the decision-making process.

4. *Affection* is a most effective means through which values may be shaped and shared. As teacher, pupil and parent come to understand and respect each other, affection will most likely result.

5. The pupil's *skills* in many areas are assessed according to his abilities. Evaluation and recognition of these skills are primary purposes of the three-way conference. Skill in communication cannot be overestimated. In this respect, values are shaped and shared through the evaluative process and decisions regarding the child's progress and direction.

6. *Well-being* thrives in a healthy atmosphere of interchange of ideas concerning a child's progress where concern is demonstrated for the child by the two institutions which form his present and mould his future: the home and the school. Such focus on the child's physical, emotional, social and intellectual development add immeasurably to the child's well-being. There are certain inherent safeguards for the well-being of the adults involved in the encounter, as well. Values are shaped and shared through this type of confrontation.

7. The value of *rectitude* is shaped and shared in the teacher-pupil-parent conference. Responsibility for one's behavior in thought and action is an index of a high status in rectitude. Acceptance of responsibility resulting from small-group planning is a means by which the enhancement of status in rectitude can be achieved.

8. *Wealth* is involved. Though not especially shared in the problem-solving process, it may be a result of some value shaping. To the extent that the child is allowed an environment in which he may eventually choose an occupation and the opportunity to explore and seek the areas for which he is best suited, the teacher-pupil-parent conference may provide value shaping toward honest and

productive employment. Obviously, the services of the teacher and parent in the pupil's interest represent a form of wealth for him.

The teacher-parent-pupil conference can be the most exciting educational innovation teachers discover. That it is an innovation is a startling indictment of American public schools in failing to bring to fruition this means of promoting the realization of human dignity. That such a conference is not yet accepted widely is an indictment of our present educational plans. That it *will* be accepted is a promise so long as democratic teachers are motivated by value shaping and value sharing for the realization of human dignity for every human being.

SUGGESTED INTERVIEW QUESTIONS TO BE USED BY TEACHERS, COUNSELORS, AND ADMINISTRATORS IN THEIR CONFERENCES WITH PARENTS

Parents have many different reasons for talking with teachers, counselors and administrators. These questions are not prescriptive but should serve only to suggest to school personnel some of the approaches that might be used to draw parents into helpful discussion about their children. Those who use this list should not hesitate to add other questions and to share their own contributions with all of the others engaged in the project. Obviously, not all of these questions could ever be used with any given parent. The professional teacher, counselor, or administrator will select those pertinent to given situations.

Power

1. How are important decisions reached in your family?
2. Do you have a rule that each person may be heard on questions which the family will discuss?
3. Do you think your child feels he has a fair part to play in the decision making in his classroom or in play situations?
4. Do you feel your child is dominating with other children or unduly timid?
5. Does your child often express a desire to be a leader and to be elected by his peers to leadership positions?
6. What ambitions do you have for your child that would place him in positions of authority; does your child accept these ambitions as his own?
7. Does your child often appear to feel hurt because he is passed over when class officers are elected?
8. Has your child expressed any dislike for other children who hold leadership positions?
9. Basically, does your child prefer to lead or to follow; is he equally happy either to lead or to follow?
10. Do you think your child feels he lives under too many rules?
11. Does your child seem afraid of his teacher, the assistant principal, or the principal?
12. Do you feel that discipline patterns at home differ from those in the school; if so, how does this appear to affect your child?
13. From what your child says about his classroom, what one thing do you think he would like to change in it?

Respect

1. Do you agree that the greatest goal in school is to help children attain human dignity through wider access to things people need and want such as respect, affection, good health and other values?
2. Does your child give you any evidence that he is considered a real person at school?
3. Does your child have some friends or associates for whom he appears to have great respect; what seems to account for this?
4. What kind of obedience do you expect from your child–are small children in your family to be "seen and not heard"?
5. Can you suggest some ways in which we could help your child to achieve everything which his ability permits?
6. Can you cite things your child does for others that you think shows respect? Have you told him you admire him for this?
7. Do you think that it is helpful for your child to take part in group activities at school?
8. When children in your home speak, do adults listen?
9. What do others feel about your child; what are the things they like or dislike about him?
10. Do you ever help your child to feel respected by giving him something useful to do in the home activities which can earn some appreciation by the other family members?
11. Do you believe in allowing a child to "be his age"?
12. What limits do you set for your child with regard to discipline, exploration, and play?
13. Do you compliment your child on his good behavior or work well done?

Wealth (Economic Security)

1. Do you feel that the school makes too many demands on your child for money?
2. Does your child make wise use of the money he is given?
3. Do you think that a good education helps one to earn money? Does your child know your feelings about this?
4. Does your child have an allowance?
5. Does your child make too many demands on you for money?
6. Would you like the school to teach children how to manage money in a free society?
7. Does your child complain about the clothes he must wear to school?
8. Are there constant demands to buy articles of clothing which other children wear to school; does your child feel happier when he is dressed like other children?

Enlightenment

1. What does your child tell you about what he learned at school?
2. Does your child have a time and place for effective study at home; do you help him study; do you ever do his work for him?

3. Do you like to see your child participate in extracurricular activities?
4. Would you like to know some of the reasons why schools organize learning activities as they do?
5. Do you ever go with your child to a library or museum?
6. Do you ever take sight-seeing trips with your child and discuss points of historical, governmental, or cultural interest with him?
7. Would you like to know more about what a school day is like for your child; what does he like and dislike about his schedule or program?
8. Do you feel your child should be learning more in school; in which areas?
9. What kinds of books does your child like to read?
10. Do you believe that the school is a proper place to talk about democracy and the improvement of living?
11. Would you cooperate in any program of the school to increase the sharing of human values in your neighborhood?
12. Do you deliberately try to stimulate interest and broaden the background experiences of your child by taking him on trips to various places, such as to the zoo, airport, a farm, a cruise on the lake, etc.?
13. Do you buy your child his "very own" magazines and books?
14. Does it sometimes seem to you that a child's argument is his way of trying out new ideas?
15. Do your child's interests tend to be like yours? Do you react enthusiastically to his constructive interests?

Skill

1. What special talents does your child have?
2. What out-of-school skills does the child have?
3. Does he try to improve these skills voluntarily?
4. Do you feel your child needs any remedial instruction in the skills area?
5. Which skills do you think the school should stress?
6. Do you think your child should know not only *how but why* he is being asked to work on a skill?
7. Do you think the school should stress skills in thinking?
8. Are social skills taught at home? Do you think they should be taught at school?
9. When children bring work home from school such as paintings or spelling tests, do you take time to examine them?
10. Do you look for little signs of progress each day or do you expect your child to meet a certain standard?
11. Do you put words in your child's mouth or do you let him find his own words?
12. Does your child find it difficult to be compared with other children in skill development?
13. Would you like to have your child compared with other children and the results published for all to know?
14. Do you deliberately speak clearly and distinctly to your child in order to help him learn to speak clearly and distinctly?

15. Do you encourage him to build his vocabulary by playing word games with him or discussing new words or ideas that appear in his reading or on T.V.?
16. If your child is being taught reading, writing or arithmetic differently than the way you were taught, how do you feel about this?
17. In helping him with homework, do you sometimes find that your directions sound strange to your child?
18. In teaching your child how to manage his money do you also help him to learn skills in arithmetic?

Well-Being

1. Does your child sometimes appear to need to be a child and sometimes a grown-up?
2. Does your child have any health or physical problems which cause him to be less effective in school or feel unhappy?
3. Does your child appear to feel tired when he comes home from school?
4. Would you like to discuss any of your child's health problems with the school nurse?
5. Would you like to discuss any of your child's problems with the school psychologist or case worker?
6. How do you think your child feels about his own ability; does he seem to believe he is getting a fair chance to develop it?
7. What does your child talk about most when he talks about school; tell about the favorable as well as the unfavorable things?
8. With whom and what does your child like to play at home?
9. What pets does the child have at home; how do you feel about the keeping of pets?
10. What do you and your husband (or your wife) enjoy doing with the child; do you set aside some definite time for play or having good times together?
11. Does your child have any particular trouble with another child in which he needs help?
12. What lunch arrangements do you make for your child? Does the child ever complain about these arrangements?
13. Does your child have frequent headaches?
14. Does your child sleep well or is he disturbed by "bad dreams"?
15. Does your child cry a great deal without apparent good reason? If so, what do you do about these occasions?

Rectitude

1. What are some of the ideals which you hold up to your child as being most important in life; do you believe the school can hold up these same ideals, too?
2. Do you believe that children should be taught to share values with others?
3. Can you cite things your child does for others that you consider to be "good"?
4. Could you suggest ways in which the teachers in this school could show their interest and concern in children and parents of this neighborhood?

5. What responsibilities does the child assume in helping the family with its routine chores; does he do this willingly?
6. Do you sometimes feel that your child is too young or immature to accept responsibilities assigned to him?
7. Does your child think of himself as a nice child, a good child, a naughty child, an ugly child; do you agree with him?
8. Does your child seem to stick with what he starts?

Affection

1. Does your child appear to like anyone at school very much?
2. Does your child have any close friends; discuss what you consider are the reasons why your child prefers their association.
3. Do you have to be away from your child at a time when he is at home?
4. Does your child cry or complain when you have to leave him?
5. Does your child ever appear to feel that no one cares about him?
6. Have any members of your family died in recent years? How did your child feel about it?
7. Are either of you stepparents to the child? If so, are there stepbrothers or stepsisters? Do the children appear to share affection?
8. Are either of the child's parents away from home for long periods of time?
9. Do grandparents or other close relatives live in the home?
10. How do you let your child know you love him?

SUMMARY

Newer methods of reporting the learner's progress are evolving in accordance with the newer emphases in evaluation which place more responsibility on the student. The central purpose here is to strengthen the young person's status of rectitude by building in his experience both the advantage and the necessity of his taking a realistic view of himself, his progress, and his responsibility for steering his own course within the congenial and interested guidance of his teacher and parents. It is felt that enlightenment is served through the investigative process of the reporting conference. Further, goal clarification is a new and built-in feature of the reporting medium. It is hoped that other value statuses will be enhanced by all participants in the conference. For instance, respect enhancement for all concerned is an expected outcome of sincere deliberation in the conference. Power sharing is an inherent feature of the process. Skills of communication are a by-product or may be the result of prior preparation by the learner. Encouragement and merited praise of progress by the adults will help to enhance well-being and respect. Factual, realistic exploration by the participants, while important in the long term for the maintenance of self-enlightenment and well-being should not, however, be pursued so relentlessly as to sacrifice too much in the category of affection. A general rule for adults to follow appears to be that a minimum climate of affection be maintained through troublesome periods of the young person's development.

Index